DKR

JENNA HAYS McEACHERN

with

EDITH ROYAL

DKR

The Royal Scrapbook

UNIVERSITY OF TEXAS PRESS | AUSTIN

Hook 'Em,
Jenna McEachern

THE PUBLICATION OF THIS
BOOK WAS MADE POSSIBLE BY
THE GENEROUS SUPPORT OF
JEANNE AND MICKEY KLEIN,
OF ELLEN AND EDWARD
RANDALL III IN HONOR
OF THEIR DEAR FRIEND
ELEANOR MOSLE HILL, AND
OF ALICIA B. HAYNES IN
HONOR OF HER DEAR FATHER,
J.P. BRYAN, WHOM SHE LOVES
AND ADMIRES.

Copyright © 2012 by Jenna Hays McEachern

Printed in China
First edition, 2012

Requests for permission to reproduce material from this work
should be sent to:
    Permissions
    University of Texas Press
    P.O. Box 7819
    Austin, TX 78713–7819
    www.utexas.edu/utpress/about/bpermission.html

♾ The paper used in this book meets the minimum requirements
of ANSI/NISO Z39.48–1992 (R1997) (Permanence of Paper).

LIBRARY OF CONGRESS CATALOGING-IN-PUBLICATION DATA

McEachern, Jenna Hays
  DKR : the Royal scrapbook / Jenna Hays McEachern with
Edith Royal. — 1st ed.
     p.   cm.
  Includes bibliographical references.
   ISBN 978-0-292-70493-0 (cloth : alk. paper) —
ISBN 978-0-292-73916-1 (e-book)
   1. Royal, Darrell.   2. Football players—United States—
Biography.   3. Football coaches—United States—Biography.
I. Royal, Edith.   II. Title.
  GV939.R69M34   2012
  796.332092—dc23 [B]
                     2012012161

*To Darrell, who rescued me
from an Oklahoma cotton patch*
EDITH ROYAL

*To Pee Wee and the Big Coach,
with my love and admiration*
JENNA HAYS McEACHERN

───────

1946 - 3rd ____

CONTENTS

Home place - 12 mi North of Gould
Okla, on Salt Fork of Red River

PREFACE

For as long as she can remember, Edith Royal has been a saver of "stuff" and a documenter of events, unaware that she was actually an archivist. As a teenager, when she so carefully bound in blue satin ribbon the latest letters from her boyfriend, she could not have known that one day all those saved things—newspaper clippings, ticket stubs, family photos, funny letters from friends—would serve a larger purpose. She couldn't have imagined that sixty years later, researchers and writers would pick through those photos and scrapbooks, searching for clues as to what had made her husband successful, unique, revered. She never dreamed that anyone outside of their family would care, or would thank her for being a "pack rat." "I just thought I was saving history for my family, for the children and grandchildren Darrell and I might have one day," she says.

I first knew of Darrell Royal from my father, a successful high school football coach in southeast Texas. I knew that Coach Royal was larger than life: handsome and witty, his "Royalisms" were repeated so often that today they are part of our state's, as well as the sport's, lexicon. He was innovative and forthright, the picture of integrity, and he welcomed high school coaches to his practices, his film room, and his office. And he always—always—remembered their names.

Royal was the head coach at The University when I arrived in Austin in 1972. I was an intern in the Sports Information Department, so whenever I was trying to avoid either actual work or the wrath of my boss, Jones Ramsey, I'd cut over to the coaches' offices, where I'd visit with Bill Ellington, Leon Manley, or Coach Royal. Anytime I stuck my head in his door, Royal, the head coach and athletic director of The University of Texas, responded in the same way: "Well, hello, Jenna. Come in and have a seat. You have time for a visit?" Never did he make a visitor feel as if he were too busy.

I met Edith a year or so later. She sat in a side room of the KTBC television studio, embroidering while she waited for Darrell and Bill Worrell, a Houston sportscaster, to finish taping a weekly segment of *The Darrell Royal Show*. I was nervous about meeting her, and I expected an aloof celebrity. What I found instead was a woman who laughed easily and was willing to befriend a silly twenty-year-old coed. I now know that she is a keeper of people as well as things. A few years ago, Edith brought me treasure: files of letters and drawings and poems that young fans had sent Coach Royal during his years at Texas: "I don't know what we can do with these, but I wanted you to have them." I wasn't her first choice; Bud Shrake had held onto them for years, but he was busy with other projects and never found time to publish the letters. He finally returned the file to Edith, who gave it to me. "Let's do a book," I suggested. When Coach Royal's players planned to honor him with a party to celebrate his eight-fifth birthday, Edith and I asked Royal's friends and former players to write him letters recounting some special memory. The overwhelming response provided more letters for "The Book." With the help of Edith; my agent, Kathleen Niendorff; the book's creative director, Randy McEachern; and Bill Bishel, Allison Faust, and Dave Hamrick at the University of Texas Press, "The Book" of letters morphed into a more intimate glimpse into Royal's life. Over the past two years, Edith and I have met over breakfast or at our favorite junk store every couple of weeks, and truth be told, we did a lot more laughing than working. The book progressed, and I became enthralled with her stories of life with Darrell, and I knew no book on the Coach would be complete without including more of Edith. The book shifted shape again, into what you now hold in your hand, a scrapbook full of DKR's quotes, Edith's recollections, and family photos never before published—a private glimpse into the very public lives of one of Texas' best-loved and most influential couples. The world did not need another football book about Darrell Royal, and this is not intended to be a biography, but a scrapbook of his and Edith's lives as they were intertwined with football, friends, and family.

Future historians will be indebted to Edith for saving the things she saved, because she and her husband became almost mythic in reputation. Two impoverished teenagers, products of the Dust Bowl and the Depression, they started out with little more than big dreams and a deep devotion to each other and then grew into a couple of great influence and power. Their celebrity and prestige originally sprouted from his position as head football coach at The University of Texas, where he enjoyed unmatched success. But through the years, their reputation flourished as a result of their generous gifts of money, time, heart, and spirit, as well as their willingness to help others find a job, find sobriety, or find their way.

This book is really a love story, recording the devotion between the Royals and their friends, the Royals and the Longhorn Nation, the Royals and their family, and of course, the love between two kids who laughed and loved and bickered and bore unbearable pain as they forged an almost seventy-year union. This book is Edith's love offering to Darrell.

Finally, this scrapbook is my love letter to Darrell and Edith. I've been blessed to call them my friends.

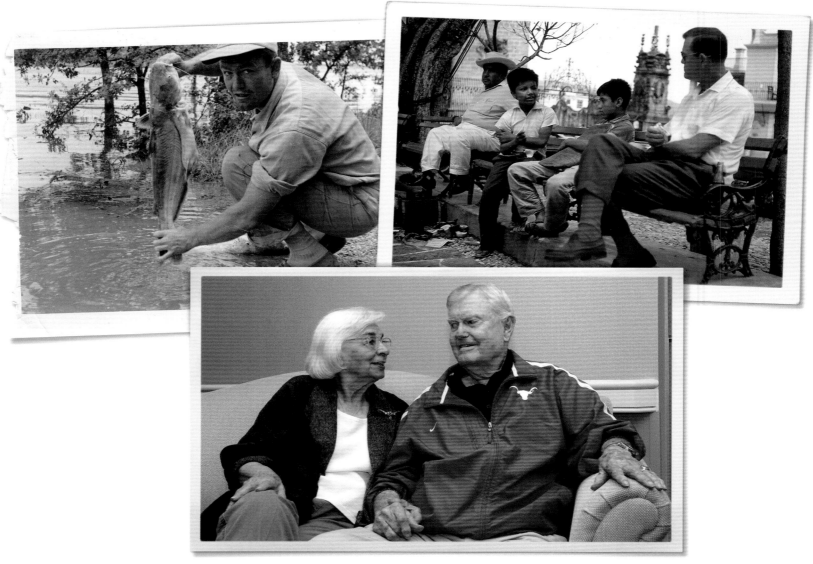

Photography by Rick Henson

ACKNOWLEDGMENTS

I am grateful to Edith Royal for her friendship and generosity of spirit, and for sharing her memories, mementos, and confidences. I am humbled by her trust. Darrell Royal was a demigod for coaches across the country, and they, along with his former players, carry to future generations his message of pride in one's self and integrity above all else. As a Longhorn, I am grateful that he was ours for twenty years. Mack Royal shared 10,000-plus family photos that he had laboriously digitized over the years. I enjoyed meeting Mack for Mexican food and hearing his perspective on life as a Royal.

Whenever people learned that this was a project honoring the Royals, they became eager to lend their names, quotes, artwork, and photos. I am grateful to a large group of photographers, foremost among them Rick Henson, who was a godsend. The others are Amber Snow, Jerry Hughes, Susan Sigmon, Mack Royal, Cindy McWilliams, Charla Wood, Russ Smith, and Carrell Grigsby. Thanks also go to Governor Rick Perry, Bill Caldwell, Jim Bob Moffett, Earl Campbell, and especially Rich Hull, Murray Olderman, Bob Taylor, and Dan Jenkins for their generosity. John Wheat and the staff at the Dolph Briscoe Center for American History were of invaluable help and exhibited great patience. Marty Akins and Hays McEachern helped me decipher the wishbone offense, and Ryan Haenes "rescued" some of the Royals' family photos that seemed unusable.

Thanks are also due to those who have previously written on the Royals; some of the quotations and anecdotes in this book first appeared in their works, the most important of which are listed in the Selected Sources section. Every effort was made to give proper credit to photographers and artists and to seek the holders of copyrights, but time has erased the identity of many. Much of the material in this book came from articles in the Royal archives, which had been cut out and pasted into scrapbooks, so attribution became impossible.

Saundra Goldman kept me focused with her literary advice and psychological counseling, and designer Derek George created a work of art from the hodgepodge he inherited. This project would never have achieved liftoff were it not for Kathleen Niendorff. I took her a pile of kids' letters and admitted that I had not the first idea what to do with them. She has been everything a consultant, agent, and friend should be. Years ago, Bill Little grabbed my hand and dragged me in the direction I needed to go. I write books because he told me I could. I am so indebted to every player and friend who wrote Coach Royal and was willing to have his or her words shared. The outpouring was so great that only a small portion could be published here. Please visit www.burntorangebooks.com to find other letters and memories of the coach. I am still surprised, thirty years later, that I ended up with Randy McEachern, all-around great guy, and three wonderful children, Bailey, Hays, and Lester.

And finally, thank you to Annie and Jackie for reminding me what real heroism looks like.

D

K

R

DARRELL K ROYAL

TEXAS MEMORIAL STADIUM

"Just remember, the cream always rises to the top." Royal often repeated this saying to encourage his players, promising that there would be rewards for those who were persistent, hard-working men of character. His own athletic and coaching careers bear witness to the truth of the saying. Photo by Susan Sigmon, The University of Texas at Austin.

Chapter 1

THE ULTIMATE COMPLIMENT

A man famous for his clever words, Darrell Royal was rarely at a loss for them. But now he was flabbergasted. In all his seventy-two years, he had seldom been as stunned as he was at that moment. The two men sitting across from him in his living room waited for his response to their request. As he struggled to comprehend what they were saying, Royal could only stammer, "My gosh, are you asking for my approval?" The men said that they were. "Well, yes, of course!"

* * * * *

It was 1996, and Darrell Royal wasn't much given to worry. He looked out over the open rolling hills of Barton Creek Country Club and heard the wind chimes sounding softly through his sliding-glass door. He knew every contour of every fairway and green on the golf course outside the window. Although he still worked for The University of Texas as special assistant to the president, it had been twenty years since he had left behind the pressure of being head coach, and life was good, peaceful, satisfying. He was curious, though, why his two bosses—UT chancellor William Cunningham and Robert Berdahl, the president of The University—had asked to meet with him. He wondered why they

*As he found it: Aerial view of Memorial Stadium,
as it looked in 1957, Royal's first year at Texas.*

had not asked him to come to campus for this meeting. Instead, they were coming to him. Afterward, Royal joked that he thought he must have been in some kind of trouble. But when the three men were gathered in the Royals' living room, surrounded by framed photos, autographed footballs, and awards for a life well lived, they came out with it.

The University of Texas Board of Regents had voted to add "Darrell K Royal" to the name of Texas Memorial Stadium. Cunningham and Berdahl were there to ask Royal's permission to make the change.

The first time Royal saw it in print—"Kickoff is 7:20 p.m., August 31, 1996, at Darrell K Royal–Texas Memorial Stadium"—

he was shocked, as he was when he saw it for the first time on the Jumbotron in the stadium. The magnitude of the gesture overwhelmed him: "I thought, 'This is really something. It may be referred to this way forever.'"

Football is big business at The University of Texas. The UT Athletics Department is unrivaled; it is one of the most successful college athletics programs in the country, and easily the most profitable. There are orange-bloods who complain that UT's advertising, licensing, and marketing circus has become more important than the football game itself. The football field, the athletic complex, the locker room, the trophy room, the north end zone, the academic center, the club on the west side of the stadium, the hall on the east side, the practice facility, and the weight room all bear the names of loyal and generous donors. And this, as much as any other accolade, speaks of how beloved and revered Darrell Royal still is. Mickey Herskowitz, a sports columnist for the *Houston Chronicle*, wrote in 1996: "Keep in mind, Royal didn't buy the naming rights. They gave it to him from deep in their hearts." It was a merited tribute for the man who arrived in December 1956 to take over a Texas football program that had

> **"Naming the Darrell K Royal–Texas Memorial Stadium represents nothing more than a small down payment on our debt of gratitude to you and Edith for all you have done for The University."**
>
> —William Cunningham, former UT president and chancellor, in a note to the Royals

been battered by the worst season in school history. Royal methodically and with integrity rebuilt the program into one that commanded respect, even awe, on the national stage. He took the Longhorns to conference championships and national championships and left us with his enduring "Royalisms." He is recognized as one of the most brilliant and innovative coaches in the history of the game. And with the addition of his name to the stadium, things had come full circle for Royal.

Dr. John Genung, who played quarterback for Royal (1960–1962), recently wrote his coach this note: "The boys who played for you knew you did it the right way. That your way was correct—that it could be done with honor and hard work and fairness. When it was over you could look yourself in the mirror and know that it was right—you were the reason why, the cause of it all. Thanks, Coach."

> **"The smartest coach I knew. Not even close."**
>
> —Dan Jenkins on Darrell Royal

Under Royal, the Longhorns did not lose a game in Memorial Stadium from 1968 until midway through the 1976 season, a forty-two-game home winning streak. (1977 Cactus, Texas Student Media)

Houston Chronicle *story by Mickey Herskowitz, announcing the renaming of Memorial Stadium as Darrell K Royal–Texas Memorial Stadium. (Darrell K Royal Papers, Dolph Briscoe Center for American History, The University of Texas at Austin [hereafter, DKR Papers, DBCAH], di_07343; reprinted by permission of the Houston Chronicle Publishing Company)*

Burley Royal, Darrell's dad, said, "I never had to get after Darrell much. He wasn't a rowdy kid . . . never was one to start things, but if they wanted to box, he'd box with them. And he never would say anything mean about anyone, even if he didn't like them," 1932. (Royal Family Archives)

Darrell K Royal - born Hollis Ok

A rare photo of young Darrell, left, standing still and wearing shoes, with Don Fox, a lifelong friend, 1933. (Royal Family Archives)

Darrell K Royal, bundled up against a cold Hollis winter, 1926. (Royal Family Archives)

Chapter 2

FAVORITE SON

Darrell K Royal. The *K* is just an initial, not an abbreviation. *K* is in honor of his mother, Katy Elizabeth, who died when he was just four months old.

Darrell Royal plays a crucial role in the folklore of Hollis, Oklahoma, where he was born in 1924. Hollis, which Royal called "a great little place to grow up," basks in the glory of its favorite son. The sign on the Hollis High School stadium boasts: "We're proud of Hollis, hometown of Darrell Royal." In 2003, the football field at Hollis High School was officially named Darrell K Royal Field.

But back in the 1930s, he was just a freckled-faced, barefoot little boy, tagging along with his older brothers and working hard to keep up with them. They had no money, but they did have an abundance of energy and competitiveness. When he was just a toddler, Darrell started carrying a ball with him: an old Clabber Girl Baking Powder can with tape all over it to cover the sharp edges. "I just ran everywhere I went. I was never without a ball or a bat."

Darrell "played up" with his older brothers, and this was one source of his fierce competitive streak, having to compete with the older boys. But on his own, even as a child, Darrell drove himself to perform better, to surpass his previous mark. He drew lines in dirt roads to aim for, and when his jump eventually reached that line, he would erase it with his foot and draw another one just a little farther away. He competed with himself, by himself, "just learning to do it a little faster and better." Darrell couldn't bear to be called in for supper or for bedtime; he never was ready to stop. On Saturdays in the fall, he organized neighborhood football games in the yard.

> **"God gives talent, size, speed. But a guy can control how hard he tries."**
>
> —Darrell K Royal

Darrell "played up" with his brothers Glenn (second row, second from left), Don (third row, third from left), and their older friends. Darrell (front row, right) poses with his brothers' football team and Coach Dean Wild (far right), 1935. His dad, Burley Royal, recalled, "He got kicked around a lot, but he always stayed in the game to the end." (Royal Family Archives)

The kids would put the radio outside and tune it to the Oklahoma Sooners broadcast. As the radio blared "Boomer Sooner," the future college all-American pretended that every time he ran with the ball he was scoring a touchdown for Oklahoma.

If Darrell played hard, he worked even harder. In the late 1930s, Hollis was at the heart of the Dust Bowl; relentless winds churned the dry soil, lifting thick red clouds of dust and rendering farmland useless. At night he slept with a wet washrag covering his face to keep the red silt out of his nose and mouth. The Royals' house stood next to the highway, and every day Darrell watched the cars leaving town, headed west, loaded down with every stick of the families' furniture, the canvas water bags slapping against the side of the truck. Darrell was pretty much on his own from the time he could walk, and he had always worked—shining shoes, throwing newspapers on a paper route, feeding newsprint into the presses after hours. He eventually had to quit his paper route in order to help the family pull bolls of cotton, fifty cents for a hundred pounds. "He was smaller than a lot of 'em," his father, Burley Royal, remembered, "but he could do a day's work with the best of them."

Burley hung on in Hollis during most of the Depression and made it through the Dust Bowl. He worked several jobs to feed his family, including WPA projects, but in 1940, after Darrell finished junior high, he couldn't hang on any longer. He built a crude trailer to pull behind the family's Whippet sedan, loaded up the furniture, filled the canvas water bags, and headed to California with his wife and two youngest sons. "We must have had twenty flats on the way to California." Darrell said. They landed in Porterville, in the San Joaquin Valley, and lived in what Darrell called an old shack. The fourteen-year-old landed jobs as a fruit picker, a construction worker, a wheelbarrow pusher, and, because farmers believed putting a touch of olive oil on the end of figs would cause them to ripen faster, a fig painter.

Darrell started high school in Porterville. He had waited with great anticipation for the day he could finally play high school football, but when he showed up for practice, he wasn't allowed to try out for the A team. The teams were divided by weight, the coach told him, and Darrell was just too little. "Well, now, couldn't you just let me *try*?" No, the coach thought not. Rules were rules. Darrell was welcome to try out for one of the smaller, less competitive teams, but that page was not in Darrell's playbook. He had endured poverty, neglect, lack, dirt, and bitterly hard work. He had lived through ill treatment at the hands of his stepmother and the

shameful humiliation of being called "Okie." But when his dream of playing varsity ball evaporated, it was too much to take.

Dean Wild, an assistant coach at Hollis High, had written Darrell a letter earlier, inviting him to come home to Hollis to play ball. The coach promised Darrell a job, lunch every day, a place to stay, and a chance to play varsity ball. Coach Wild's invitation and his letter served as a compass for Darrell, pointing him back home, where he belonged. After yet another blowup with his stepmother, it didn't take much for the eager teenager to convince "Pop" to let him hitchhike back to Oklahoma. Burley tucked thirteen dollars in Darrell's pocket and wished him well. He carried all his possessions—his clothes and his baseball glove—in a gutted Victrola box. In his back pocket he carried the creased letter from Coach Wild.

He found a ride east with an acquaintance of his dad, but the trip was a disaster: the driver liked to pull on the bottle. After several near wrecks, Darrell jumped out and rode his thumb the rest of the way. Once back in Hollis, he stayed mostly with Grandma Harmon, his mother's mother. Sometimes he stayed with his coach, occasionally with an aunt, but home base was Grandma's house.

Back in Hollis, his fairy-tale journey would begin, and he would meet, in his words, "the only girl I ever cared about." Joe Bailey Metcalf, an assistant coach at Hollis, called Royal

the workingest kid you ever saw. He'd stay after practice to work on his punting, then he'd run over to sweep out for Bill Hall. Darrell was always wound pretty tight and never had much time for sitting around doing nothing.

The 1941 Hollis High School Tigers. Darrell, front row left, is #11. (Royal Family Archives)

> **"Darrell always had a bigger time than anybody; he was a leader in everything—including the mischief. He was mischievous, but never mean."**
>
> —Joe Bailey Metcalf

He was a study in perpetual motion. He fed paper into the printing press of the local newspaper for twenty-five cents an hour. He swept and mopped Bill Hall's Ford dealership and cleaned the grease racks at five every morning. On Saturdays he shined shoes at Cecil Sumpter's barbershop. He even put in time as a short-order cook. He never had time for wasting time.

Just as when he was a barefoot little boy trying to keep up with his older brothers, Darrell pushed himself to improve, pushed himself toward his goals. One of his heroes was "Indian" Jack Jacobs, a punter for the Sooners. As he listened to the broadcast of the Sooner games, he envisioned Jacobs's form. He imagined his steps, the drop of the ball, and then spent hours after practice trying to get those moves down, competing not just against other athletes but also against his own last mark. Whether he was studying his competitors in order to improve his shoe-shining technique, using his paper route to learn to pass more accurately, or setting up his own track-and-field course to compete against himself, his will to improve was legendary. He surveyed his shortcomings, observed people he wanted to emulate, and then disciplined himself to refine his skills. He worked so hard that his classmates and teammates looked up to him. His strength of will, his presence, helped him develop into a leader. "Everyone respected him, even when he was a little kid. Adults would listen to him; he always talked sense," Metcalf said.

And in spite of how books and interviews later romanticized his early life, Edith painted this picture:

> It was awfully hard, just a real hard childhood. He was a poor boy, and he was so lonely. Honestly, he was neglected. I think that drove him harder than a lot of the others. He wanted so much more than he ever had in Hollis.

As was all too common for children of that era, he was forced to grow up too soon, with suffering everywhere he turned. His mother had died of cancer when he was four months old, and because that was considered a shameful way to die in 1924, Darrell's family allowed him to believe that his mother had died giving birth to him. He bore that burden most of his life, believing until he was an adult that he was to blame for his mother's death.

As a result, Royal was highly sensitive, even thin-skinned,

although he was able to shed that prickliness in later years. The "Okie" experience stung mightily, as did the poverty. In his words: "I'm not saying we had it as bad as blacks or Hispanics; it wasn't close to what they experienced. But when people called us 'Okies,' it was said with spite. People hated us, when all we were trying to do was find honest work." Burley and his children worked hard, and their pride wouldn't let them accept "commodity clothes," the government-issued overalls that marked one as poor.

Darrell, back in Hollis where he belonged, led the Hollis High Tigers to an undefeated season and a mythical state title. (Royal Family Archives)

* * * * *

In later years, Darrell Royal remarked, "I studied those people I admired . . . tried to do as they taught." Those people—his father, his high school principal, his football coaches—along with the harsh conditions of his early years, shaped the boy who would be known throughout his life as a compassionate champion of the underdog.

Edith Marie "Pee Wee" Thomason, of Harmon County, Oklahoma, 1944. (Royal Family Archives)

> "I really didn't have other girlfriends.
> She's the only girl I ever cared about."
> —Darrell K Royal

Chapter 3

A LITTLE COUNTRY-TOWN COURTSHIP

She had never seen a football game. He had never had a girlfriend. Both of those things were about to change. He was the best athlete in Hollis, and something of a celebrity around town. But, Edith confessed, "I didn't know enough about football to be impressed. He was cute. But I thought *all* boys were cute. He was shy, not pushy, and I liked that. I thought that would be a challenge. I didn't think I had a chance after I found out all the girls in high school liked him. But he kept coming back."

Darrell's senior portrait, 1943 Tiger *yearbook. (Royal Family Archives)*

In 1941, Edith "Pee Wee" Thomason was visiting a girlfriend in Hollis when she spotted Darrell Royal. She and her friend were skating at a traveling skating rink. Darrell and his brother Glenn were hanging around watching the two girls skate. When the girls finished, Darrell and his brother walked the girls home.

"As we walked home that night, the other couple did all the talking. Darrell and I just kinda lagged behind and looked at each other," Edith remembered. Darrell's take on the situation was a little less sentimental. "Well, it was one of those love-at-first-sight deals. We started dating, and that was pretty much it. We pretty well knew we'd get married." So did everyone else, it seems.

In the 1943 Hollis High School annual, beside his senior photo, some clever yearbook staffer wrote:

*"D" is for Darrell, the Pride
of the School.
Reckon some day we'll lose
him to Gould?*

Edith's family farmed cotton in Harmon County, on the Salt Fork of the Red River, about twenty miles out in the country. She went to high school in Gould, eight miles from Hollis. Neither the Royals nor the Thomasons owned a telephone, and Darrell didn't have a car, so the two never knew when they would see each other next. Darrell said that happened only on "butter and egg days," when farmers took their produce or dairy into town.

Edith later recalled in *The Story of Darrell Royal*:

I never knew when we'd go to town. War rationing had just begun, and we didn't have good tires. Sometimes we didn't have enough gas to get there. But he knew and I knew if we were going to go into town, it would be on a Saturday. So I'd just always keep my eyes open for him, and he'd be keeping his eyes peeled for me, and we'd just find one another. We went to the movies together, or just walked around town, or rode with a friend who had a car. It was a little country-town courtship . . . they're all alike.

They had been dating about a year when he graduated from high school and joined the service. There was never any question about it; there was a war on and he knew it was his duty. He enlisted in the U.S. Army Air Forces (USAAF). The night before he was to catch the bus to report to Fort Sill in Lawton,

Oklahoma, Darrell borrowed a friend's car and drove out to the cotton farm to visit Edith. They parked on a country road and talked about their future.

Almost seven decades later, Edith is sitting in a local coffee shop, thumbing through old photo albums. She takes a sip of coffee and finally says, "Darrell was always so careful, so guarded with his feelings. He really was scared to expose himself to any kind of hurt. Matter of fact, he stayed that way for most of our lives. He never really opened up about how much he cared until much, much later. I guess that's why I felt like I had to do the pursuing," she laughs. But even today he remembers the white dress with navy blue polka dots she wore that night he asked her to wait for him. "It wasn't a proposal," he revealed to Bill Little, former UT Sports Information director, in 1999. "Well, it was to me—but I asked her if she'd wait on me till I got back. You know, I knew I wanted to marry Edith about a year after we met, but I wasn't going to bring it up until I had a reporting date." Edith remembers, "We just talked. He asked me to keep a trunk that had his football jacket in it. I figured that even if he didn't come back for me, he'd come back for that Hollis High School letter jacket." When Darrell indicated that he wanted her to be there when he got out of the army, "I was thrilled," she laughed, "because he didn't like to make commitments."

Edith posing in front of her family's farmhouse, as best friend Billie Nell Albright looks on, about 1942. Edith recalls that after Darrell left for the service during her senior year, "Every day I'd walk that two miles in all kinds of weather down that dirt road to check the mailbox, hoping for a letter. There were about ten mailboxes mounted on a big wagon wheel, and come rain or shine, I'd hike up there to see if there was a letter for me. I wrote to him several times a week. I'd get one from him every once in a while, which I read over and over and over again, I took those letters and tied them up with a blue satin ribbon like I'd seen them do in the movies, and I put them away so nobody else could find them. I saved those letters for a long time. But Darrell doesn't like to save things like I do. He was so cautious when he wrote me, and the letters didn't say anything embarrassing, but when he realized I'd kept them all, he eventually talked me into throwing them all away. He thought they were silly. You know how boys are. I sure wish I had them today."
(Royal Family Archives)

Royal's official Army Air Forces portrait,
1943. (Royal Family Archives)

"You've got to be in a position for luck to happen.
Luck doesn't go around looking for a stumblebum."

—Darrell K Royal

Chapter 4

OFF WITH ONE HELLUVA ROAR

Royal earned his high school diploma in 1943, and after asking Edith to wait for him and getting the answer he had hoped for, he was off to the U.S. Army Air Forces. He was first stationed in Miami Beach. As his class was finishing basic training, their records were lost, so the whole group was required to redo the training. Royal later recalled: "I was young enough and strong enough that going through basic a second time really didn't bother me. We had a basketball there and a hoop . . . outside our hotel, so I used to spend a lot of my spare time down there shooting baskets." Royal found opportunities to compete even in basic training. He received a reprimand from a first lieutenant after talking a fellow trainee into seeing who could launch a dummy grenade farther. He went from basic training to gunnery school in Harlingen, Texas, then to Davis-Monthan Air Base in Tucson, where he was assigned to a flight crew as a tail gunner on a B-24. When his crew

"I had been eating catch as catch can for a long time. That [his stint in the USAAF] was the first time I can ever remember having three meals a day where I could eat all I wanted. Even that shit-on-a-shingle was great to me. I loved that breakfast, had all the milk I wanted. And boy, I loved that gravy."

—Darrell K Royal

was picked for weather- and photoreconnaissance training in the spring of 1944, they were sent to Will Rogers Field, just outside Oklahoma City.

By then, Edith had graduated from Gould High School, moved to Oklahoma City, and found a job mending flight suits at Tinker Field. One sweltering July afternoon in 1944 while Royal was on furlough, he and Edith put on their Sunday best and, with two witnesses in tow, walked from Edith's apartment to the First United Methodist Church, where they were married in the Reverend Hooten's office. After the quick ceremony, they took a bus to Altus, Oklahoma, and stayed in a hotel on their wedding night. Their friend Don Fox retrieved them early the next morning and drove them to Hollis for a few days, and then it was back on the bus to Oklahoma City. Edith was nineteen and Darrell was barely twenty. "All I owned was my ass and hat," he joked years later. But he had an understanding wife, tremendous athletic talent, and a dream of one day being a successful coach.

"We lived on Dewey Street in Oklahoma City in a house that was divided up into apartments," Edith remembered. "Two other couples lived in apartments in the same house. Come to think of it, I don't think either couple was married—wartime, you know." Edith continued to live on Dewey Street in Oklahoma City and work at Tinker. Royal's crew prepared for bombardment, photo, and weather reconnaissance, but the USAAF lost a promising B-24 tail gunner when Sergeant Darrell K Royal had to have an emergency appendectomy. While he recovered in the hospital, his squadron shipped out to Guam. Royal never saw overseas duty.

Edith was four months pregnant with their first child when Darrell was transferred to Tampa's Drew Air Force Base.

> **"Statistics dictate that we should have waited. But it was wartime, and no one knew how long you'd be gone, or if you'd even see one another after that next shipping out."**
>
> —Darrell Royal to Donia Crouch,
> *Texas Twosomes: Married for Life*

Edith was four months pregnant with their first child when she joined Darrell at Drew Air Force Base in Tampa, Florida. (Royal Family Archives)

Edith was four months pregnant with their first child when she joined Darrell at Drew Air Force Base in Tampa, Florida. (Royal Family Archives)

She talked the doctor into letting her take the train to Tampa. "It was my first trip to the South," Edith remembers. "We got on one of those troop trains and went from Oklahoma City to Tampa, Florida. The train didn't have a dining car, so we got off at these small town depots to eat. I quickly discovered grits and lots of flies."

Royal intended to try out for the vaunted Third Air Force football team, the Gremlins, stationed at Drew. He pleaded with Edith, "Whatever you do, do not have this baby on the 19th of July. That's tryout day." Marian K Royal was born on July 19, 1945, of course, but she proved to be his good luck charm: he made the team.

One sportswriter said at the time, "In high school . . . observers believed his athletic future lay on the gridiron, but Service League basketball has changed the minds of many who have watched him play."

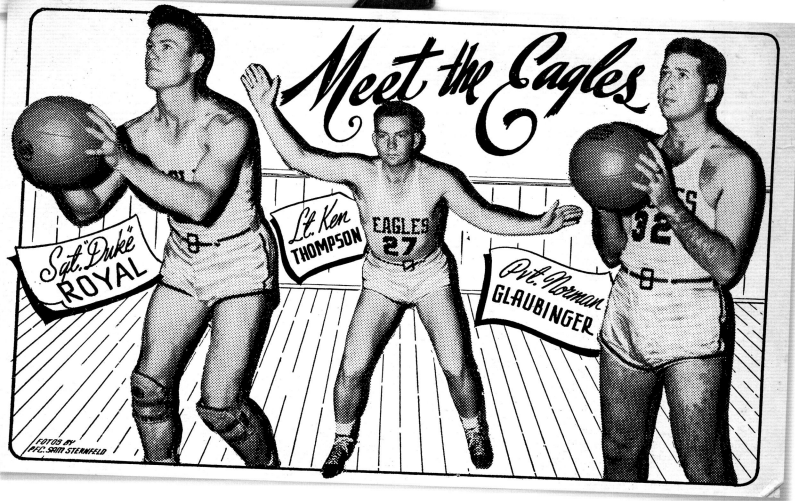

Darrell was a star in any sport he tried. After football season ended, "Duke" Royal starred on the Third Air Force Eagles basketball team. (Royal Family Archives)

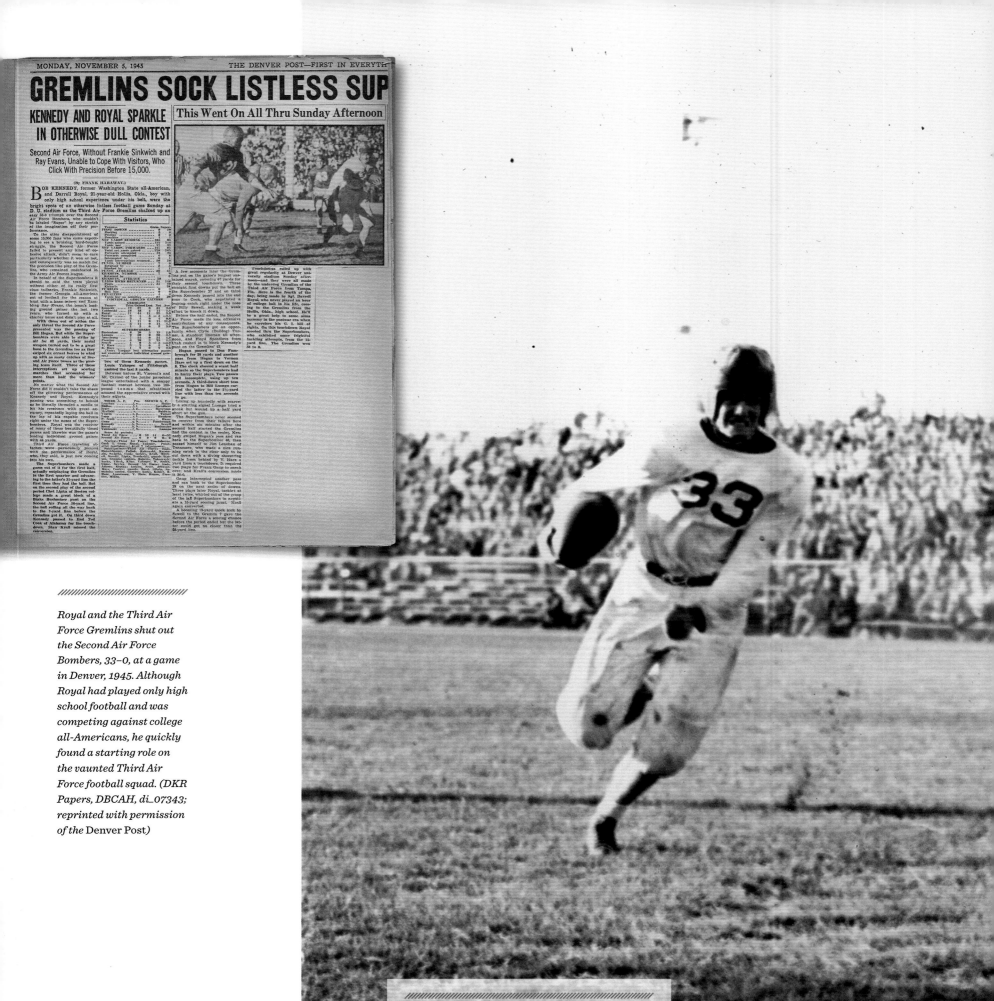

MONDAY, NOVEMBER 5, 1945   THE DENVER POST—FIRST IN EVERYTH

GREMLINS SOCK LISTLESS SUP

KENNEDY AND ROYAL SPARKLE IN OTHERWISE DULL CONTEST

Second Air Force, Without Frankie Sinkwich and Ray Evans, Unable to Cope With Visitors, Who Click With Precision Before 15,000.

This Went On All Thru Sunday Afternoon

////////////////////////////////////

Royal and the Third Air Force Gremlins shut out the Second Air Force Bombers, 33–0, at a game in Denver, 1945. Although Royal had played only high school football and was competing against college all-Americans, he quickly found a starting role on the vaunted Third Air Force football squad. (DKR Papers, DBCAH, di_07343; reprinted with permission of the Denver Post)

//

"Duke" Royal, #33, leaves the Keesler Field tacklers in the dust, 1945. (Royal Family Archives)

His heart was in football, however, and it was at football that he excelled. Royal's teammates were older and bigger than he was, and all of them had college experience. Many had been all-Americans before enlisting in the USAAF. Yet in spite of his lack of experience and size, Royal made his mark and made it quickly. He was talented enough to play—just a couple of years out of Hollis High—on one of the finest football teams assembled during the war.

Playing at a scrawny 150 pounds, Royal was "nimble, smart, and fired up." According to Mack Royal: "Dad's spirit made him bigger." He made an immediate impression on his superiors and an early impact on the field. One sportswriter wrote that Royal demonstrated a "know-how which will put him up with the leading candidates for wing . . . Royal's youthful drive . . . makes him a threat to veteran backfield starters."

Although his Hollis friends knew him as "Katy," his service nickname was "Duke," and the Tampa sports pages were full of articles singing the praises of "Duke" Royal: "[Royal] heads the list of 3rd Air Force players who have advanced rapidly . . . That is one guy that has the go in his game." By the time his service

career was over, he had come to the notice of the best college football programs in the country, and the recruitment of Darrell Royal began.

His childhood dream of scoring touchdowns for the University of Oklahoma had not changed, but that didn't stop him from visiting other colleges. Edith and Marian waited things out in Hollis. Darrell and Edith still had no car, so he hitchhiked to and from recruiting visits. Edith later recalled:

> The colleges gave him travel money, but instead of taking a bus, he'd hitchhike home and pocket the money. One time I was looking for him, and he'd gone to visit . . . I think it was Tennessee. That secretary said, "Well, he was here, and we gave him bus fare to get home, but someone saw him out on the highway . . . I believe he intended to hitchhike home." After his recruitment was over, he'd saved enough money to buy us a used Chevrolet Coupe.

He received offers—with the pot sweetened—from Florida, Auburn, Alabama, USC, Texas Tech, Georgia, Tennessee, Cornell, South Carolina, and many others. Despite pressure from those schools to make a commitment, he was waiting on OU. The coaches had guaranteed Royal a full scholarship, which would cover housing, food, and tuition, but that didn't come close to what other schools were offering.

Before the NCAA adopted its "Sanity Code" in 1948, which was designed to rein in coaches and alumni and return college football to amateurism, colleges did as they pleased, and the sky was the limit as far as what they could offer prospective players. South Carolina was willing to make "a scholarship proposition you can hardly turn down." The Cincinnati coach promised to "beat any offer that you have." USC insisted that "it is a 'must' that you come to school out here," and to sweeten the offer, ended the letter with "P.S. Baseball officially starts March 1st." As the deadline for committing drew near, Royal, back in Hollis with Edith, delayed making a decision. He had a wife and a child; he would be crazy not to go where the money was. But he had always dreamed of being a Sooner.

Finally, he and Edith convinced each other that they could somehow struggle through. With Edith's blessing, Darrell walked to the nearest telephone and called Jim Tatum, the coach of the Sooners, and accepted OU's offer of a standard scholarship. Tatum was thrilled. He had played his cards right and had come up with a Royal flush.

///

After Royal's discharge, it seemed every college in the country wanted him. Here is a sampling of letters of interest from Cincinnati, Dayton, Georgia, South Carolina, Southern Cal, Alabama Polytechnic (Auburn), Oklahoma, and Florida. (Royal Family Archives and DKR Papers, DBCAH, di_07344)

Sgt. Richard "Pruit" Ankney
Branch # 3 Box # 1402
Drew Field, Florida

Sgt. Darrell Royal,
Hollis, Oklahoma,
Dear Sgt.:

The coach of Cincinnati has just talked to me and
he has ask me to tell you that he will beat any offer that
you have. I tried to get you round trip fares to Hollis
once a year and they will give it and a good deal besides.
The University of Dayton in Ohio will do the same. Today
I talked to Jim Van Sistine and he told me that he thought
that you would be wise to go to a smaller shhool. He said
that he had introduced you to Jeff at U.S.C. . If you are
interested in going to Cincinnati and you can call long
distance (collect) to John Wiethe 1109 Enquirer Bldg.
Cincinnati 2, Ohio. He can also get you a job through
the summers. Dayton is willing to do everything too.
Both places are good places to go to college and also
get a lot a angles for future work.

I will be glad to hear from you and if you would rather
send me the number and I will have him call you.

As ever

"Pruit"

Dick

December 6, 1945

Cpl Darrell Royals
Sqdn. F - Football Team
Drew Field
Tampa, Florida

Dear Darrell:

I have spoken to Coach Butts in reference to you. From
all indications he is interested in you coming to Georgia.

A full scholarship will be offered to you and I assure
you that you will be doing the right thing. Let me know as
soon as possible what you think of the idea, and maybe we can
work out something good for you.

If you do decide to visit the University of Georgia,
Coach Butts will arrange for your expenses. I hope you can
make it and we will be looking forward to your visit.

THE UNIVERSITY OF GEORGIA
DEPARTMENT OF ATHLETICS
ATHENS, GEORGIA

UNIVERSITY OF SOUTH CAROLINA
DEPARTMENT OF ATHLETICS
COLUMBIA, S.C.

January 19, 1946

S/Sgt. Darrell K. Royal
Hollis, Oklahoma

Dear Darrell:

Certainly hope you have not made any committments
as to where you expect to attend school on your separation
from the Army.

My plans are more than likely to go to work at
the University of South Carolina on or about the first of
ruary. Spring football will start here on March 1, at
ch time the Spring Quarter will open.

I hope you now have sufficient points for release
March 1, or September 1, and I feel sure that we can offer
a scholarship proposition that you can hardly turn down.
ld like for you to make arrangements to leave home from
furlough in sufficient time to visit us here at the
rsity of South Carolina in Columbia. Your expenses

THE UNIVERSITY OF SOUTHERN CALIFORNIA
DEPARTMENT OF INTERCOLLEGIATE ATHLETICS
UNIVERSITY PARK
LOS ANGELES 7, CALIFORNIA

OFFICE OF THE DIRECTOR

February 7, 1946

S/Sgt. Darrell Royal
38407419 U. S. Army
Hollis, Oklahoma

Dear Darrell,

I was wondering if you had received and dis-
patched your application for admission along with
the transcript of your grades.

I was talking to Boob Myers last Saturday
and he tells me that it is a must that you come
to school out here. As I mentioned in my last letter
the housing situation here is acute but we can
readily find accommodations for you. Do you think
you will be able to enter in the semester beginning
March 1st?

Drop me a line and let me know the current
situation.

Sincerely,

By Raoul Dickson

officially starts March 1st.

UNIVERSITY ATHLETIC ASSOCIATION, INC.
UNIVERSITY OF FLORIDA
GAINESVILLE

March 15, 1946

Mr. Darrell Royal,
Hollis, Okla.

Dear Darrell:

After accepting the job as head coach of the University
of Florida I made a trip to Tampa to see you, but was inform-
ed that you had been separated a few days before.

I am sorry that I did not have an opportunity to talk
over attending the University of Florida, and other information relative to scholarship.

My plans are to be in Texas soon after spring training
and I would like to contact you at that time. Please let
me know at your earliest convenience if you will be in Hollis
at that time.

With kindest regards and best wishes, I remain,

Yours very truly,

R. B. Wolf, Head
Department of Intercollegiate Athletics

Alabama Polytechnic Institute
Auburn, Alabama

DEPARTMENT OF PHYSICAL
EDUCATION & ATHLETICS
CARL M. VOYLES, DIRECTOR

October 26, 1945

Mr. Darrell Royal
3rd Air Force Football Team
Tampa, Florida

Dear Darrell:

Your name has been given me by an Auburn alumnus. I
understand that you haven't been to college and I would like to
invite you to visit Auburn so that we may show you the school
and try to interest you into coming to college here.

In a way of introduction - I graduated from Oklahoma
A. & M.; coached high school ball at Altus, Oklahoma, and coached
at Southwestern Teachers College. I know quite a few boys in Hollis
Oscar Abernathey, the banker there, is a good friend of mine. I
expect your coach and a few men who played football at Southwestern.

Darrell, I would like to hear from you and have you to
pay us a visit if you can.

Very truly yours,

Carl Voyles
Carl Voyles
Director of Athletics

CV:ec

INTERCOLLEGIATE
ATHLETICS

THE UNIVERSITY OF OKLAHOMA
NORMAN · OKLAHOMA

February 12, 1946

Sqd. F 3ol Beam
Drew Field
Tampa, Florida

Dear Darrell:

Since writing you February 8th, I have had a telephone conversation
with Jim Tatum, and he is particularly keen to have you come to
Norman to talk the situation over with us prior to your making your
final decision on attending any other school.

The alumni of the University of Oklahoma, as well as the entire
coaching staff, are very much interested in you and your academic
and athletic future. I am confident that we will be able to make
satisfactory financial arrangements so that you can enter school.

Looking forward to hearing from you in the near future and to seeing you soon, I am,

Sincerely yours,

Walter S. Driskill
Assistant Coach of Football

WSD:djs

Edith and Darrell on the OU campus, 1948. Edith enjoyed his celebrity and enjoyed being part of the team. "Every afternoon, I'd get Marian and Mack all dressed up, and we'd stroll to the Campus Corner drugstore to meet Darrell and drink malts. We had a good time." (Royal Family Archives)

Darrell, Marian, and Mack, 1947. Many of his teammates were married, but Darrell was the only Sooner with a wife and two children. For big "away" games, Edith's mother drove to Norman to stay with the children so Edith could travel with the other wives to watch the team. (Royal Family Archives)

"Darrell was one of the most intelligent, dedicated players I've ever known."

—Bud Wilkinson, head coach of the Oklahoma Sooners, 1947–1963

Chapter 5 HE KICKS WITH HIS HEAD

Norman, Oklahoma, was a small, idyllic college town. Edith and Darrell's second baby, Sammy Mack, was delivered in Norman on February 2, 1947, by Dr. Willard, the Sooners' team doctor. The Royal family was growing, and so was Darrell's reputation. He was already a local celebrity, thanks to his athletic exploits at Hollis High and with the Third Air Force.

He landed a position as a starting defensive back as a freshman, and at the end of 1946 season, the coaches chose Royal and Max Fischer as the "Best Team Players."

The Sooners had been successful in 1946, but the outlook wasn't good for the autumn of '47. Besides losing a lot of players to pro football, the team had a new coach: thirty-one-year old Bud Wilkinson, a first-time head coach who had graduated with an English degree. The Sooners won only two of their first five games, and Wilkinson said later, "I was too young, too inexperienced to be the head coach." Going into the game against Missouri, the OU fans were grumbling. In that game, Royal punted the ball out of bounds inside Missouri's five-yard line three times. The third kick went out at the two, and after the Tiger quarterback fumbled behind the line, OU recovered on the one-yard line. The Sooners beat Missouri 21–12 that day, thanks in large part to Royal's precision punting.

Many years after Wilkinson retired from coaching, Putt Powell of the *Amarillo Globe-News* asked him to choose the most important single play of his coaching career. Wilkinson wrote: "I guess you would have to classify Darrell's three punts which kept Missouri backed up, together with Frankie Anderson's tackle which forced the fumble, as being the most decisive, important plays of my tenure at Oklahoma. I say this because of the effect this victory had on our team's morale and fan support. We did win the rest of our games." For the rest of his life, Bud Wilkinson believed that Royal played a significant role in saving his coaching career.

Although the OU football program and newspaper articles

fudged on Royal's weight, he played at 150 pounds all four years. Still, Royal established himself as someone who could not be kept off the field. He punted, he returned punts, he held for extra points, he played defensive back, and he ran with the ball. And he detested being out of the game.

By the time he was a senior, Darrell had been a three-year starter. Still, Sooner fans were concerned about the '49 season, Royal's last year. Who would replace the amazing Jack Mitchell, widely thought of as the best quarterback in Sooner history? Many OU fans and sportswriters believed that while Royal was an accomplished athlete, he just didn't have the same mastery

over the quarterback position that Mitchell had. The doubters needn't have worried. In the season opener, according to the *Oklahoman*, "'Little Darrell Royal' fooled the Boston College Eagles so completely on handoffs, quickies and laterals" that soon the question became "Who's better—Royal or Mitchell?"

He ran the split-T to perfection. He never left the field unless the Sooners had already salted the game away. And although he was quiet and reserved, his teammates followed him and had faith in him.

After an undefeated regular season, Oklahoma prepared to face Louisiana State University in LSU's backyard, the Sugar

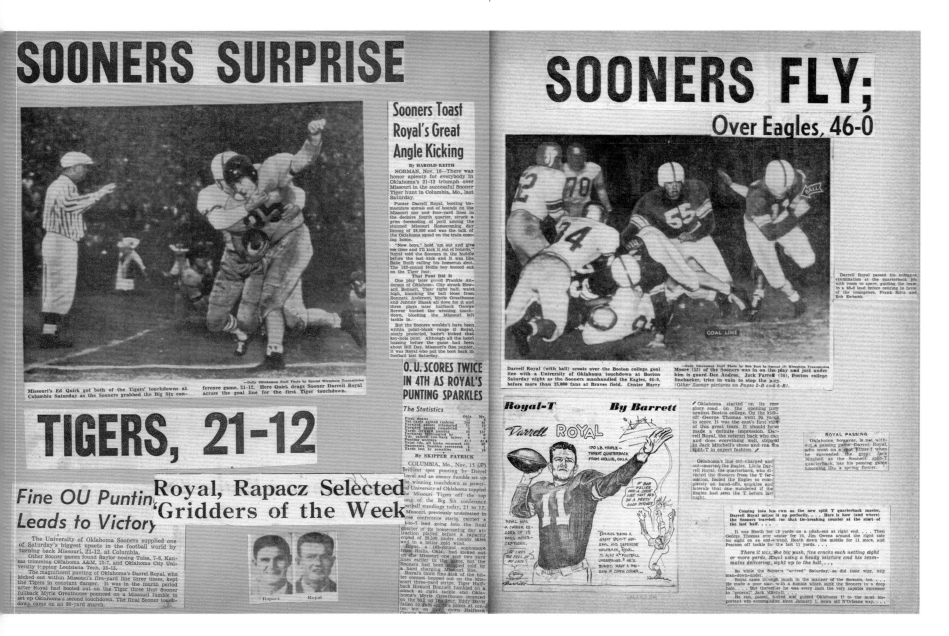

Royal's punting exhibition was pivotal in OU's defeat of Missouri in 1947, a victory that Bud Wilkinson said saved his job. (DKR Papers, DBCAH, di_07342; © 1947, Oklahoman)

Royal had big shoes to fill when he took over for all-American quarterback Jack Mitchell in 1949. He rose to the occasion with a masterly performance and a victory over the Boston College Eagles. (DKR Papers, DBCAH, di_07348)

OLDERMAN

NEA

Darrell Royal's "O" card, indicating that he was a football letterman at the University of Oklahoma. (DKR Papers, DBCAH, di_07374)

Darrell poses outside Oklahoma Memorial Stadium before a 1949 practice. (Royal Family Archives)

Darrell Royal's caricature, photograph, and name dominated Oklahoma sports pages, but his on-the-field dramatics weren't the only reason people were drawn to him. Hal Middlesworth wrote in his column "On the Level" that Royal was "such a standout guy, you ache for him to make good . . . he's one of the best all-round football players ever . . . a real gentleman." (Royal Family Archives; reprinted by permission of Murray Olderman)

Edith's caption: "Biloxi, Miss. Buena Vista Hotel—Played LSU in Sugar Bowl. I went to Havana, Cuba with the team. LSU-0, OK-35. After game, Darrell played in 1st ever Sr. Bowl '50." "I think I made the suit I'm wearing in this picture," Edith recalls. (Royal Family Archives)

Edith and Darrell enjoy a team banquet at the 1950 Sugar Bowl in New Orleans with friends Wade and Jean Walker (left) and Joe Legunec and Virginia Herman (right). (Royal Family Archives)

> **"Don't matter what they throw at us. Only angry people win football games."**
>
> —Darrell K Royal

Bowl in New Orleans. The team stopped over in Biloxi, Mississippi, to conduct practices before moving on to New Orleans.

In what Walter Stewart called "one of the angriest sports rhubarbs of the year," a furious Bud Wilkinson charged LSU with spying on a closed workout while Oklahoma was preparing for the bowl game. LSU denied it, of course, but Wilkinson was not a man given to histrionics or false accusations. The spying incident turned out to be immaterial to the outcome of the game. Walter Stewart wrote in the *Memphis Commercial-Appeal*, "In being hamburgered 35–0, LSU took the most vicious beating in the sixteen-year history of the Sugar Bowl." And the star of this historic victory was "little" Darrell Royal.

Roundy Coughlin, a sportswriter for the *State Journal* of Madison, Wisconsin, who eschewed punctuation, wrote: "This guy Royal he called a beautiful game for Oklahoma. His quarterbacking really was on the thinking side." And, of course, there were his "booming angled punts." Darrell punted eight times that evening; not one was returned.

"Magnificently lucid and economically complete": years later people would attribute much of his coaching success to just

> **"Darrell Royal is the best football player I've ever seen for his weight . . . what a punter he kicks with his head."**
>
> —Roundy Coughlin

Moving from halfback, Royal took just one snap at quarterback in the 1949 Sugar Bowl. His 43-yard pass to Frankie Anderson was OU's lone pass completion of the game. No. 5 Oklahoma defeated No. 3–ranked North Carolina.

Edith wasn't bothered by the attention lavished upon her husband by sportswriters, fans, and overeager coeds: "No. Much of that was just for publicity. As a matter of fact, girls who threw themselves at him always turned him off. He was more attracted to tomboys, women who played golf and were athletes." (DKR Papers, DBCAH, di_07378)

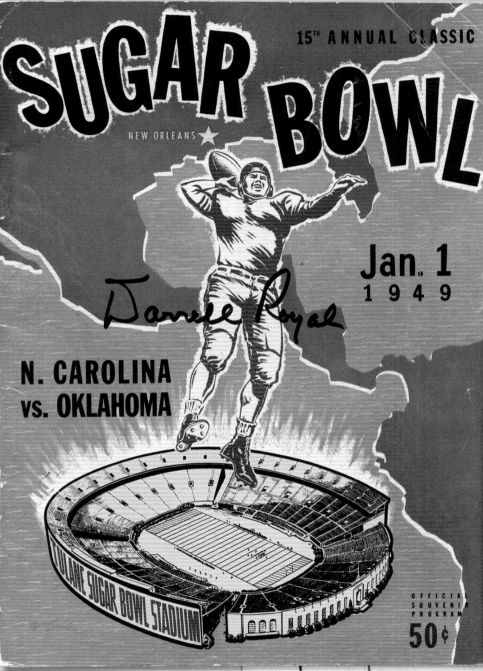

Young fans get their Sooner hero's autograph, 1949. (Royal Family Archives)

'Coffin Corner' Royal Also Holds Running, Interception Records

By ROY ANGEL

When a long Sooner kick goes bounding out on the opposition's 2-yard line, Oklahoma fans don't have to ask who kicked the ball. They know it's Darrell Royal, Coach Bud Wilkinson's fiery half-back-quarterback from Hollis.

Greatest Sooner Kicker

Royal is one of the greatest Sooner spot punters of all time, but that isn't all he can do. In fact, if there's anything he can't do and do well, it hasn't been discovered.

You'll see the wiry 165-pounder in there on defense batting down passes, intercepting passes, tackling hard and running back punts.

And if you look again, the versatile Royal will be in there running the team from quarterback slot, firing a pass or clicking off yards on the ground. He even holds the ball for place-kick specialist Les Ming.

Three Records Held

Royal holds three all-time Sooner records. He has intercepted more passes than any other Sooner in history, 13. He is tied with Jack Jacobs and William Conkright for most pass interceptions in a single game, three.

His 96-yard return of a punt against Kansas State two weeks ago was the longest return every made by a Sooner.

Royal is the only Sooner ever to have been chosen as the nation's "Back of the Week." The Associated Press acclaimed Royal as the outstanding back for his sensational performance this year against Kansas State.

Seven Punts Go Out

All Royal did in that affair was run for two touchdowns and pass to two more scores. On top of that he kicked all seven of his punts out of bounds.

When the Sooners and Missouri clash at Owen Field November 6, Coach Don Faurot and his Tigers will have no trouble recalling Royal.

It was against the Missourians last season that he punted so spectacularly that Oklahoma was able to keep command of the game all the way and win 21-12. Royal's precision boots nailed the Tigers deep in their own territory time after time.

Leading Big Seven

This season Royal has shown that he's plenty dangerous on either end of the punt. He leads the Big Seven in punt return average, returning four kicks for 146 yards for a 36.6-yard average.

He is fifth among loop punters, compiling a 37.7-yard average on 29 kicks. He is also high among the list of leading passers, completing 12 of 25 tosses for a net gain of 183 yards.

In his first season as a varsity player Royal stood out. He and Max Fischer were voted by the coaching staff as the best team players on the powerful 1946 squad.

Played at Hollis

Royal played his highschool football at Hollis where he led Coach Dick Highfill's Tigers to an all-victorious season in 1942. He was later named all-state.

When you see the Homecoming clash next Saturday, just look for

A record holder then and now: More than sixty years later Royal is still in the Sooner record books for punting, punt returns, and interceptions. He is considered one of the greatest all-around players in Sooner football history, 1949, Oklahoman. (DKR Papers, DBCAH, di_07346)

DARRELL ROYAL

OKLA. SOONERS' 165 LB. TRIPLETHREAT HALFBACK —FROM HOLLIS, OKLA.

AND THIS ONE MAKES ME AN EVEN BIGGER THIEF!

HE HOLDS O.U. RECORD OF 13 INTERCEPTIONS (1946-47)

HE'S ONE OF THE NATION'S TOP SPOT-PUNTERS

AH-TH' LAD MUST BE SLIPPIN' HE ONLY PUT IT OUT ON THE FOUR THIS TIME

CONSISTENTLY KICKS 'EM OUT NEAR THE GOAL LINE

BARRET '4

—Daily Oklahoman Staff Photo

Sarge Dempsey, equipment man for the Oklahoma Sooners, gives out a grin as big as OU's 41-7 victory over Missouri as he gets ready to help quarterback Darrell Royal doctor his ankles following Oklahoma's conquest of the Tigers Saturday

> **"Darrell Royal . . . owns one of the most brilliant masses of football cerebellum we've seen caged in one skull . . . Never witnessed better play selection, and that night he gave us a clinical critique which was magnificently lucid and economically complete. He'll make someone a game-winning coach."**
>
> —Walter Stewart, *Memphis Commercial-Appeal*

those traits. It is a rare thing for a man to know unwaveringly what he is destined to do. But Darrell K Royal, while surely not able to predict the titanic success he would one day achieve, knew absolutely what he would do when he graduated. He knew it as a child, he knew it as he was proposing marriage to Edith, and he knew it while he studied at OU: "Pro ball's not for me. I want to coach."

The Sooners lost only six games, and won the last twenty-one, during Royal's time at OU (1946–1949). He received all-American honors in 1949 as quarterback, and although the Sooners went undefeated that season, they were denied the AP National Championship. Royal sat at his breakfast table in the autumn of 2010, thumbing through the brittle pages of scrapbooks from his college days, when a friend asked, "Y'all were undefeated in '49, weren't you?" "Yes, we were." "So why did Notre Dame win the national championship? Why did y'all end up number two?" He glanced sideways as a sly grin crept across his face. "Oh, it's just that same ol' Notre Dame deal, I guess."

Canada calling: In 1950, Royal turned down the then-princely sum of $400 a game to play for the Toronto Argonauts. (DKR Papers, DBCAH, di_07345)

Darrell and Edith on a vacation in Craterville, Oklahoma, 1950. The Royals had built a cozy life in Norman, living in the cocoon of family and friends for four years, but they were about to spend eight years crisscrossing the country as Darrell's coaching career advanced. (Royal Family Archives)

Royal's Teacher's Contract with the City of El Reno, Oklahoma, 1950. (DKR Papers, DBCAH, di_07371)

TEACHER'S CONTRACT
ACCEPTANCE

To the Board of Education of the City of El Reno, Oklahoma (head football coach)

I have received notice of my election as **teacher** in the El Reno City Schools for the school year 1949 -19 50 at a salary of **four thousand five hundred** Dollars ($ 4500.) per year, subject to the conditions hereinafter specified, to which terms and conditions, I agree, and which shall constitute a contract between said Board of Education and myself; provided that neither the School District nor any member of the Board of Education shall be liable for the difference between the total amount of the teacher's contract and the amount of the budget made and approved for this purpose.

I agree that the year's salary shall be divided into — equal parts, and that one-— will be paid at the end of each month.

The salary as specified herein is subject to adjustment at the discretion of the Board of Education, upon final completion and approval of the budget. If Federal Aid becomes available during the fiscal year, salaries will be adjusted in keeping with the regulations of the State Board of Education covering the distribution of such funds.

I hereby warrant that I am qualified for the position to which I have been appointed, and that the statements made in my application heretofore filed with the superintendent are true and correct and if I am unable to meet the requirements of the Board, I agree that the Board may cancel this contract at any time.

I agree that I will obey all rules and regulations of the Board now in force or that may hereafter be adopted during my term of service. I agree to co-operate with the Superintendent, Principal, and my fellow-teachers, and that the Board may revoke my appointment or cancel this contract at any time when I am found to be out of harmony with the school and its policies.

Dated this 13th day of February , 19 50   Signed: _Darrell Royal_

OATH OF ALLEGIANCE

STATE OF OKLAHOMA, CANADIAN COUNTY, SS.

I, **Darrell K. Royal** , having been employed by the Board of Education of the City of El Reno, Oklahoma, do solemnly swear (or affirm) that I will support, obey and defend the Constitution of the United States, and the Constitution of the State of Oklahoma, so help me, God.

Subscribed and sworn before me the 13th of February , 19 50   _Darrell Royal_   Teacher

Walter Wilson   Clerk

NOTICE: If this contract is not signed and returned by the Superintendent by , the Board will consider the place vacant.

EL RENO AMERICAN 6-49-300W 509

Resigned March 13, 1950, to go to N. Carolina State

THE NEWS AND OBSER

State Names Darrell Royal

From El Reno High to North Carolina State: The headline in the Charlotte News and Observer announcing Royal's hiring. (DKR Papers, DBCAH, di_07379)

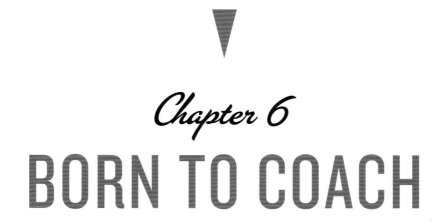

> "I've wanted to coach since I
> could tell a ball from a pumpkin."
> —Darrell K Royal

Chapter 6
BORN TO COACH

He always knew that he wanted to coach. Throughout his four years of playing for the University of Oklahoma, he became a keen student of the game of football. He studied everything his coaches did. He spent hours talking football with the Sooner head coach, Bud Wilkinson, and he paid particular attention to the way Bud interacted with his players. Royal was given permission to sit in on coaches' meetings. "I went to school with guys who, after they finished college, did not know what they wanted to do. I knew where I was headed all the time."

Well, not exactly.

Royal and Edith always figured he would end up as a high school head coach, and he swears that would have suited him just fine.

He accepted his first head-coaching job at El Reno High School on February 13, 1950, with the proviso that if a college came calling before June, El Reno would let him out of his contract. He pledged that he would not leave after June; he knew that trying to find a coach so late in the year would put the school in a bind.

Just one month after signing on with El Reno, Beattie Feath-ers of North Carolina State telephoned Royal and offered him the job of coaching the freshman backfield. Feathers intended to install the split-T offense, first with the freshman team, then the following year with the varsity. And who better to teach them than the all-American quarterback who had operated the split-T to perfection.

Royal had been at N.C. State for one year when Buddy Brothers called from Tulsa, wanting to interview Royal for the varsity backfield job. Brothers offered the young Royal the job right there at the interview, and Royal accepted. It was a raise, and it was a step up. Edith started packing. But the very next day, Bud Wilkinson called. There was an opening on the Oklahoma staff, and Wilkinson wanted to bring Royal back to his alma mater. Royal told Wilkinson what had just transpired in Tulsa, and then he called Coach Brothers. Royal told him of OU's offer, and he made it clear that he hoped Brothers would let him out of his commitment to come to Tulsa. After all, anyone would understand that this was the chance of a lifetime for Royal. Nothing doing. Brothers reminded Royal that he had committed to take the Tulsa job and that he expected Royal to honor that commitment. Only a day and a half had passed since the interview, and Royal had not signed a contract. Still, Brothers thought a deal was a deal, and Royal had to agree. He reluctantly turned down Wilkinson and Oklahoma and his dream job. It was not the last time Oklahoma would call, and it was not the last time Royal would say no.

"Isn't that something?" Edith marveled years later. "At the time, we thought it was the end of the world, but as it turned out, having to say no to the OU job ended up being the best thing that ever happened to us." Coach Brothers gave Royal freedom and

autonomy in running Tulsa's offense. The Hurricanes enjoyed a successful season, and it was another great learning opportunity for the twenty-five-year-old Royal.

Soon, the telephone rang with another offer.

Murray Warmath, the head coach at Mississippi State, called to offer Royal a job as backfield coach. Royal and Edith had been in Tulsa for just one season, and the raise in pay wasn't enough to warrant a move. Nevertheless, Royal knew that moving from the Missouri Valley Conference to the Southeastern Conference was a professional move up.

Darrell Royal accepted the head-coaching job in 1953, with the Edmonton Eskimos of the Canadian Football League. He had been out of college for just three years and had had four jobs.

When the Vancouver sportswriter Jim Brooke met Darrell, his first thought was, "Well, well. Jack Armstrong, all-American boy." His opinion was unchanged after their interview was concluded. There was no artifice in Royal, just the straightforward, earnest manner that would stay with him throughout his life.

Royal Resigns At State;
Former Star For Oklahoma At Edmonton

From Mississippi State to Edmonton, 1953. (DKR Papers, DBCAH, di_07350)

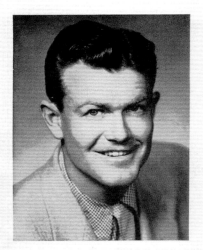

Darrell Royal

Don't let that charming smile and that soft Oklahoma drawl fool you, beneath Darrell Royal's personable exterior there lies a will of iron.

The Eskimo coach is a perfectionist and, while he's not the ranting, shouting type, he believes in drilling the troops until they do it right.

Fans who watched the Eskimo pre-season drills, came away with the opinion that they'd witnessed the best-organized football practices in the west. This is a tribute to Royal's gridiron know-how and the application of that savvy.

At 28 the former Sooner quarterback star is by far the youngest coach in the Western Conference. But he promises to make up in wisdom what he lacks in years.

Royal was an outstanding field general at Oklahoma and although he graduated with a business degree, he has decided to make coaching his life-long profession.

Royal will stand or fall with the split-T formation, which he is introducing to Canadian pro football.

Before signing with the Eskimos last winter, Royal, married and the father of two children, he served as backfield coach at North Carolina State, Tulsa University and Mississippi State.

He has already garnered a reputation as a teacher of young players and the veterans respect him for his methods of instruction.

The youthful looking Edmonton mentor may teach some of the older coaches in the conference that football is a young man's game.

DARRELL ROYAL

Royal was getting noticed in the coaching ranks and by sportswriters, and not just for his football acumen. Melvin Durslag of the Los Angeles Herald-Examiner *was impressed with Royal: "Attired in a good suit, socks that match, and a neatly knotted tie . . . he is the antithesis of the lovable slob image of a coach." Royal's fastidious appearance was more like that of an executive than a coach. (Royal Family Archives)*

In spite of having never seen a professional football game, Royal was hired as head coach of the Edmonton Eskimos of the Canadian Football League. (Royal Family Archives)

"Through mutual agreement, Coach Darrell Royal has become an emigrant.... The coaching abilities of the parting mentor are held in highest esteem ... A man would be hard-pressed to dig up one fan in the city of Edmonton who has anything but the best to say of the ex-coach."

—Red Smith, *New York Herald Tribune*, 1954

////////////////////////////////////

From Edmonton back to Mississippi State, 1954. (DKR Papers, DBCAH, di_07352)

Remarking on the "by gollys" and the "cotton pickins" scattered through the interview, Brooke called Royal a "country boy with Park Avenue talents and instincts." His speech was peppered with aw-shucks expressions. "Golly Ned!" "Golly Pete," or a strong "Gosh all Friday!" were the harshest exclamations he uttered back then. Once, in a pileup during a Mississippi State practice, a lineman cursed a blue streak when one of his teammates fell on his leg. "Let's watch your language, son," Royal admonished. "Cussing won't do any good."

Darrell had never seen a professional football game in his life, yet in Edmonton he would be coaching men who were his age or older, several of them former teammates. Still, Royal felt confident and sufficiently prepared to be head coach. His instincts proved to be right. The Eskimos won their division with a 17-5 record.

And then the telephone rang.

Three colleges approached him about jobs that year, and all three were schools where he had previously worked. But Mississippi State, in the highly regarded SEC, offered Royal the chance he had been looking for: to be the head coach at an American university. Two years remained on his contract with Edmonton, and

"You've got to think lucky. If you fall into a mud hole, check your back pocket—you might have caught a fish."

—Darrell K Royal

the club initially balked at releasing him from his obligation, but Royal finally convinced the board of directors that college football was where he belonged.

Mack Royal says his dad always thought several moves ahead as far as his career was concerned: "He knew he'd been lucky and blessed, but he also worked hard and stayed optimistic." And he was making all the right moves. Coach Royal swears that none of it was by design. He never had written goals—he was just hustling, learning more football, and keeping his eyes open for opportunities, improving his field position with each move.

Noting Royal's rise through the coaching ranks, Jim Brooke commented, "Some people are lucky. And others are like Darrell K Royal."

It was in Starkville, Mississippi, that Royal met Mike Campbell. He was the head football coach at Carr Central High in Vicksburg. His winning record and his cerebral approach to the game of football caught Royal's eye. He would hire Campbell for his University of Washington coaching staff, and for the next twenty-one years, Campbell's defensive genius would be the counterpart to Royal's brilliantly innovative offensive mind. Like Hewlett and Packard, or Rodgers and Hammerstein, Campbell and Royal were good separately, but together they were magnificent, game changing. Their friendship and their like-minded

TEXAS MEMORIAL STADIUM

TEXAS MEMORIAL STADIUM

ATHLETICS

Edited by Bill Crook and Nan Werner

Page 361

philosophy of football were the pillars upon which some of the greatest teams in college football history were built. Royal believed that hiring Campbell was "the best thing to ever happen to me," adding, "Mike was as good a football man as I've ever been around." Edith says, "I think they got along so well because both appreciated the talent of the other. They had supreme confidence in one another. They discussed strategy and game plans, but Darrell just left the defense in Mike's hands. And it certainly paid off."

During their time at Texas, the Longhorns were so dominant that one clever sportswriter wrote, "Two things in life are certain . . . death and Texas."

The two men spent more time with each other than they did with their families. They grew into the best of friends, and so did their wives, Mary and Edith. They reared their children together. Both intelligent men of unquestioned integrity, Campbell and Royal shared a sharp wit, a folksy and unique way of making a point, and an acute curiosity about the world outside football. Pick a topic—just about any topic—and you would find they knew something about it.

In July 1955, the Royals drove from Starkville to San Antonio, where Darrell was to make a presentation at the Texas High School Coaches Association coaching school. After the clinic, Darrell suggested that he and Edith drive an hour north to Austin, just to look around. Edith remembers:

> We came to Austin to look at the campus. We drove all around the stadium; it was not impressive, just concrete, weeds, and barbed wire. And when we drove into Austin, it was dry and kind of ugly. Town Lake was not Town Lake yet, with the trails and such. Austin was not a particularly pretty place. Why he wanted this job, I just didn't know. But I knew that he did.

He had grown up six miles north of the Red River, so even as a young boy, Royal knew about Texas Longhorn football. And after competing against Texas for four years while at OU, he was in awe of the place and the program. He allowed himself to daydream a little: What would it be like to be the head coach at The University of Texas? And how could he get there?

After the tour of Austin and the Texas campus, it was back to Starkville. They stayed at Mississippi State for two seasons, a record for the Royals. And then the telephone rang.

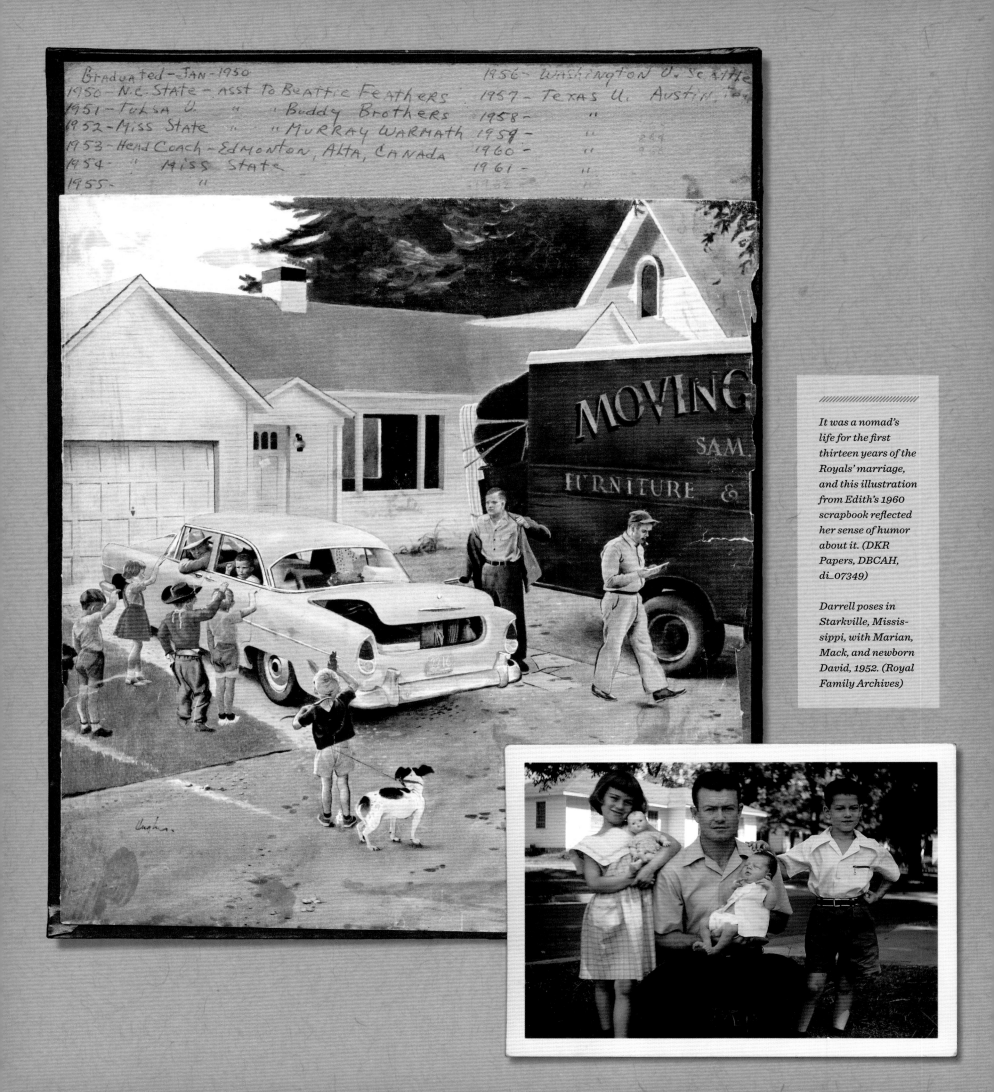

Graduated-Jan-1950
1950-N.C. State - Asst To Beattie Feathers
1951-Tulsa U.   "   " Buddy Brothers
1952-Miss State   "   " Murray Warmath
1953-Head Coach - Edmonton, Alta, Canada
1954- " Miss State
1955-   "

1956- Washington U. Seattle
1957- Texas U. Austin, Tex
1958-   "
1959-   "
1960-   "
1961-   "

It was a nomad's
life for the first
thirteen years of the
Royals' marriage,
and this illustration
from Edith's 1960
scrapbook reflected
her sense of humor
about it. (DKR
Papers, DBCAH,
di_07349)

Darrell poses in
Starkville, Missis-
sippi, with Marian,
Mack, and newborn
David, 1952. (Royal
Family Archives)

People could not believe that Darrell Royal accepted the University of Washington job. The former Huskies head coach, Johnny Cherberg, had been fired during a scandal over a slush fund set up by some alumni to pay players. Dissension had set up camp in the team, and there were almost as many problems at UW as there were players.

Yet Edith never questioned her husband's strategy or his sanity. Whenever the telephone rang with a new offer, she smiled and started collecting packing boxes. As she noted years later, "Darrell and I discussed all his job offers. I knew what he was thinking all along, knew what he was aiming for. We really were a partnership . . . partners in almost everything."

Edith and her husband were yin and yang, complementary pieces composing a whole. She is an open book; he is hard to read. She is patient; he is restless. "He turns the pages of a magazine like someone's timing him with a stopwatch," said a friend. Even after thirty years of retirement, he still gets into that firehouse mode without even realizing it. Edith says, "Sometimes I just look at him and say, 'Darrell, you don't have to make kickoff anymore.'"

> **"If you want to go crazy in a hurry, try changing coaching jobs every year."**
>
> —Darrell K Royal

The Royals were not received warmly at Washington. The UW faculty, disgusted with the excesses of the football program, rose in revolt when Royal was hired for $17,000 a year. It was a battle that Royal would fight for the rest of his career: administrators and faculty complaining about the money spent and the emphasis placed on athletics, particularly on football. The *Daily of the University of Washington*'s poll of the faculty found that 79 percent felt football should be deemphasized; 81 percent felt Royal's salary was too high. One professor wrote anonymously: "Three-and-one-half PhDs with . . . experience superior to our new coach could be hired for his salary. . . . We're all . . . stupid, spending years preparing for an education in specified fields when a man with nothing but brawn and no brains can get $17,000 for chasing a bunch of ninnies around a field with a ball." Carl Walters of the *Jackson Clarion-Ledger* wrote, "Royal is envied—which means he is disliked—by four-fifths of the faculty and . . . they won't extend a helping hand in any way." And this was before he had even arrived on campus.

When they did arrive, the Royals and the other coaches' families moved into the temporary barracks that served as faculty housing. They were not welcomed by their neighbors when they arrived. "The faculty didn't like us one bit, nor did they like us living there. They thought we were rich, remember?" Edith said. Later, they moved from the barracks to the banks of Lake Washington, where every morning Edith drank her coffee on their back patio and watched the rowing crews train in the shadow of Husky stadium.

Adding to the Royals' difficulties, *Time* magazine's April 23, 1956, issue gibed, "Washington was apparently still more interested in victories than its reputation, so it hired young Coach Darrell Royal away from Mississippi State." The article went on to compare Royal's salary with those of professors at Washington.

Washington had half a dozen black players on the team, and because Royal was coming from the Deep South, there were worries about how those players would be treated by the new coaching staff. No one seemed to have uncovered the fact that Royal had coached and socialized with black players in Edmonton, Canada. "If it weren't so insulting, it would have been humorous," Edith said. "We had just moved from Starkville, where we were viewed as being suspiciously liberal! Yet before we even got to Washington, we were suspected of being racists."

Back in Mississippi, a few sportswriters let him have it. Carl Walters wrote that Royal "resigned his Mississippi State post just before spring [practice] was supposed to get under way, repudiated his contract, and lit out for the Northwest." Royal later explained his decision: "The main reason I left Mississippi State was that Washington was a school that had enjoyed more success . . . I felt, and still feel, there are some natural advantages to being at state universities. I decided *that* after coaching at North Carolina State, Mississippi State, and Tulsa—competing *against* state universities. I wanted to coach at a place that had "the" in front of the name." Royal made it plain to the Washington boosters, alumni, and faculty that coaching this team was *his* job. Everyone else was to stay away until he asked for help. Royal's sincerity, his willingness to tackle tough subjects, and his professional appearance and demeanor soon won over the people in Seattle and, finally, the faculty.

The team was another matter. Royal had inherited an undisciplined program, and morale was at rock bottom. He started salvaging things by simplifying the offense and the defense. He installed organized and efficient practices, and he believed in—demanded—hard work from his players and staff. He enforced a "no swearing" rule and attempted to rebuild a strife-torn program with his get-tough policy. "Don't bitch; transfer" became his platform.

Yet he seemed to know innately when to let up on the boys. One evening after an especially grueling practice, he lined up the players for wind sprints. The boys were dog tired and too spent even to complain. "Come on, hustle up," Royal yelled. "On your marks, get set . . . Okay. That's all. Take your showers." "Perhaps then and there," according to the *Minnesota Tribune*, "he

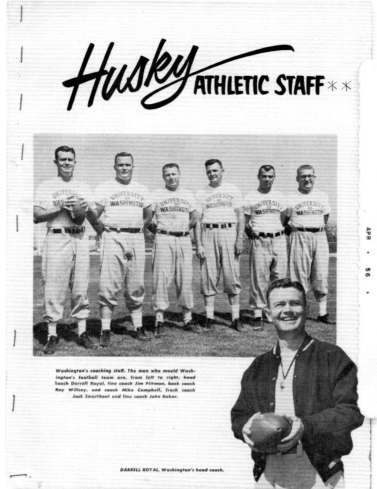

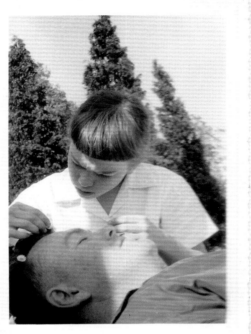

Washington's coaching staff. The men who mould Washington's football team are, from left to right, head coach Darrell Royal, line coach Jim Pittman, back coach Ray Willsey, end coach Mike Campbell, frosh coach Jack Swarthout and line coach John Baker.

DARRELL ROYAL, Washington's head coach.

Darrell Royal's 1956 University of Washington coaching staff. (DKR Papers, DBCAH, di_07353)

Marian enjoying a rare stolen moment with her daddy in Seattle, 1955. (Royal Family Archives)

established himself first in the hearts of Washington, the last place so many other coaches would choose to go."

Royal still studied other coaches and grilled them, not about *X*s and *O*s, but about their psychological approaches to and their relationships with their players. He was still a student of the game, yearning to know more. Clark Shaughnessy, the former Stanford coach and later a Chicago Bears assistant, who possessed a great offensive mind himself, was reading a magazine article one day, an analysis and explanation of the split-T offense. Shaughnessy remarked to a friend and fellow coach, "I don't like the split-T, but this young fellow sure knows his business." The author of the article was Darrell Royal.

In the 1956 season at Washington, Royal went 5-5. He had miraculously calmed the waters, gaining the respect of the faculty and the cooperation of the alumni. He brought stability back to the football program and, perhaps most importantly, erased dissension from the team. One sportswriter commented, "Seldom has any coach ever taken a place by storm as rapidly as Royal has done at Washington." And then the phone rang.

He was leaving again, and again he would be missed. George Briggs, the UW athletic director, expressed the disappointment felt by the Husky community: "I regret this loss very much. I feel Darrell is one of the outstanding young coaches in America. He

has my very best wishes for success at Texas." Dick Day, an all-Coast guard for the Huskies, called Royal the "best coach I've ever been under." The father of another player wrote:

Dear Darrell: We just now heard the news over our television station. Our entire family deeply regrets to hear the news of your resignation. We will, however have the happy thought that your one year at Washington gave our son the opportunity to have been coached by, we feel, the finest coach in America. From remarks made by him, we know that he is proud that he was able to play football under your administration, and that he has the highest regard for you as a man, friend, and coach.

More than five decades later, in a West Austin coffee shop, Edith took a sip of coffee, then turned a crumbling scrapbook page. There, in two-inch-high letters, the December 19, 1956, edition of the *Seattle Post-Intelligencer* announced that Darrell Royal was leaving Washington—after just one year—to go to The University of Texas. "I was very happy in Washington," Edith said. "I was happy everywhere we lived. I would have been happy to stay, but when it was time to go, I was packed and ready. I just trusted Darrell and trusted that each change we made was a step up in his career. Besides, this time we were headed toward home."

Darrell Royal Quits UW; Gets Texas Job

Longhorns Hire Him Away From Huskies

BY MIKE DONOHOE

Football coach Darrell Royal has been hired away from Washington by the University of Texas.

The surprise announcement came from Austin, home of the Longhorns, Tuesday afternoon.

Royal makes the move to the Lone Star State after serving less than a year of a four-year agreement at $17,000 per annum at Washington.

HOWEVER, THOSE CLOSE to the coach have felt all along Royal would be receptive to a top offer. Last fall, when it was general knowledge in the coaching fraternity that Ed Price was in his final campaign as head coach at Texas, Royal told this writer:

"Now there's a job. That's going to be a real plum."

The point being discussed at the time was coaching security, salaries and the restrictions placed on coaches' off-campus activities (recruiting) by the Pacific Coast Conference.

Royal was in Austin Tuesday and met with Dr. Logan Wilson, the Texas president; the athletic council and the Texas board of regents. He was one of 11 coaches interviewed out of a list of 100. Royal was not an applicant for the Texas job. The Longhorns sent for him.

The Husky coach told The Post-Intelligencer he was accepting the Texas job because "well, it's more like home down here. It's close to the homes of my parents and my wife's parents.

"There wasn't any other job or offer that would have taken me away from Washington. I was happy there. So were Edith (Mrs. Royal) and the kids. The Seattle people have been wonderful to us."

Royal was asked if the Texas position involved a raise in salary and he answered "Yeh, a little."

The mentor will return to his home in Seattle this week and make arrangements to move his family to Austin. He will also talk things over with his staff of assistants — line coach Jim Pittman, end coach Mike Campbell, defensive line coach John Baker, backfield coach Ray Willsey and frosh coach Jack Swarthout. Pittman and Campbell come north with Royal from Mississippi. Willsey, formerly of California, played pro ball under Royal in Canada. Swarthout, ex-Montanan, coached at Hoquiam High before coming to Washington. Baker, an all-time USC star, is the lone holdover on Royal's staff from the Cherberg regime.

Regarding his assistants, Royal said:

"I'm hoping some of them will come to Texas with me."

ROYAL, WHO STARRED on the Oklahoma teams of 1947-48-49 (making All-America in his final year), moves in for the second year behind a coach who left a dissatisfied campus. Price, whose Texas team compiled a record of one won and nine lost, was hanged in effigy three times during Texas' worst season in history. Johnny Cherberg, who was fired early last year after a Husky athletic blowup which was the direct cause of PCC investigations and

(Continued Page 22, Column 3)

DARRELL ROYAL
Pulls A Shocker

THE WEATHER

MOSTLY CLOUDY, occasional light rain or drizzle. High 50; low 44. S. winds 10-22 mph. YESTERDAY'S WEATHER: High, 52; low, 48. Record low, 12, December 18, 1924. (Table, P. 35.)

VOL. CLI, No. 110

Players Laud Former Coach

(Continued from Page 22.)

for his leadership," Snider said. "It was a shock to hear he went to Texas. I hope Washington gets a T-formation coach."

DICK DAY, who was named to the Associated Press All-Coast team as a guard, said "we all thought a lot of Royal."

"Best coach I've ever been under," was the remark lineman Don Armstrong made when he was told that Royal will coach at Texas.

Cherberg, who is preparing to take over as lieutenant governor soon, said:

"Royal's going to Texas is a surprise. There wasn't even a rumble about him leaving as far as I'm concerned. I know what Washington should do now. They should hire the best man for the job. He's right on the campus. That's Johnny Baker. He knows the game. He's well liked. He's loyal. Baker was loyal to me and he was loyal to Royal. He knows the state. Baker's a good recruiter, not only here but in California."

Dick Leon, president of the ASUW, which pays the coaches' salaries, said, "It was his decision. He sure made it. There wasn't any trouble at Washington."

The ASUW Board of Control, which must place any stamp of approval on whomever is to be the next Husky football coach, will probably go along with whatever choice athletic director George Briggs makes. Leon said, "We have all the confidence in the world in Mr. Briggs. He says that something should break next month."

Coach Quest

(Continued from Page 22.)

to best represent the University of Washington."

Briggs added that when Texas went after Royal, it vindicated Briggs' judgment of Royal as a man and a coach. "I'll look for a new coach who has the same capabilities," he said.

THE ATHLETIC director said the new coach will have the authority to hire his own assistants and added, "I presume Royal has a similar stipulation in his agreement with Texas."

All of Royal's assistants remain on the ASUW payroll until the termination or renewal of their current agreements. The head coach, however, is severing relations with Washington as of Tuesday but will be on hand to clean up unfinished business later this week,

---

CHARACTER

Seattle

MAin 2000   The

Post-

22

The

What W

Story In

Which high year in Seattle was the Big St the blood press

FLYING
They Held

the big stories

Bill Munc trophy he had the decision wa and later Stan right finally pr cey returning shiny mug und Gold Cup story

Equal in developments.

headlines were all over, both gone, the Husk were slapped and athletic d months before

The rest of

The Pete the Olympic G

Seattle's basketball cha

Luke Sew firing, the hiri place through Jansen were e

Seattle's realm, with J Lesser making

Wilt the UW beating

Shanty wi

The high nament, with Irvine, rolling

Jim McCa weight boxing Golden Gloves

We just Ballard's win the Harry Ma basketball de

They Didn

Peter Wh red mustachio town from Me

The glob largest newspa

AMERICA FIRST · ACCURACY · ENTERPRISE

Intelligencer | **SUNRISE**

of the Great Northwest

Intelligencer Sports

...d., Dec. 19, 1956   M

Royal Quits UW For U. Texas Job

Resigns U.W. Job

...orning After

> ...p   Cup, Grid Rows
>   Win In Walk

...oyal Brougham

...on sports event of the fast-fading ...sted more people the most? Which ...at made the pulse beat faster and ...mp?

Rating the 10 top news stories is an annual custom of this corner. If it creates as much discussion among the fans as it did in the sports department of your morning paper, the fat is in the fire.

In 1956 it was a tie, stand-off, photo finish, dead heat for first place.

The Gold Cup squabble and the Washington football rhubarb led all the rest by a margin as wide as the ocean. In fact, they were ...e decade.

...tter disappointment at losing the ...so fairly; the long suspense while ...g reversed; death of the Slo-mo IV, ...' sudden passing; then—justice and ...g like in the story books, with Mun- ...newly adopted home with the big, ...arm—these were all a part of the

...interest were the explosive football ...ng over from the year before, the ...ing like firecrackers. When it was ...y Cherberg and Harvey Cassill were ...l eventually three other PCC schools ...uspensions, a new coaching regime ...r installed at Washington. It was ...own was back to normal.

...n rank something like this— ...nacher, Nancy Ramey showing in

...l team winning the National AAU ...ship in Denver.

...tormy reign with the Rainiers, his ...Lefty O'Doul, Seattle taking second ...tching of Elmer Singleton and Larry ...ts of the baseball story.

...te dominance of the women's golf ...e Gunderson, Anne Quast and Pat ...national headlines.

...ois and Derby's 92-yard run.
...the Seafair Trophy on the lake.
...a in the state prep basketball tour- ...n High and its great scorer, Earle ...gh to the title.
...inning the National Amateur heavy- ...and the great showing of the Seattle ...in Boston.
...t find room for the Longacres Mile, ...e Thanksgiving Day football game, ...s-Ez Charles fight and the varsity ...f Doug Smart and Elgin Baylor.

...nt To Be Liked

...he man from London with the fierce ...word walking stick, stopped off in our ...ne to rest his writin' fingers.

...ting sports expert of the world's ...London Daily Mirror, talks inter-

Move Unexpected

(Continued from Page 1)

from Oklahoma" moved them up in class.

HIS SUDDEN JUMP from the Pacific Northwest to deep down in Texas was a shocker.

Apparently, George Briggs, UW athletic director, was the only man in authority at Washington in whom Royal confided before he left for Austin.

Briggs said:

"Darrell asked for permission to talk to the Texas people and I gave it to him. I regret this loss very much. I feel he is one of the outstanding young coaches in America. He has my very best wishes for success at Texas."

Briggs pulled a shocker on the so-called "inner circle" of Husky athletics last February by going to Mississippi State to sign Royal. Groundwork had been laid by Briggs' predecessor, Marvey Cassill, and it was generally considered at the time that Joe Kuharich, coach of the Washington Redskins, had agreed to desert the pros and come to Seattle.

ROYAL HAS DONE quite a bit of moving around since he was graduated from Oklahoma in 1950. That fall he served as an assistant to Seattle Feathers at North Carolina State. The following year he was backfield coach under Buddy Brothers at Tulsa U. Then he coached a year at Mississippi State, in 1953, helping Murray Warmath introduce the Oklahoma Split T. In 1954 he went into Canadian pro football, guiding Edmonton to a 16-5 record and the Western Division championship. The next year, when Warmath left Mississippi State for Minnesota, Royal came back to State, receiving a five-year contract at $15,000 per year, plus a rent-free home and utilities. He was with the Maroons for two years, earning a 6-4 record each season in the tough Southeast Conference, mefore Briggs talked him out of Dixie.

APPARENTLY, the Texas people had to do some talking to lure him out of the Northwest. It had been previously announced that, with athletic director Dana X. Bible and coach Ed Price both retiring, the jobs would be combined at a salary of $16,000 a year. The announcement from Texas said Royal would coach, at an undisclosed salary, and Ed Olle

Quits Washington For Texas Job

DARRELL ROYAL, Washington's football coach, resigned unexpectedly as Husky mentor Tuesday to take the post of athletic director and head grid mentor at the University of Texas. Royal coached Washington one year and gave up a four year contract.

The Austin American
Wednesday, December 19, 1956 Austin, Texas—Page 29

OKLAHOMAN DARRELL ROYAL
New grid coach for Longhorns

UT Selects Royal As New Mentor

(Continued from Page One)

me. I know it is a big challenge and it is a tremendous opportunity. I am pleased and flattered that Texas would select me for the position," the boyish-looking Royal said.

Royal, who played his high school football at Hollis, Okla., was a halfback and then quarterback on the Oklahoma teams of 1946-47-48-49.

He was a 1950 bachelor of science in business graduate but went into the coaching profession. He served a year as North Carolina State freshman backfield coach, a year as Tulsa backfield coach and then a season as the Mississippi State backfield coach.

Since then he's been on a dizzy spiral up the coaching ladder, moving into the Texas job, rated one of the top coaching plums in the nation, less than seven years after playing his last game for Oklahoma.

Royal's first head coaching job was in the Canadian league with the Edmonton Eskimos in 1953. He won 17 and lost five games.

He was called to Mississippi State in 1954 to replace Murray Warmath, who had moved to Minnesota. He had 6-4 records in 1954 and '55 both with Mississippi State, each time breaking even in Southeastern Conference games.

He was called by Washington after the big blowup there last winter and broke even in 10 games. His Washington Huskies had a 4-4 won-lost record in the turbulent Pacific Coast League race although handicapped by a team that had some half-year seniors. Washington tied for fourth place with Oregon behind Oregon State, Southern California and UCLA.

Royal, who developed into a fine split T quarterback his last season and carried the Sooners to an undefeated season, is an outstanding disciple of the split T and he plans to continue to use that formation at Texas.

Price too used the split T but Royal probably will boost the number of run-or-pitch options to make it look more like the Oklahoma and Texas A&M attacks.

Royal has been given a free hand to name his entire football coaching staff but said Tuesday he was not yet ready to name his staff.

Still left dangling were the seven members of Price's staff. Chances are only a few of the junior members will be retained. The seven are J. T. King, Charley Waller, H. C. (Bully) Gilstrap, Mike Michalske, Gover (Ox) Emerson, Bob Schulze and James (T) Jones.

Royal said he would have "the same-sized staff" and may bring a few members of his Washington staff along. His helpers at Washington were Jim Pittman, John Baker, Ray Willsey, Mike Campbell and Jack Swarthout.

Here at Texas Royal inherits the bulk of the Longhorns squad that won only one game and gave Texas its worst football season in history.

The Longhorns will have back 31 of their 35 lettermen and have a promising freshman crop coming up.

Olle, 52, has served as business manager of athletics since 1929 and will continue to do so. His contract, like all those at the University other than that of the football coach, will run from year to year.

Olle coached the Texas basketball team during the seasons of 1932-33-34 and his 1933 team, led by Price and Jack Gray, won the Southwest Conference championship. Olle served as business manager even while coaching the basketball team.

He was a three-sports letterman at Texas, in football, baseball and basketball. An infielder, he captained the 1927 baseball team and played professional ball with San Antonio in the Texas League in '27 and with Bisbee, Ariz., in the Arizona State League in 1928-29.

Olle got his bachelor and masters in business at Texas in 1929, He played his high school sports at Flatonia High School and his junior college ball at Texas Military College at Terrell.

The naming of Olle and Royal brought to an end a month and a half of work by the athletic council and an advisory committee of the regents.

At first the searchers tried to coax established big-name coaches to accept the combined jobs of football coach and athletic director, but failing in that turned to a young coach on the way up.

Royal was one of three men whom the group interviewed here since they started their intensive drive Sunday to finish up the job quickly.

He arrived here Tuesday and after a favorable interview was quickly hired and signed.

Although his salary was not disclosed at the time, it will probably become known in short order since it will be published in the next University budget.

Royal, who had permission from Washington to come here for an interview, leaves behind a rebuilding job he was able only to start.

He inherited one of the messiest athletic programs in the nation on Feb. 28 when he signed a four-year $17,000 per annum contract.

The Washington athletic program erupted last winter when the team asked that Coach John Cherberg be fired. First an aide under Cherberg, Jim Sutherland, was fired and then shortly hired as head coach by rival Washington State.

Cherberg was given a vote of confidence and was then forced out. There also came the disclosure of a huge illegal slush fund, operated by Roscoe (Torchy) Torrance, a Seattle businessman.

Finally came a complete housecleaning, in which Henry Cassill went out as athletic director and George Briggs was imported from the University of California to replace him. The hiring of Royal as coach completed the lineup.

However, the illegal Washington recruiting under the Cherberg regime drew a two-year probation term for Washington. The penalty keeps any Husky team from winning a Pacific Coast Conference championship this year and next and also keeps all Washington teams or players from participating in post-season activity. Washington is also deprived of its annual split in Rose Bowl proceeds, which amount to around $26,000 annually, for two years.

At Texas Royal inherits a recruiting program that was scrupulously clean under Price during his six years as football coach.

Although his last year reaped only a 1-9 record, Price still stepped out with a winning record. His overall six-year record was 33-27-1 and his SWC record 20-15-1, which none of the other conference schools topped during his tenure.

Price has been offered a teaching post with the University but has not yet accepted or refused it. He is thought to be considering private business offers and coaching possibilities in addition to the Texas professorial post.

HE BRINGS RAIN

Happy Royal Split T Tutor

Darrell Royal, poised and confident as an Oklahoma split T quarterback, laughingly claimed credit for the rain that fell here Tuesday.

"I brought it with me from Washington," the handsome 32-year-old Royal, who had just been named University of Texas football coach, said Tuesday night in a short and hurried press conference.

"When I went to Washington the sun shined for a week, something that hadn't happened there for a long time. They gave me credit for that and since I apparently brought the rain here with me, I guess I'll take credit for that too."

Royal, who dealt the Longhorns misery as a University of Oklahoma back in 1948 and 1949, said he had no definite plans other than saying he planned to stick with the split T he has used at all of his other coaching assignments.

"I'll use the split T but I don't that '47 game with Texas only for limited play on defense because of an ankle injury.

The 1948 and '49 games both produced 20-14 victories for the Sooners. Royal started at halfback but stepped in and out at quarterback in the '48 games and then started the '49 season as quarterback but didn't get rolling until the Texas game. He had an unsure first half, Texas fans recalled, but got rolling in the second half carried the team to an undefeated season and a 35-0 victory over LSU in the Sugar Bowl.

Royal has been cited as an All-America and he was asked which selections he made.

"That isn't hard," he said. "There weren't many. International News Service and Paramount News."

Royal went to North Carolina State in 1950 as freshman backfield coach. Beattie Feathers, currently an assistant coach at Texas Tech,

As for the Rice-Baylor game Saturday that could give the Southwest Conference championship to Texas with a Baylor victory, Royal drew a parallel with the early days when he took up golf.

"A FELLOW told me that you can't be pulling against the other fellow to miss a putt. You've got to make your own. If you want a championship you've got to play for it instead of depending on someone else to win it for you."

ROYAL'S RECORD

Here's the record compiled by Darrell Royal's teams at Mississippi State and Washington:

WASHINGTON
1956 (Won 5, Lost 5)

UW		Opp.
53	Idaho	21
14	Minnesota	34
28	Illinois	13
20	Oregon	7
7	Southern California	35
7	California	16
20	Oregon State	28
9	UCLA	13
34	Stanford	13
40	Washington State	26
222	Totals	206

MISSISSIPPI STATE
1955 (Won 6, Lost 4)

MS		Opp.
14	Florida	20
13	Tennessee	7
33	Memphis State	0
14	Tulane	0
20	Kentucky	14
26	Alabama	7
20	North Texas State	7
26	Auburn	27
7	Louisiana State	34
0	Mississippi	26
173	Totals	142

1954 (Won 6, Lost 4)

MS		Opp.
27	Memphis State	7
7	Tennessee	19
46	Arkansas State	13
14	Tulane	0
13	Miami	27
12	Alabama	7
0	Florida	7
44	North Texas	26
25	Louisiana State	0
0	Mississippi	14
188	Totals	120

Wilkinson Gives Royal Best Wishes

BARTLESVILLE, Okla., Dec. 18 (UP) — Oklahoma football coach Bud Wilkinson wished his former pupil, Darrell Royal, "all the luck in the world," Wednesday night in his new coaching assignment at Texas, one of Oklahoma's oldest and bitterest rivals.

Wilkinson and Line Coach Gomer Jones of the national champion Sooners were here Tuesday night to attend an appreciation banquet.

When told of Royal's appointment, Wilkinson replied: "What can I say? He is a fine man and a great player and I wish him all the luck on the world."

Jones said Texas was "very fortunate" to get Royal, "and he will do a very fine job for them." Jones was one of several possibilities mentioned for the coaching job.

Wilkinson, who recently put a damper on reports that he was seriously interested in the Texas coaching job, inherited Royal from former Oklahoma coach Jim Tatum. He tutored the Hollis, Okla., high school star through three fruitful seasons.

UT Officials Praise Royal

By CHARLEY ESKEW

A young and personable Darrell Royal joined the University of Texas athletic family Tuesday and everyone in the group felt he is the man to put Longhorn football fortunes on the rebound.

Ed Olle, a veteran University official, was named to become the next athletic director at the same time the school's board of regents and athletic council signed Royal to a five-year-contract as head football coach.

"Royal," said Tom Sealy of Midland, who heads the board, "was selected on the basis of the success he has achieved and his standing within the coaching profession." The new mentor, 32, moves here after head-coaching positions with the 1953 Edmonton team of the Canadian professional league, the 1953-54 Mississippi State teams and the 1955 Washington University team.

"Two of the nation's foremost coaches personally advised us that Royal is one of the most respected and brilliant coaches in collegiate football ranks," said Sealy.

At first it was believed the University would combine the jobs of head football coach and athletic director, replacing outgoing Dana X. Bible and Ed Price, and offer both to one man at a salary approaching $20,000. The University chose to leave the two positions apart, said Sealy, because "It was the feeling of all concerned that . . . it was the best interest of the university to adopt a policy of filling the posts separately."

"Mr. Olle," said Sealy, "was selected because of his long, faithful and efficient association with the department of intercollegiate athletics." Olle will continue as business manager of athletics as well as become athletic director. He takes over the second position Sept. 1 when Bible, who came to the University in 1937, goes on modified service.

Bible said of the new leaders, "You can be assured the University athletic program will be in capable hands. Royal is one of the comers in the profession and we have heard worlds of praise from the people who have been associated with him."

"The University," said Bible, was "fortunate to attract such a promising young coach. He is rapidly making a name for himself in the highly-competitive field of coaching."

Bible said he was looking forward to modified duty at Texas since the press of business would be lessened and there would be more time "with the grandchildren."

Of the appointment of Olle, he said, "I am personally pleased to see a man appreciated and rewarded for his long years of faithful and meritorious service for the University."

Price, pondering whether to continue coaching or accept an administrative job with the University, said Royal was "a very good selection. I've known Darrell as

(See OFFICIALS, Page 34)

Headlines in the Austin American, *December 19, 1956, the day after Royal was named head coach at UT. (DKR Papers, DBCAH, di_07389;* © Austin American-Statesman*)*

> **"Luck is what happens when preparation meets opportunity."**
>
> —Attributed to Seneca the Younger, first-century Roman philosopher;
> adopted by Darrell K Royal, twentieth-century American philosopher

Chapter 7
GONE TO TEXAS

When Royal first arrived at the University of Washington, Ed Price, the head coach of the Texas Longhorns, was struggling in what would be his final year at UT. Royal told Mike Donohoe, a Seattle sportswriter, "Now *there's* a job. That's going to be a real plum." One short year later, after rehabbing the Husky football program and winning over the Washington fans, Royal was climbing the ladder once again. This time, he reached for the plum and grabbed it.

Royal says it happened this way: "The University of Texas had a list of 125 candidates, and my name wasn't on it. That's how much all that daydreaming helped me." The story is well known: after Price was fired, D. X. Bible, the legendary football coach and athletic director at The University of Texas, called Duffy Daugherty at Michigan State to gauge his interest in the job. There wasn't any. Texas then ran after Bobby Dodd at Georgia Tech. He wasn't interested either. Bible was becoming frustrated. None of his leading candidates wanted the job. He called Daugherty back to ask whether he knew of a young coach, someone on the rise, a winner who had yet to be "discovered." Daugherty suggested they look at Washington's young coach. In a separate phone call,

Bible received the same suggestion from Bobby Dodd: take a look at Darrell Royal.

About this time, Southern Methodist University, a Southwest Conference rival of Texas, contacted Darrell to see whether he might be interested in coaching there. Royal told the athletic director, Matty Bell, that he was interested, but privately, he still had his sights on coaching at a state university. He had no concrete reason to believe he might be in the running for the Texas job. Nevertheless, he was really sweating it out, what with SMU's sudden interest in him. He didn't want a repeat of the predicament he had found himself in when he committed to Tulsa one day and then was offered a job at Oklahoma the next.

One night in December 1956, Edith and Darrell had already gone to bed when the phone rang. The telephone operator announced, "Long distance calling for Darrell Royal." Then there it was, the booming voice saying, "Coach Royal, this is D. X. Bible of The University of Texas." Although he has told the story dozens of times since that night, Royal retells it the same way every time, still with a trace of amazement in his voice. "I'll never forget that phone call. I covered the mouthpiece of the receiver with my hand and said, 'Edith, this is it! It's The University of Texas.'" The date for the interview was arranged. On the night before Royal was to arrive, Bible told his wife that he would have to wake up early in the morning—he was going to the airport to pick up the next University of Texas football coach.

The two headed first to a meeting of the Athletics Council, but before they went in, Royal asked Bible to list everyone who would be in the interview room. He wanted their names and positions; he wanted to know what each man looked like and how each should be addressed. The gentlemen of the Athletics Council were blown away. The next stop was the office of Logan Wilson, president of The University. Wilson detailed the school's newly instituted—and controversial—academic standards. He was proud of these high standards, but they were so stringent that they had been blamed for much attrition on the football team. He had been hung in effigy the previous football season. Wilson laid down the law to Royal: "We are going to adhere to those standards and to the rules." Royal had no problem with that.

Things progressed quickly. He had not yet been offered the job, but the process was going so well that he felt increasingly confident. After meeting with the board of regents, Royal was asked to wait outside their room while they made their decision. Royal quickly found a pay phone to tell Edith that the job was his—start packing. By the time Royal made it back to Seattle to gather his things, two of his assistant coaches, Jim Pittman and Mike Campbell, were already on the road to Texas.

When asked about salary, Royal told the regents in earnest, "I'm not going to be hard to get along with on salary. Just don't embarrass me by asking me to come for nothing. And remember, all this is a matter of public record, so make sure you don't embarrass yourself either." Texas offered $17,500, five hundred dollars more than he was making in Seattle. And that was how Darrell K Royal became, at age thirty-two, the deliverer of the Longhorns.

After meeting Royal for the first time, the *Austin American* (December 19, 1956) reported: "If we had to limit ourselves to one word . . . it would be 'sincerity' . . . freedom from hypocrisy, disguise or false pretense . . . not smooth or glib, not a hard-bitten taskmaster like Bear . . . His straight forward approach is more impressive than either Bud or Bear."

Eight jobs in eight years: Royal had established a reputation for being unstable, indecisive, and even, to some, disloyal. At Washington, there were those who resented his not honoring the rest of his contract. For the most part, however, everyone was excited about this decision. Former bosses, former players, and even the people from his home state of Oklahoma were happy for his success. He even received a congratulatory telegram from eight "Hollis boys," Sooner fans all, when he got the job at hated rival Texas. "Whatever Darrell did," Edith observed, "they were always proud of him in Hollis."

On the family's cross-country car trips, most of which were taken as they moved from Norman to Raleigh to Tulsa to Starkville to Edmonton back to Starkville to Seattle, and, finally, to Austin, Edith encouraged the children to look up from their comic books and notice the beauty outside their car: "Look, kids! Look out your windows at this country. We might not come this way again." She said it so often, it became a kind of family joke. This time, however, it rang true; the Royals really were about to take their last cross-country car trip.

Edith was anxious to get closer to home. As Darrell noted later, "When I got back to Seattle, Edith already had the moving van there, with everything boxed up. We didn't even have any place to sit." He was impatient to get to Texas, too. There was work to be done and a couple of his coaches were already waiting for him in Austin. But before Darrell and Edith left the West Coast, they had a promise to keep. Ever since they moved to Seattle, Marian, age eleven, Mack, nine, and David, four, had been begging to go to Disneyland, and their parents promised that one day they would take a family trip there. But Darrell and Edith had assumed that they would be in Washington for years, so the trip to Disneyland got postponed. Finally, without divulging the plan to the children, Edith and Darrell turned south in their black Chrysler sedan with the red pinstripes and Mississippi plates and detoured to Anaheim on their way to Texas. Edith will never forget that trip. "Every time they asked where we were going, we just told them it was a surprise. Darrell and I were excited just imagining how thrilled they would be. I'll never forget the whoop Marian let out when she saw the sign that said, 'Disneyland, 10 miles.'"

Darrell and Edith had driven around Memorial Stadium in 1955 and quietly dreamed about being part of such a grand university. As they drove into Austin and passed by the stadium in December 1956, they knew this was it. This job represented the realization of years of dreaming. As long as Darrell could make the Longhorn nation happy, this would be the last move they would ever make.

He had found his dream job, yet there were a few nightmarish aspects looming. He was dismayed to discover Memorial

University president Logan Wilson presents the Longhorns' new head coach with a "good luck" plaque, 1956. (Royal Family Archives)

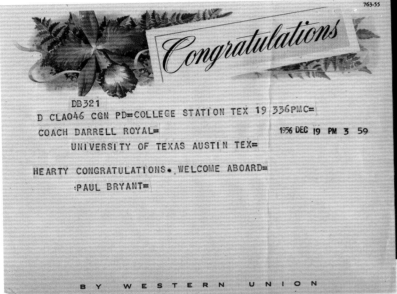

Paul "Bear" Bryant, then head coach at Southwest Conference rival Texas A&M, welcomed Royal to the conference with this telegram. (DKR Papers, DBCAH, di_07339)

> **"He fit Texas to a 'T,' literally. His way of doing business, his persona, his values— he was everything that Texas needed."**
>
> —Keith Jackson, the famed ABC sportscaster, in the documentary *The Story of Darrell Royal*

Stadium in shoddy condition. Years later, Royal's memories of the substandard facilities were still vivid: "The field had a chain-link fence around it, with weeds growing all along it. The practice field was just a big field of goat-heads, or sticker burrs. All of this had a depressing effect on my coaches, but I told them at least we had some things we could improve on."

As soon as the family unpacked the car, he set about his work. And what a lot of work there was to do. The whole complex was embarrassing: dressing rooms needed updating, there was only one secretary for all the coaches, and all the assistant coaches were in one room. Each coach had a phone on his desk, but they had no privacy, so whenever coaches were talking to a recruit or his parents, there might be a dozen conversations going on in that same room. Royal later recalled, "My desk was an old broken metal thing." All of the facilities were subpar, at least according to the standards Royal had in mind for UT. As he later

explained: "I knew that any time I made a correction . . . I was on the correct side. I wasn't overbearing . . . We just couldn't tolerate it the way it was."

"I always tried to stay 100 percent in the guidelines, in the chain of command," Royal said in *Coach Royal: Conversations with a Texas Football Legend*. "My guideline was to [report to] the athletic director . . . to the Athletic Council, to the president, and to the regents. And when I wanted something, I didn't go to the regents and let it come back down. That makes everybody . . . mad—and when you lose, they will get your ass." He was adamant about going through the proper channels, but he was not patient about seeing results. Everything was about to get an overdue overhaul—and fast. Royal oversaw enormous changes in and around the Athletics Department. He added a new "T" room underneath Memorial Stadium where players could study during the week and former lettermen could congregate during home games. He had finally gotten new offices and secretaries for the coaches. The remodeled press box was more welcoming to members of the media. The stadium and the practice field got

> **"Being the football coach at Texas is like being the president of U.S. Steel. And Darrell could run U.S. Steel."**
>
> —Former rival and longtime friend Frank Broyles, head football coach at the University of Arkansas

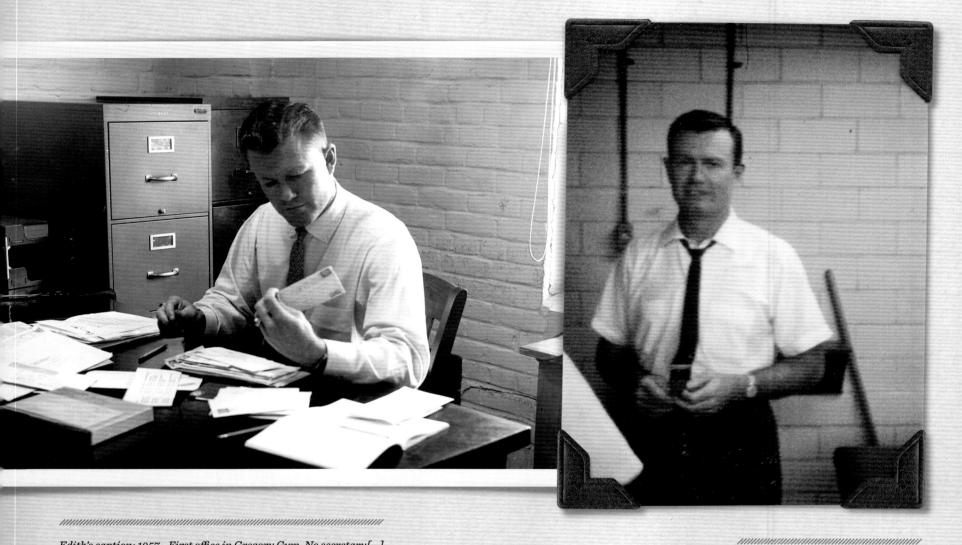

Edith's caption: 1957—First office in Gregory Gym. No secretary[—] Broken furniture—Age 33—Loved his job!" (Royal Family Archives)

Royal in the outdated Longhorn locker room, 1957. (Royal Family Archives)

new turf, the players got new workout equipment, and the stadium got new concessions, stands, and landscaping.

Not all of those changes were well received. In 1962, Royal changed the game uniforms from bright orange back to the "burnt orange," or Texas orange, of the Clyde Littlefield era (1927–1933). It stood to reason that a school with UT's unique history and unique mascot should have a color unique to its program. Alumni unfamiliar with the history sent outraged protests to the administration, demanding a return to the "true school colors."

> **"Hell, no. I'm not gonna candy this thing up. These are work clothes."**
>
> —Royal's response when someone suggested he add a burnt orange stripe on the outside of the Longhorns' uniform pants

In 1967, after an eight-month study, a committee recommended that burnt orange be the official color of The University.

Royal didn't limit his work to just Xs and Os. He immersed himself completely in the community of burnt-orange bloods, who were thirsty for a winning program. There had been little stability in the football program since D. X. Bible retired as head coach in 1946. Royal met with alumni groups—"Goodness knows how many March 2 [Texas Independence Day] meetings I went to"—spoke at high school banquets, and visited with as many current players, faculty members, and high school coaches as possible. His staff traveled to track meets all over the state of Texas; at the time, there was no limit on recruiting visits. Schools recruited year-round. Dan Jenkins wrote in *Sports Illustrated* that when Royal arrived at Texas in 1957, he was

> cautious, grim, tense, self-conscious, ambitious. If he had a sense of humor, it failed to show. The team he inherited had a 1-9 record the previous season and Oklahoma had beaten Texas for five years straight . . . He did not even have a secretary. Was any of that supposed to be funny?

Royal made an immediate impression on the players he inherited from Ed Price. Bobby Lackey, a UT quarterback from 1957 to 1959, recalled: "When we had our first meeting with Coach Royal, you just knew things were about to change. He had a charisma and cockiness that rubbed off on you. He was sure of himself at a young age." Jim Bob Moffett, who played tackle on the 1959–1960 team, noted: "He was bigger than life . . . Here was a guy who'd been all-American at OU, coaching at Texas." And Bobby Gurwitz, who started at halfback (1958–1960), remembered: "Coach Royal changed a lot of things when he came to Texas, and one of the first was that he brought discipline to the program. He cleaned up the

"You don't take over a team that has lost nine games and inherit a warm bed."

—Darrell K Royal, when asked in 1957 about the outlook for his first team at Texas

dorms. Anybody who didn't want to behave, didn't want to act like a gentleman, didn't want to obey the rules, they were gone."

Workouts at the practice field down by Waller Creek were grueling; the competition among teammates was tough. But players always knew where they stood. Each day before practice, the trainer taped the new depth chart to the inside glass of the trainer's office. Players could see at a glance whether they had moved up or down in the lineup.

"What you came to understand," Gurwitz said, "was that if you went all the way for Coach Royal, he'd go 110 percent for you. If you didn't, just turn in your jersey . . . It was all about work habits, sticking to something, having a plan." The results of Royal's "sic 'em" football philosophy were immediate: aggressive defensive attacks, emphasis on the kicking game, a simplified offense. He knew that a confused player could not be an aggressive player.

The players weren't the only ones putting in long hours. The schedule Royal established for his team of coaches and himself during the season was grueling. He left nothing to chance, overlooked nothing. Monday brought another week of practices, press conferences, recruiting calls, and Longhorn Booster Club appearances. During the week, the coaches broke down film, assessing the strengths, weaknesses,

The 1957 Longhorn coaching staff invigorated the program, taking a 1-9 team to a 6-4-1 season. (1958 Cactus, Texas Student Media)

Left to Right: Darrell K. Royal, Raymond L. Willsey, Harold Jack Swarthout, William Mike Campbell, James Carroll T. Jones, Robert Clayburn Schulze, James N. Pittman, Charles Norris Shira.

and tendencies of their next opponent. They reviewed film to evaluate their own players.

They were up early on game days to eat with the team in the dining hall of Moore-Hill dorm. Before night games, Royal drove the two miles home to catch a game on television and maybe a nap. Then, back to campus: eat the pregame meal, cross the street to Memorial Stadium, get uniforms and game faces on.

After his postgame press conference at the stadium, he and Edith, UT staffers, sportswriters, and friends gathered at suite 2001 of the Villa Capri Hotel for a more informal get-together. Most Sundays the Royals attended church with their children, then Darrell was off to tape his television show at station KLBJ. Sunday afternoons were for watching more film and planning strategy with his coaches.

In Royal's first season at Texas, the Longhorns finished with a 6-4-1 record and took second in the Southwest Conference. In spite of a 39–7 flogging in the Cotton Bowl at the hands of Ole Miss, morale and expectations were sky high. Royal had taken the state of Texas by storm, and he impressed the national media as well. After just one season at Texas, Royal was named to *Playboy*'s 1958 preseason all-America team as coach of the year.

It took Royal three years to climb to the top of the conference. Texas tied for the SWC championship in '59, but UT lost to Syracuse in the Cotton Bowl. The following year, 1960, the Longhorns tied for second in the conference and ended the season by tying Alabama 3–3 in the Cotton Bowl. That was as close as the legendary Bear Bryant ever came to beating Darrell Royal.

* * * * *

As Royal's popularity grew, he became more in demand as a public speaker. Royal pushed himself to polish that craft. He owned two books on the subject of delivering effective speeches, and Edith remembers how he studied those books over and over, practicing, making notes in the margins. He pushed himself to be better, and eventually became a poised speaker, blending humor with motivation.

But this confidence didn't come easily for the shy Royal. While an assistant coach at North Carolina State in 1950, he had been asked to speak at a high school sports banquet. He came prepared, of course, and knew precisely what he would say. But when the time came to address the audience, he choked. He could not remember one word he had planned to say. He ended up offering a red-faced "I'm sorry," and suffered in shame through

> **"The basic formula of winning football is so elemental. You can cloak it under fancy names, sew ruffles on it, run it up the flagpole, but it's just as simple as a screwdriver . . . It's the team with pride that rakes in the chips."**
>
> —Darrell K Royal

the rest of the banquet. Afterward, the booster club representatives presented Royal with a pair of cuff links. Embarrassed and disgusted with himself, on the drive home he pulled his car over, got out, and threw the cuff links as far as he could. He either had to defeat this terror or get out of coaching. Since coaching was his dream, he had no choice. He had to tackle his dread of public speaking.

He turned to his friend Bill Alexander, an Oklahoma City preacher who was a dynamic public speaker. Alexander gave Darrell a poem to memorize, and Royal studied the poem as if it were a playbook. When he felt he had the delivery down, he called Alexander and announced that he was prepared to perform. Royal recited the poem over the telephone. Rather, he sang it: "Ta-*da* duh-*da* duh-*da* duh-*da*."

"Good grief," Alexander said, "you're supposed to be telling a story, not singing a song." Darrell went back to the drawing board, this time considering the meaning of the poem as he memorized the words and the cadence. The poem, "The Bridge Builder," by Will Allen Dromgoole, tells of a lone traveler who crossed a churning river, then turned around and built a bridge across that same river. Observing this work, a fellow traveler asked why he built a bridge over a river he would never cross again. The bridge builder answered:

> *"Good friend, in the path I have come," he said,*
> *"There followeth after me today,*
> *A youth whose feet must pass this way.*
> *This chasm that has been as naught to me*
> *To that fair-haired youth may a pitfall be.*
> *He, too, must cross in the twilight dim;*
> *Good friend, I am building the bridge for him."*

The coach can recite it to this day.

By the time Royal came to UT, he was an accomplished motivational speaker. In 1959, Putt Powell, a sportswriter for the *Amarillo Globe-News*, reported on one of Royal's performances:

> Persons attending the first annual Tascosa High School Football Banquet last night might have been hearing a coach who will rank as one of the all-time greats. . . . He certainly looks like the hottest young coach in the business right now . . . It was amazing the way he won the guests at the Tascosa banquet. He had the players practically on the edge of their seats. Some of the red-hot Oklahoma Sooner followers looked like they were ready to drop their Big Red allegiance.

One of the most dramatic changes
Royal's staff made was the effi-
ciency with which they practiced.
Royal ran his practices like Henry
Ford ran his assembly line. He
stood atop his iron tower to get a
bird's-eye view of both offense and
defense. Drills were structured,
sequential, timed. At the blow of an
air horn, players changed stations.
They knew exactly where to go and
what to do next. Simplification and
repetition—there was no standing around, no wasted motion.
(Royal Family Archives)

Left to right: *Edith with her younger brothers, Charles Ray and Billy Wayne, 1931. Edith says, "I was always a caretaker, from the time I could hold my baby brother on my hip. I just went straight from taking care of them to taking care of my own family. It may sound simple, but I was Darrell's wife and the kids' mother and that's what I wanted to be."* (Royal Family Archives)

Edith and Darrell at a meeting of Texas Exes in Dallas, 1966. Edith was the consummate coach's wife, splitting time between traveling with Darrell and anchoring things at home in Austin. (Royal Family Archives)

"I'm aware that some people see me only as Coach Royal's wife, and that's perfectly all right with me. That's what I am. That's how I got here. Sometimes—now, later in our lives—he reminds me that I'm the only girl he's ever loved, and he thanks me for staying with him through all we've been through. I just tell him, 'Well, you got me out of that cotton patch, so thank *you*.'"

—Edith Royal

"There must be a special place in heaven for coaches' wives."

—Paul "Bear" Bryant, legendary coach of Texas A&M and Alabama

▼

Chapter 8

COACH ROYAL'S WIFE

Edith Royal loved the football life. She had never seen a football game until she was sixteen and started dating Darrell, but from her first game in Hollis, Oklahoma, until he retired as UT athletic director at the age of fifty-five, it was the only life she knew.

She is Darrell Royal's wife. She is Marian, Mack, and David's mother. She is "Mama Edie" to her grandchildren, Christian Kazen, David Kazen, Sammy Royal, and Elena Royal Trombetta, and to countless other friends, orphans, college students, and musicians she has "adopted" over the years. Finally, she is "G-G" to her twin great-granddaughters, Isabella Marian and Alexandra Jeanne Kazen. She is perfectly content with those titles.

She never attended college and never particularly cared to. She hasn't held a paying position since she was pregnant with her first child. Married to a man who was idolized by millions, she has shared him with football fans and country music lovers and golf fanatics across the world. Many women would have been intimidated, but while she is immensely proud of being the partner of Darrell Royal, she moves with the confidence of someone who knows her worth.

Her friends will tell you she is so much more than just a wife. She has been Darrell's patron, his administrative assistant, and his financial adviser; she worked out the details of their life so he could concentrate on his. Darrell brags, "She was an excellent coach's wife. We had eight jobs in eight years . . . She never hesitated to move, never complained. She was an understanding travel companion. There's just not a lot of wives who'd put up with having eight jobs in eight years."

"And while I'd like to stand up here and humbly accept these honors, I must follow the lead of the man whose birthday you honor on this occasion and tell the truth. Without this little lady sitting beside me, there wouldn't be anyone in this room who would even know my name. I'd like to present the best thing to happen to this football coach, or any other . . . my wife, Edith."

—Darrell K Royal, accepting the Mr. South Texas Award
at a George Washington's birthday celebration, 1972

Left to right: *Darrell, Edith, Gregory Peck, Veronique Peck, and Doris Day, 1964. Darrell and Edith lived in two different worlds. One was a public sphere of privilege and photo ops and private jets. The other world they inhabited—the real world—included budgets, carpools, doctor's appointments, and the dry cleaners. When the doctor's office called to verify the dates of the family's smallpox vaccinations for an upcoming vacation to Cuernavaca, Edith scribbled the information on the first piece of paper she could find: the back of a personal letter from their friend, Academy Award–winning actor Gregory Peck. (Royal Family Archives)*

When Texas played USC in Los Angeles in 1967, the legendary actor John Wayne visited the Longhorn sidelines to watch practice. (Royal Family Archives)

Edith's delights are her twin great-granddaughters, Isabella and Alexandra, who share a July 6 birthday with "Daddy Darrell." (Royal Family Archives; photo by Cindy McWilliams)

Edith beams at her husband after the Longhorns presented him with his first bowl game victory, a 12–7 win over Ole Miss in the 1962 Cotton Bowl. Celebrating with the Royals is Colonel D. Harold Byrd. (Royal Family Archives; photo by James Langhead)

We spent 3 days as guests of Peck's
Universal Studios on set of
"Send Me No Flowers" w. Rock Hudson   Feb. 1964

Gregory   Veronique
Peck   Peck

Doris
Day

Admitting to a case of
nerves before football
games, Royal said:
"I'm the world's biggest
coward. I run scared all
the time. As Eisenhower
said, 'Just before the
election, the opposition
looks twelve feet tall.'"
(Royal Family Archives)

Darrell

Mortgage	218.00
Insurance	109.00
Church	100.00
Phone	15.00
utilities	25.00
Plymouth (Gas oil mtn.)	20.00
laundry & cl.	10.00
drug	10.00
haircut & shines	5.00
Yard mtn. charity	
dentist, gifts, toys	
Sunday school, meals out,	
clubs, home repairs.	
investment club	50.00
clothes	50.00
	612.00

Once a year

Car ins. about 150.00
license plates 35.77
Insurance 1959 - have pd. $260.
taxes-
Sept. 5 2-2000
N.Y. Life -20-743-40L }400 - 106.84
2-5000
Sept. 5 22-481-913 }-912 - 314.00
20-002
Aug 30. 25-500-343 - 437.20

Edith

Gro. meals out - school parties lunches and milk	135.00
Clothes for 4	100.00
Chrysler (gas oil mtn.)	20.00
Maid and sitter	75.00
movies, mag., papers	5.00
school bus	5.00
beauty parlor 6.00 & haircuts 2.50	8.50
gifts, linens, books	
records, clubs, postage	
film, dishes & home	
furnishings	80.00
school supplies	1.50
Childrens allowances	10.00
dancing lessons	10.00
	450.00

Blue Cross 3 times year 143.00
tires and seat covers 100.00
Income 1458.37
tax 212.50
6 months a yr. 89.50 89.50
1156.37
1062.00
Savings 94.37

Edith, with Lan and Kathryn Hewlett, helping out at a University of Texas faculty tea, 1967. She relished being a coach's wife and faculty spouse, even though it meant juggling her roles as mother, housewife, community activist, hostess, and school volunteer. (Royal Family Archives)

Today, Edith swears it was no struggle.

There was nothing to complain about. I was as excited as he was about new opportunities, about football season, and about their success. I felt very much a part of things, like a teammate. I knew my job was important, and he knew it, too. *My* job was to take care of everything else—everything—so he could do *his* job. I see now that I gave him lots of freedom to do whatever he needed or wanted to do. He didn't have to worry about anything at home or me or the kids, because he knew I was taking care of it. I was the worrier of the two. The only thing that worried him was losing football games. And, from the vantage point of sixty-six years later, I guess it worked, although there were times I wasn't too sure it would.

Darrell grew up kicking a football, and I don't know what he'd do if they didn't have such jobs for grown men! I wouldn't change any of it. It's all I've ever known. It's all he ever wanted.

A coach's wife must possess a thick skin. Before luxury suites ringed the top tier of Memorial Stadium, the coaches' wives sat in the stands with the spectators. A "good" coach's wife did not respond when fans called her husband an idiot for punting on third down. She ignored it when the newspaper or anonymous letter writers insisted he was playing the wrong quarterback.

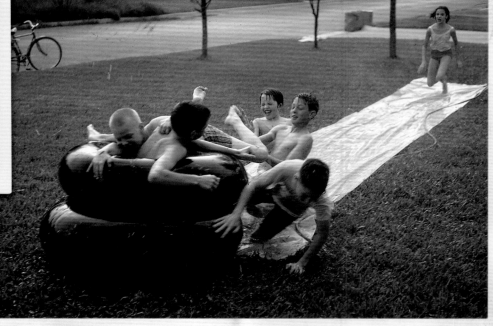

When a reporter called the Royal's home to announce that Darrell had been chosen the 1963 coach of the year, eleven-year-old David Royal answered the telephone and scribbled the message on a yellow scrap of paper for Edith to find. (Royal Family Archives)

A "good" coach's wife did not get her feelings hurt when fans or admirers overlooked her or crowded her out of the way. Edith swears:

> I never let any of that stuff upset me when things got bad. I believed in Darrell and figured he knew what he was doing. I just let that stuff roll off my back. But thank heaven we didn't have the Internet message boards back when Darrell was coaching. That stuff can be destructive.

Through the years, through every move, Edith saved everything. Her worn scrapbooks are full of reminders that even celebrities with seemingly glamorous lives still must deal with the aggravations of everyday life. Edith's kitchen in their home on Belmont Parkway was a study in organized clutter. Opened mail stacked on the kitchen counter by the phone was intermingled with church bulletins, PTA notices, and scribbled reminders. The phones rang constantly, and the mail sometimes served as a message pad when scratch paper couldn't be found.

For all the fame and all the fawning that came with being a Royal, Edith tried her best to maintain a semblance of normality when their children were living at home, but it was tough to have a "normal" life considering the adoration that was showered upon their father. Nonetheless, Mack remembers: "We really were a happy family. We kids were disciplined and well mannered. We knew that when Dad was on the phone at home, we were to quiet down. When it was time to move to another town, we moved without complaint. Mom did all that. She made us all feel we were an important part of Dad's job. We were happy, and a lot of the credit for that goes to Mom."

As youngsters, Marian, Mack, and David were surely aware that they received more attention and more perks than their friends did, but it wasn't until they were older that they understood that their father was "DKR." One night around the supper table, Darrell told Edith and the kids about his latest trip. He had just returned from Del Rio, Texas, where he spoke at a local

David and his friends set up a slip-and-slide in the front yard of their house on Belmont Parkway. The Royals' neighborhood was full of kids, and they usually found their way to the Royals' house. (Royal Family Archives)

Darrell poses with (clockwise from left) Sammy Royal, David Kazen, Christian Kazen, and Elena Royal Trombetta. Edith and Darrell are never so happy as when they are surrounded by their grandchildren. (Royal Family Archives)

Marian, David, Edith, Mack, and Darrell, boarding a plane for a trip to Houston in the airplane of their friend Johnny Holmes. (DKR Papers, DBCAH, di_07354)

To: AUSTIN, TEXAS

Even before winning his first national championship, Royal was one of the most recognized faces in the country. This envelope, postmarked "Los Angeles" and containing no mailing address other than Darrell's photograph and "Austin, Texas," made it to the Royal home on Belmont Parkway. According to Edith, "He just never understood that he was famous. He is surprised to this day when someone wants his autograph. It's always been like that. We remember what we came from." (Royal Family Archives)

chamber of commerce banquet. The owner of the local theatre had picked up Royal at the airport in an orange convertible with the top down, and he insisted that Royal sit on the back of the car and wave as they paraded through downtown Del Rio. Darrell refused at first, but finally, as they neared the hotel where he was to stay, Royal relented and rode the last few blocks sitting on the back of that orange convertible. As they turned the corner, Royal heard, then saw, the Del Rio High School band playing "The Eyes of Texas" on the steps of the hotel. The mayor and city and county officials were there, waiting to shake his hand and have their pictures taken with him. The spectacle had embarrassed Darrell. Six-year-old David Royal listened pensively, then asked innocently, "Daddy, who did they think you were?"

On game days, the kids stepped softly around Darrell. He was

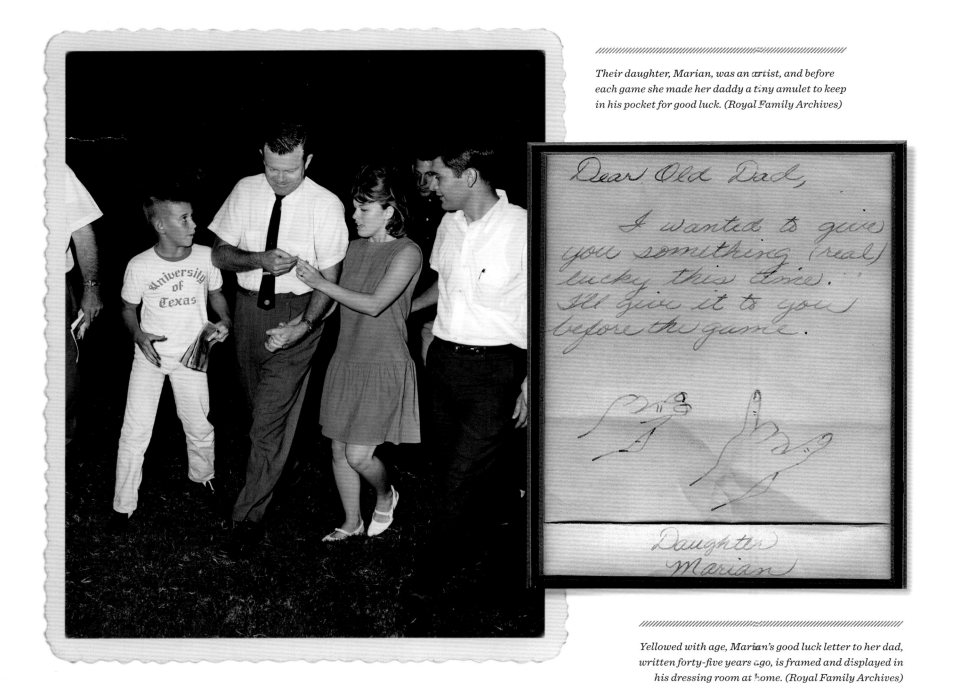

Dear Old Dad,

I wanted to give you something (real) lucky this time. I'll give it to you before the game.

Daughter
Marian

tightly wound, single-minded, going over plays and schemes and situations. Yet even though they knew when to leave their father alone, the whole family was involved in his job. David Royal sold programs at Memorial Stadium for years. His parents hoped it would teach him math, but "he never seems to come out with the right change at the end," Edith claimed. Darrell gave Mack, and later David, full access to the sidelines, to the locker room, to the team buses. Memorial Stadium was their playground, their backyard, and if they wanted to see their dad, Memorial Stadium was where they needed to be. Sometimes before games, Darrell gave Marian diagrams of specific plays to look for. Against Texas

Tech in 1960, he gave her a diagram of the opening play. As the game began, Marian nonchalantly explained the unfolding pass route—which resulted in a Texas touchdown—to her date. Darrell and Edith made sure the whole family was part of the team.

* * * * *

Edith laughs easily. Her hair is soft and white, uncomplicated, and she wears makeup only on special occasions. Her eyes are as blue as they were the day she met Darrell. She has as many fans, it seems, as her husband does. Her friends idolize her. She is a kind

woman who doesn't hand out unasked-for advice. But if you ask, and if she answers, it won't be sugarcoated or sanitized. She pays attention. She listens, and she remembers.

What kind of daddy was DKR? Edith answered the question recently and answered it honestly.

> You know, he was rarely there. He was at the stadium or recruiting or at a speaking engagement or an awards banquet or a celebrity golf tournament. When he was there, he was on the phone either to fans or friends, musicians, or other coaches. He left his assistant coaches alone at night, but he'd talk to coaches from other schools till all hours. I don't like to talk on the phone, but Darrell loved it. He still does.

Even today, when their phone rings, Edith has to be quick on the draw to answer before Darrell does.

She explains that his life's work was a twenty-four-hour-a-day passion.

> And the hours he spent watching film! He'd get up and study film in the middle of the night. I'd wake up at 2:00 a.m., and he'd be in there, breaking down the film play by play and making notes. When things got bad, when he was so tense and focused on football that he couldn't see anything else, I just left him alone, let him have his space. He talked to people on the phone all night long. He just did whatever he needed to do, and we let him do it at our house. I did anything that he needed me to do to support him. The children did, too. When they'd start whining about him not being there, I'd say, "Well, your daddy has to do this or that. It's part of his job." And they just adapted, although I know they wanted more of his attention.

> Every once in a while—not very often—I'd get on him about spending time with the kids. When David Royal was playing Pee Wee football, I told Darrell it seemed to me that David knew nothing about the game. I suggested that Coach Royal might want to teach his boy something about football. Darrell puffed up and said, "Well, that's nonsense. Of course he knows football." So, after Pee Wee practice one day, Darrell got David in the car and said, "David, do you know what a first down is?" David smirked, "Sure, Daddy. It's those lines that go across the field!" Darrell grimaced a little, embarrassed. But he still didn't teach his boys anything about the game. He never wanted to push it on them.

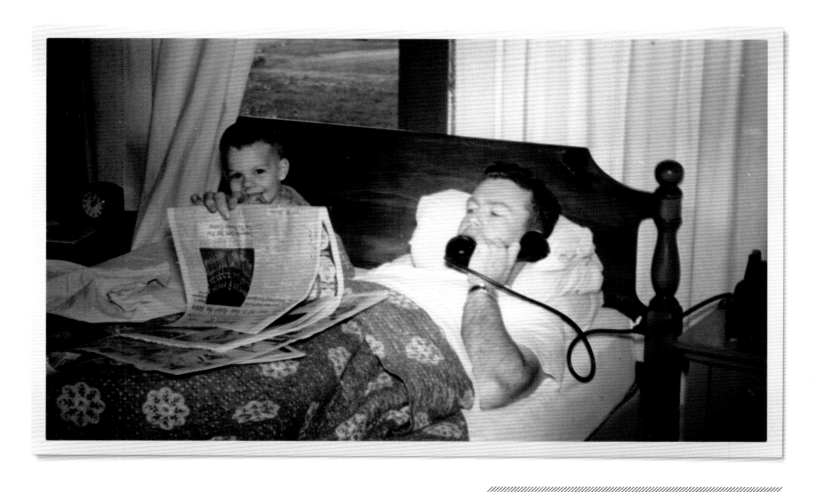

Darrell multitasks, talking football while watching son David and catching up on the news, 1954. (Royal Family Archives)

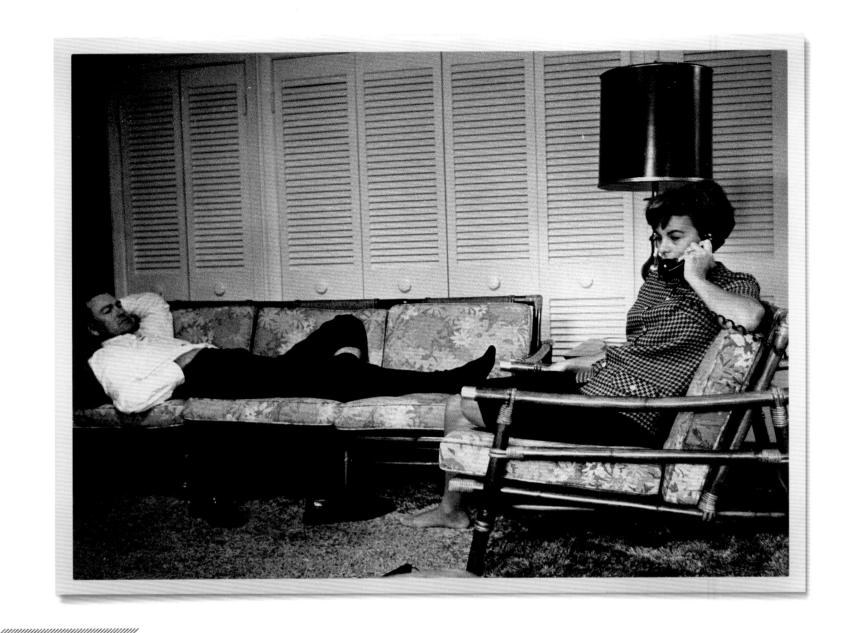

Gift giving is one of her greatest joys, and the presents are thoughtful and meaningful. She is generous with her own possessions, and she believes in regifting. If she owns something that she thinks will be perfect for one of her friends, off it goes to a new home. One friend, a football fan, admired Edith's football-shaped key holder while they were eating breakfast. Before she could blink, Edith's keys were off and she offered the key holder to her friend: "Let's trade." Last year, Edith's friends wanted to throw a birthday party for her. Edith consented, but with one condition—she was the only person permitted to bring presents. She presented a crystal delphinula seashell to a friend who loves the beach. A hand-painted scene of Kenya went to a friend who had recently returned from Africa. "You can't imagine what fun it was to go through my things and choose just the perfect gift for each friend!"

Although some may call her an angel or a saint, she is one with a mischievous soul. There is the story of the night three decades ago when she and a girlfriend jokingly threw their bras onstage as their friend was performing. Or the one about the day she was riding horses with a group of women. They were all sweaty, hot, and smelling of horses. They came back to a friend's swimming pool, and when three friends disrobed to go swimming, Edith peeled off her clothes and jumped in, too.

Edith tells this one on herself: Walt Garrison, the former Dallas Cowboy running back and a cowboy in real life, was a longtime spokesman for Skoal smokeless tobacco, or snuff. Edith found herself fascinated with the ritual of snuff dipping and peppered Walt with questions about it. Finally, she said, "Show me how to do that. I want to try it." Walt refused, saying, "Now, Edith, it'll just make you sick to your stomach. Everyone gets sick the first time they try it." Edith insisted he show her how to put the dip "between your cheek and gum," so he relented. She sat and practiced spitting, and pretty soon the room started spinning. She was determined, however, not to give him the satisfaction of being proved right. So she sat with him for an acceptable amount of time, spit the snuff out, and casually announced that she was going up to her hotel room for a nap. She recalls: "I was sick as a dog and sprawled out on the bedcovers. When Darrell came into the room, I warned him, 'If you so much as touch this bed, I'm going to throw up. And if you dare tell Walt Garrison I got sick to my stomach, I'll never speak to you again.'" Walt bragged on Edith after that, "Man, she's tough. She's the only person I've ever known who didn't get sick the first time they dipped."

* * * * *

Edith is passionate about her "other" life's work—promoting education about drug and alcohol abuse and recovery. When the Palmer Drug Abuse Program first opened a chapter in Austin in the early '70s, Darrell was asked to serve on its board of trustees. He declined; he simply had no time for it. When Edith studied the program, however, the precepts of PDAP appealed to her, particularly the principle of carrying love and understanding to others in trouble. She accepted. "They asked for Darrell, but I said, 'I'd *love* to,' and they got me instead," she chuckled. She served on PDAP Austin's first board, became its chief fund-raiser, and eventually became president of the board. Along the way, she

"Regarding Edith Royal: she is a living saint."

—Bob Lively, author, columnist, preacher, and former chaplain for Austin Recovery

educated herself about the illness of alcoholism and drug abuse and has, through her compassionate and nonjudgmental ministry, helped countless friends, and friends of friends, attain sobriety. She sums it up this way: "I do think alcoholism and drug abuse are two of the biggest problems in our nation. I've seen so much of it, so much destruction. I'm really grateful when people finally want to get sober and they ask Darrell and me for help."

She has been called an angel by the many troubled souls she has steered toward recovery. Edith continues to spread the message of Alcoholics Anonymous and Alanon. She served on the board of the Austin Recovery Center for years and recently led the charge to raise money for expansion of its facility. The 55,000-square-foot Edith Royal Campus at Austin Recovery in northeast Austin honors her contributions to the recovery community here in Austin.

In addition to the Austin Palmer Drug Abuse Program and Austin Recovery, Edith helped found the Children's Advocacy Center in Austin, which is dedicated to reducing the trauma of victims of child abuse. She delights in her church work and serves that community as an elder. In 2009, the Girls Scouts of Central Texas awarded her its Women of Distinction award for being a role model for women's leadership and success.

"Just a wife and mother" indeed.

In 1996, Edith and Darrell were the first couple to receive the Harvey Penick Most Worthy Citizen for Excellence in the Game of Life award, bestowed by Caritas Austin. Photography by Carrell Grigsby.

Royal reacted with disbelief when the Longhorns were picked number four in the 1961 preseason polls: "Gosh, that's stronger than Sadie's breath!" (University of Texas Sports Photography)

Chapter 9

THE FLIP-FLOP

Stubborn as he could be, Royal was not averse to considering new ideas. His mind churned constantly, thinking of ways to use his personnel more effectively. In 1961, he and his staff designed an offense that would get the ball into James Saxton's hands almost every play. The "flip-flop" allowed the strong-side and weak-side blockers to swap sides from play to play, allowing Saxton always to run behind the strong side. It both changed the way the players broke huddle and kept the blocking assignments uncomplicated. The offense was developed and tested by using UT Athletics Department staffers to fill in for players in August in stifling, unairconditioned Gregory Gym. The sweaty effort was worth it. From 1961 through 1964, the Longhorns' record was an incredible 40-3-1, with three conference championships and UT's first national championship.

The 1961 season featured the first all-Royal team. By then, every player in the program had been Royal-recruited, Royal-coached, and Royal-indoctrinated. With what many swear was his best team ever, the 1961 Longhorns rolled over everyone for eight straight games. Only Texas Tech scored in double digits against UT's defense, and according to Royal, the Horns were "hotter'n a burning stump" as they racked up 548 yards against the Red Raiders. After beating tenth-ranked Arkansas at Arkansas in week five, Royal was named the UPI coach of the week. "He never said anything to me," Edith said. The *Statesman* called to break the news, and Edith had to ask, "What kind of coach of the week was he—Southwest Conference or national or what?"

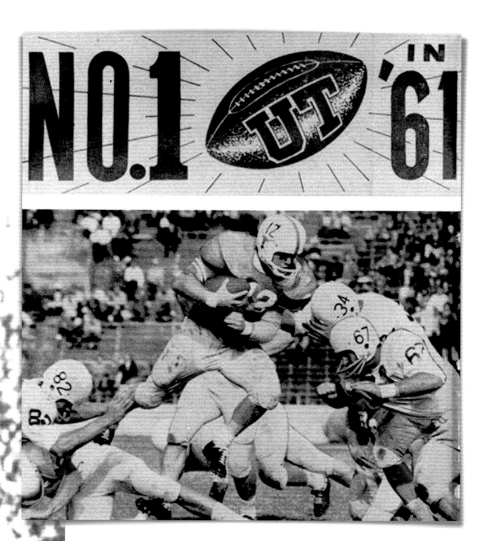

NO.1 IN '61
UT

"They're like a bunch of cockroaches. It's not what they eat and tote off, it's what they fall into and mess up that hurts."

—Darrell K Royal, after a shocking defeat by 2-4-1 TCU ruined the Longhorns' undefeated record

//

Quarterback Mike Cotten was the hero of the day as he played every offensive down in a gritty Cotton Bowl victory over Ole Miss, 12–7. (1962 Cactus, Texas Student Media*)*

In 1961, the Horns climbed to number one after winning eight straight. Texas fans' bubble burst when the lowly Horned Frogs of TCU shut out the Longhorns 6–0, slamming the door on any dreams of a national championship. (1962 Cactus, Texas Student Media*)*

After Texas beat Baylor 33–7, the Horns were 8-0 and were ranked first in the nation. Texas was steamrolling everyone. Then they plowed into lowly TCU. The Frogs had won only two other games that season. In the second quarter, TCU scored on a touchdown pass. The extra point kick was blocked, but six points were enough. UT came up empty-handed, and all dreams of a national championship were crushed. But the Horns weren't finished.

After rebounding to whip A&M 25–0, this team, the first all-Royal team, gave their coach his first bowl victory as a Longhorn by beating Ole Miss 12–7 on New Year's Day in the Cotton Bowl.

Royal was nominated for the ultimate honor—a nod from his peers—when the American Football Coaches Association nominated him as coach of the year. (Bear Bryant wound up winning the award.) In addition, the Football Writers Association of America (FWAA) named him coach of the year, to which Royal later responded: "I wouldn't be telling the truth if I didn't say I'm happy over this honor; however, I have a guilty feeling about this . . . I've been credited with a lot of things that did not originate with me. . . . I am tremendously indebted to the coaching staff and the squad for this honor."

Those were intoxicating times for Edith and Darrell.

THE DAIL

"First College I

ol. 61   Price Five Cents   AUSTIN, TEXAS, TUES

Longhorns' Roya
By City, Legislat

The success of the 1961 season brought Royal accolades at the city, state, and national levels. (Daily Texan, January 9, 1962; reprinted by permission of Texas Student Media)

Johnny Lujack, an ABC commentator and former Heisman Trophy winner, and Blackie Sherrod, a sportswriter for the Dallas Times Herald, present the 1961 Football Writers Association of America's Coach of the Year award to Royal. He became the first Southwest Conference coach to receive the honor, which he won in spite of his team not finishing number one in the nation. (Royal Family Archives)

TEXAN

Weather:
Cold, Rain
High 38, Low 34

"...ily in the South"

...AY, JANUARY 9, 1962   Six Pages Today   No...

...l to Be Honored
...ure, UT Tower

★ ...LE

The Ex-Students'
Association
of
The University of Texas

presents

the first annual

LONGHORN GRID BANQUET

honoring

**The 1961 Football Team and
Coaching Staff**

PROCLAMATION

    WHEREAS, the home-folks of the home-town of the greatest University in the greatest state in these great United States are justifiably proud of their adopted All-American son, Darrell Royal; and

    WHEREAS, the University of Texas has not only earned contemporary national recognition through the indomitable football teams under the coaching of Darrell Royal, but of infinitely greater significance, those whom his leadership has influenced have been imbued with the larger treasures of integrity by a coach who would rather lose a game than engage in unsportsmanlike tactics; who would neither make excuses for losing nor brag about winning; and who by his own example contributes to the building of stalwart character in men fully equal to their tasks but humbly mindful of their obligations as brothers in the family of God; and

    WHEREAS, in recognition of these and other extraordinary characteristics, the National Football Writers Association has bestowed upon our beloved Darrell Royal the coveted distinction of "Coach of the Year"; Now, Therefore, Be It Proclaimed,

    As a token of their esteem and appreciation, that the people of the City of Austin have specially set apart for celebration and recognition the 9th day of January, 1962, A.D. to be observed as:

        "DARRELL ROYAL DAY"

    Given under my hand and the seal of the City of Austin this 21st day of December, 1961.

ATTEST: _____
                                       Mayor

*Program from the first-ever Longhorn football
banquet, January 1962. (Royal Family Archives)*

*After Royal won the
FWAA Coach of the Year
award, Lester Palmer,
the mayor of Austin, pro-
claimed January 9, 1962,
to be Darrell Royal Day.
(Royal Family Archives)*

Sept 1 1962 American-Statesman/Bill Thompson

It's That Time Again

University of Texas football coach Darrell Royal fraternizes with sophomore wingback Jim Hudson, left, prior to the start of Saturday morning's opening of fall practice, but the smiles didn't last long. Center, Royal is lecturing to his fatigued players midway in the two-hour drill, and at right, end Tommy Lucas goes through the tortures of a "bridge" exercise to strengthen neck muscles.

The Longhorns Discover

Football Demanding Game

By LOU MAYSEL

The University of Texas football team, a superbly-conditioned group of athletes by any body's standard, found out Saturday that you can never get into good enough shape for the start of two-a-day work.

Coach Darrell Royal sent his 74 hopefuls out Saturday morning for their initial drill and although the pace was only a moderately brisk one, they were quick to learn the truism of a statement Royal uttered after the drill.

"To say the least, football is a very demanding game," Royal commented after his fatigued team had beat its retreat from the muggy drill field. There wasn't a one of the players who wasn't ready to surrender to the comparative comfort of a lengthy shower in the Memorial Stadium dressing room.

Royal had done everything he could to make the initial shock of fall football as light as possible. He had mailed his squad a vigorous training schedule that included the full run of exercises and drills for them to follow for the six weeks prior to their first exposure to two-a-day training and all who were questioned said they'd followed them religiously.

He also held the work pattern well below the all-out pace often seen on opening day but his Longhorns were beat just the same.

Their first fall exposure to two-a-day work must have come as a surprise to some of the sopho-

mores but it didn't to the veterans.

"It wasn't any shock to me. I've been here too long," said Johnny Treadwell, one of the 26 lettermen who participated in the workout. "I worked out every day this summer we were supposed to but the only way to get in shape is to put on the pads."

Even more tired, if that was possible, was guard David McWilliams, another veteran.

"I started several weeks before we were supposed to but it got me out there," he said as he sat on a table just inside the dressing room door and nursed a cooling coke in a paper cup.

"That humidity got me down," said wingback Tommy Ford, an all-out type as he stripped off his wet gear.

"I think you get just as tired no matter how hard you work out in the summer. Where it will probably make a difference is in how fast you recover," said quarterback Duke Carlisle, indicating he was beginning to snap back.

"It's the hottest I've ever been," said end Tommy Lucas, another Longhorn veteran who had two previous fall campaigns behind him. He indicated he'd hovering around the water fountain during the next few hours.

"I worked on a construction job in Houston this summer and they had three water buckets around. I never passed one up without taking a drink," he said, smiling.

The Longhorns didn't have any dropouts from the heat in the morning but there apparently was some delayed reaction since three players had to be sent in early from the afternoon drill and several more were showing signs of fatigue at the end of it.

Despite this, Royal felt his Longhorns indeed were in excellent shape.

"There were only a few of them who were dragging and even some of those who gave out were probably in good shape. Some of the others, like Jerry Cook for instance, looked like they could have gone two more hours," he said.

Royal indicated he might cut back a bit of the length of the workouts next week if the pace is telling.

Royal sent his Longhorns right into punt protection work and gave his backs and ends a liberal dose of the pass offense in the morning. The afternoon drill's team work centered on the running game.

"It was a pretty good pace for the first day but we didn't push them as hard as we have in some previous years," Royal said and, then without prompting he explained their lessons are absorbed better at a slower pace.

"You can push, push, push and after an hour they're white-eyed but after they get exhausted, they're just out there trying to survive. Or you can go slower

and they won't get so tired that they aren't interested in learning any more," he said.

The Longhorns will have a day to recover from their initial workouts, Sunday's an off day for the players but they were urged to get in some limbering up Sunday to get ready for the 8:30 a.m. return Monday, which will be Labor Day—the second for the Longhorns.

FOOTNOTES —No matter how lean a player gets during the summer work, the first workouts always see a sharp weight drop. It generally ran from around 10 pounds for the bulkier linemen and five to eight pounds for the compact backs. Biggest loser was tackle Lee Hensley, who showed a 14-pound drop on the weight chart. He went from 208 to 194. Guard Marvin Kubin showed a 13-pound drop, from 202 to 189 and even greyhound lean Ray Poage went from 201 to 190 during the first workout. The lost weight's mostly water and virtually all of it's regained at the water fountain before the next drill . . . Asked about his weight drop, tackle Scott Appleton answered in his typical, "Seven/expectanyway," but a trip to the scales pegged the loss at 12 pounds, from 235 to 223 . . . First serious injury of the fall work wasn't long in coming. Sophomore halfback Dan Burgess knocked down a shoulder during the first hour Saturday morning and will probably miss much of the fall . . . The Longhorns also noted their

first defection Saturday, even before work started. A manager checked out for Baylor, where a younger brother will be a freshman this fall . . . A big surprise in the weight department was David McWilliams, who was a 200-pounder as a schoolboy but played at a sickly-looking 185 last fall. He checked in a 195, which he probably will carry this season, but was down to 185 after each of the workouts . . . End Buddy Fults, who missed last year for a leg injury, had favorable words on the limb. "My leg still drags a little when I get tired and they told me it might be that way for a few years but it's as good as can be expected." . . .

LONGHORN ROSTER
Weak Ends — Tommy Lucas, Tommy York, Ben House, Knox Nunnally, George Sauer, Garry Brown.
Weak Tackles — Scott Appleton, Stanley Faulkner, Jim Besselman, Lee Hensley, Bo Price, Ed Pennington.
Weak Guards — Marvin Kubin, George Brucks, George Bass, Frank Bedrick, Kenneth Halm, Tim Smith.
Centers — Perry McWilliams, David McWilliams, Clarence Bray, Tommy Mankin, Rodney Kelley, Whitt Baker, Mickey Riggs.
Strong Guards — Johnny Treadwell, Glen Underwood, Bobby Gamblin, Reggie Grob, Bud Jackson, Kenneth Lee.
Strong Tackles — Ken Ferguson, Gordon Roberts, Tommy Phillips, Clayton Lacy, John Hays, Sam Parker, Larry Beevers.
Strong Ends — Sandy Sands, Buddy Fults, Charles Talbert, Kenneth Brooks, Pete Lammons, Stan Mauldin, Tony Crosby.
Quarterbacks — Johnny Genung, Duke Carlisle, Tommy Wade, David Kristynik, Currie Bechtol, Danny Barfield, Donald Walker.
Tailbacks — Tommy Ford, Jerry Cook, Hix Green, Charles Bucklew, Wayne Bates, Alan Baum, Dan Burges, Pat Byrd.
Wingbacks — Joe Dixon, Ernie Koy, Jim Hudson, Jim Cook, Bobby Nunis, Tony King, Brett Morris.
Fullbacks — Ray Poage, Pat Culpepper, Derrell Oliver, Harold Philipp, Tommy Doerr, Joe Ed Lynn, Gene Gifford.

Saturday, September 1, 1962, was a typical hot, humid day in Austin. It was also the first day of practice. Even though there was no cooling breeze on the practice field next to foul-smelling Waller Creek, there had been no problems during the first morning practice. In the afternoon session, however, three Longhorn players collapsed from heat exhaustion. By Saturday night, all three—Lee Hensley, Jim Besselman, and Reggie Grob—were said to be in satisfactory condition. Hensley and Besselman were released from Brackenridge Hospital.

Grob was a well-liked player who, through his great desire and hard work, became the first walk-on of Royal's career to earn a scholarship. At the beginning of the '62 season, Grob was listed as fourth team, behind Johnny Treadwell, Bobby Gamblin, and Olen Underwood. These heat-related problems scared the coaches. Their anxiety was made worse by the death that very day of Mike Kelsey of SMU from heat stroke. Two A&M football players and three from TCU suffered heat-related incidents on

the first two days of practice. Everyone was relieved when Grob rallied, seemed lucid, and visited with his parents, teammates, and Royal. Grob was still in the intensive-care unit on Sunday evening, but the papers reported that the threat had abated. He was rational and conversant, and his body temperature was down to ninety-nine degrees.

But things turned cruelly for the worse. Grob's progression from heat exhaustion to heat stroke to kidney failure was a seventeen-day battle, and Darrell and Edith Royal lived the major part of that battle with the Grob family. Between scheduled practices, Royal could be found at Brackenridge Hospital, standing beside Grob's parents, or at Reggie's bedside, offering encouragement. When the doctor finally told him that Grob might not survive the trauma, Royal staggered back a few steps as if he had been punched. He turned and collapsed in the arms of the defensive line coach, Charley Shira.

On September 19, 1962, in the shadow of Memorial Stadium,

Reggie Grob collapsed from heat stroke on September 1, 1962, the first day of fall practice. His condition improved over the next few days, but then began to worsen. (Newspaper clippings in DKR Papers, DBCAH, di_07317, di_07318, di_07319; © Austin American-Statesman)

"If I can tell a mother and dad that a boy has played as well as he is capable of playing, that's a greater compliment than saying he's all-American."

—Darrell K Royal

Condition Of Grob Worsens

Reggie Grob, young guard for the University of Texas football team who suffered a heat stroke Saturday, took a turn for the worse Monday and his condition was considered grave.

A terse bulletin issued Monday night by a team of specialists at Brackenridge Hospital said: "Kidney complications have arisen and his case is much more critical."

Grob, a sophomore from Spring Branch, a Houston suburb, was stricken Saturday afternoon at the end of practice and was quickly taken to Brackenridge Hospital.

Rising temperature late Saturday night prompted emergency treatment in a refrigerated jacket to bring it down and by Sunday morning he was considered out of danger from the heat stroke. However, a kidney malfunction had kept him on the critical list and lack of improvement apparently prompted the Monday night advisory.

A Dallas specialist was flown to Austin Monday to join local doctors on the case. Names of the doctors were withheld.

Grob's parents, Mr. and Mrs. Warren Grob, came to Austin Sunday and were at his bedside Monday.

Grob was one of three Texas football players stricken Saturday, but the other two, tackles Jim Besselman and Lee Hensley, both responded quickly to treatment. They were still at Brackenridge Monday night but only for observation. Their release is expected Tuesday.

The Grob case follows closely on the heels of a similar incident at SMU, where letterman center Mike Kelsey was stricken with heat stroke Saturday morning. Kelsey died Sunday morning.

UT Footballer
Stricken Grob Is Recovering

The University of Texas had a sharp scare for a few hours early Sunday morning that it might have the Southwest Conference's second football casualty this year, but by late Sunday night the threat had practically abated.

Reggie Grob, a sophomore guard with the Longhorns, was still under intensive care late Sunday for heat exhaustion at Brackenridge Hospital, but doctors seemed to think he was over the hump.

Grob, a Spring Branch (Houston) product, was one of three Longhorns who came down with heat exhaustion in the Saturday afternoon practice session.

The other two were tackles Lee Hensley and Jim Besselman. The three were taken to Brackenridge Hospital for observation and a late Saturday night advisory indicated all three were in satisfactory condition.

However, Grob took a turn for the worse overnight and was placed in a refrigerated jacket to bring his temperature down. By morning he was maintaining a temperature of 101 degrees without artificial means and was responsive to orders although under some sedation.

By nightfall Sunday Grob's temperature had fallen to 99, his blood pressure was even and he was completely rational and had conversed with his parents, Mr. and Mrs. Warren Grob, and a younger brother, Chuck.

Some minor complications still kept his case classified as serious, however. If he continues to progress, he probably will be taken off the serious list Monday.

Both Besselman and Hensley looked forward to being released, possibly Monday morning.

Grob's crisis followed sharply on the heels of the collapse of Mike Kelsey, SMU center, Saturday morning at Dallas. Kelsey died early Sunday morning after staying in very critical condition for a number of hours.

The three Longhorn opening-day casualties came as a sharp surprise since the squad had weathered the Saturday morning workout with only one dropout, halfback Dan Burgess, for a shoulder injury.

Sunday was an off-day for the Longhorns but Royal met with his squad briefly and directed the team to do some limbering-up to take the kinks out.

The Longhorns are to resume their drills Monday at 8:30 a.m. and they'll continue on a two-a-day basis, with the exception of Saturdays, for the next two weeks. Afternoon drills are due to start at 4 p.m.

WEATHER:
Partly Cloudy
Low 70, High 91

THE DAILY T

"First College Daily in the Sout

Vol. 62   Price Five Cents   AUSTIN, TEXAS, WEDNESDAY, SEPTEMBER

Death Claims Reggie Grob

By BILL LITTLE

Reggie Grob, the University sophomore gridder who collapsed on the opening day of practice, died Tuesday afternoon in a Dallas hospital.

For 17 days, the 19 year old tackle battled a kidney failure that resulted from the heat stroke Sept. 1. He died four days before the Longhorns' first kickoff of the 1962 season.

He came to the University from Houston Spring Branch without a scholarship—he earned one. He was a reserve as a freshman, but was rated as a coming prospect and had a fine spring training.

During his freshman year, he had a two point average.

Who was Reggie Grob?

Ask Ken Jacob, a fellow member of the Phi Kappa Psi fraternity.

"There was nothing he wouldn't do for a friend—like the time we were coming back to Austin after a summer rush party. Our car broke down in Katy and at 10 p.m. we called Reggie and he got out of bed, came to Katy and brought us on to Austin. He spent the night here with me and then went back to Houston the next morning. This summer he went to summer school in the morning, rushed for the fraternity in the afternoon, and worked out in the evening. He could run the mile in less than 6 minutes—and he was a lineman."

FRATERNITY TURNS

Jacob described Grob as one of the most respected men in the fraternity—he said he never saw anyone who knew him who didn't really like him. Almost 100 per cent of the fraternity will attend the funeral—and they will be officially in mourning for the next 30 days.

But the center of the University's heartbreak must focus on the practice field down on Waller Creek. Here Darrell Royal, the man who lived a major part of Grob's fight learned of the death. A phone call to Memorial Staduim sent a messenger to the field. Royal took it hard.

"It was a deep shock to me and to the squad when I told them—although I was expecting it I never gave up hope because Reggie and the doctor fought so hard. If they all hadn't been real competitors it would have been over long before now. I was expecting it for a week—but I still was shocked when they told me."

Royal told the team after practice, and gave permission to any members who wished to attend the funeral.

Bubba Phillips, Longhorn end, described Grob as well-liked, and expressed the team's sympathy.

"The whole University community is deeply distressed at the loss of an outstanding student who was as accomplished personally as he was athletically," University Chancellor Harry Ransom said Tuesday night.

IN COMA 5 DAYS

Grob, who had been unconscious for five days, was in Brackenridge Hospital here for 17 days before a plane owned by John Holmes, a member of the University Athletic Council, flew him to Dallas Monday.

Emergency surgery was performed Saturday at Brackenridge and an artificial kidney was affixed.

He was reported suffering from progressive liver failure, kidney failure, and bleeding complications.

"He put up a great fight," a spokesman at Parkland Hospital said Tuesday. "He was a strong boy, but he could not overcome the many things working against him."

REGGIE GROB
. . . . a hard fight

—Ava's University Studio Photo

Royal had to break the devastating news of Grob's death twice, first to the starters on one end of the practice field, then to the rest of the squad. It was the worst day of his coaching career. Royal prided himself on being in control of every aspect of his program. He wanted every facet to reflect the pride and greatness of The University of Texas. How horrific then, when, despite his attention to every detail, he could not prevent the death of one of his players. The guilt did not soon go away.

"That was the closest he ever came to quitting, in all those years of coaching," Edith remembers now. "After Reggie died, Darrell really did want to give it up, wanted to get as far away from it as possible. He agonized over the decision. He felt he had failed to take care of one of his players." In the midst of his agony over Grob's death and his guilt over "letting it happen," he made arrangements for the entire team to travel to Houston for the funeral.

The 1962 season opened four days later.

Royal went on a mission, a single-minded quest to speak with experts everywhere about the proper way to keep athletes safe. He spent time at Brooke Army Medical Center in San Antonio, and his relentless research with trainers and doctors across the country led him to understand better the need for salt and electrolyte replacement, the dangers of dehydration, and the need for regular water breaks. The University—and schools across the country—made immediate changes in the way that practices were conducted. Insistence upon salt tablets, checking a player's weight before and after practice, and practicing earlier in the morning and later in the afternoon, became the norm. Reggie Grob's death saddened the country. It devastated his family and friends. But the resulting education of coaches and trainers across the country surely saved the lives of other athletes.

Royal quickly earned a reputation as a "conservative" coach. His philosophy was to try for field position: "Get the ball to their end of the field and let *them* make the mistake. That philosophy puts an enormous emphasis on defense." Years later, Royal lamented the emphasis on offense at the cost of a strong defense. Laughing, he said, "Go out there and try to outscore people without a defense. See where you get. Fundamentals are still important." Following the fever of the 1961 season, in which the top-ranked Horns improbably dropped a game to the Horned Frogs, Texas looked to have another superb team in 1962.

> "People in the stands ... love to see an aggressive guy like Arnold Palmer, a swashbuckler who shoots for the flag. But in football ... when you plan to swash, you buckle instead. And that's the point when you come back and play sane, conservative-type football."
>
> —Darrell K Royal, on his affinity for playing "percentage football"

But the success that accompanied Royal's arrival had spoiled Longhorn fans. They had forgotten the dark days of losing seasons, of coaches hung in effigy from the majestic oaks on the South Mall of the campus. They had come to expect perfection.

Texas started powerfully, rolling over Oregon, Texas Tech, and Tulane, the last a 35–8 stomping that led Royal to quip: "All the white meat's gone. There's nothin' but necks on the platter." Texas got past OU in a 9–6 squeaker, and then had its hands full with seventh-ranked Arkansas. Royal had predicted the Arkansas game would be a real fight: "Playing Arkansas is like trying to throw a cat into the lake. He'll stay clung to you somehow." Texas somehow clung to a 7–3 win.

In the sixth game of the year, top-ranked Texas went ahead 14–7 over Rice, but with 10:07 left in the game, Rice scored, then made the extra point to tie the game 14–14. On Texas's next possession, the Horns were faced with fourth down and one yard to go. Quarterback Johnny Genung wanted to go for it. He assumed they would go for it. Instead, Royal sent in Ernie Koy to punt. If players and fans were surprised by Royal's move, that was nothing compared to what was to come. With five minutes left in the game, a number-one ranking on the line, and facing another fourth and one, Royal sent in the punter. Again. Fans, sportswriters, and even some of the players were dumbfounded. The game ended in a 14–14 tie, the only blemish on Texas's first undefeated season in thirty-nine years. The Horns dropped from the top spot.

In a column titled "Rice-Texas Game Produces Sorry Ending," Lou Maysel lamented that Texas had gotten too conservative, falling back on the tie and playing "not to lose." He scalded Royal in print for "playing for the break instead of trying to make our own breaks," adding, "College football has come to a sorry pass when pressure of avoiding a defeat forces coaches to pass up a reasonable gamble to try and win a game." In the *Dallas Times-Herald*, Bud Shrake faulted Royal but was not as harsh as Maysel—"Whether the Longhorn offense would have worked against Rice if Royal had let it try is debatable. But he didn't let it try on a few occasions."

The tie unleashed forces of anger that Royal had not felt before at Texas. The "conservative" label took on a negative connotation. Edith saved telegrams, some from fans congratulating Royal on the undefeated season, and others from folks with fury and retaliation on their minds. Edith kept them all.

WESTERN UNION
TELEGRAM

CLASS OF SERVICE
This is a fast message unless its deferred character is indicated by the proper symbol.

W. P. MARSHALL, PRESIDENT

SF-1201 (4-60)

SYMBOLS
DL=Day Letter
NL=Night Letter
LT=International Letter Telegram

The filing time shown in the date line on domestic telegrams is LOCAL TIME at point of origin. Time of receipt is LOCAL TIME at point of destination

1107P CST OCT 27 62 DA339

-B FWA561 NL PD AR FORT WORTH TEX 27,

DARRELL ROYAL

UNIVERISTY OF TEXAS AUSTIN TEX

MAY I CONGRATULATE YOU ON YOUR TIE I AM SURE YOUR PLAYERS FEEL
THAT YOU CALLED THE RIGHT PLAYS IN THE FOURTH QUARTER TWO KICKS
ON FOURTH DOWN WHAT IS YOUR FIELDPOSITION NOW REPLY REQUESTED

Bud Shrake

To Be Or Not to Be

EVEN IF IT HAD BEEN an ordinary football game, with nothing much involved except trying to do well enough to satisfy the alumni, many of the decisions made Saturday night at Rice Stadium would still be questioned. But it was more than an ordinary game. It was an hour in which Texas knocked itself out of a chance at the national championship, and that's how it will be remembered.

Rice played its best game of the season to tie Texas, 14-14. The Owls came back fanatically after Texas went ahead, 14-7, in the third quarter, and they refused to let the Longhorns break for a winning touchdown in the final minutes. Rice earned what it got.

The Longhorns, meanwhile, were caught up in what was probably the worst game they've played in two years. They made mistakes. They let penalties hurt them. They dropped passes, they threw the ball wildly, they fumbled, and they let the Owls hit them for an easy touchdown on a 49-yard run by Paul Piper.

But every team is going to play a bad game occasionally. The team that is No. 1 in the nation is supposed to be able to play a bad game and win, anyhow, especially when it is playing a team that hasn't beaten anybody.

But Texas didn't give itself an opportunity.

Each decision of Texas coach Darrell Royal was made under extreme pressure. Thinking back on them, after time for quiet reflection, Royal might change them and he might not. But his decisions were based on what must have been a lack of confidence in his offense and a resulting caution that took Texas out of the game.

Nobody can argue with the fact that Royal is a fine coach. His record proves it. He believes in field position and a solid kicking game and a clawing defense. This year, he believes in those things more than ever because his offense is uncertain.

That doesn't mean Royal can't coach offense. He was an offensive wizard last year when he had Jim Saxton, Mike Cotten and Jack Collins and was winning, 33-7.

Weapons Are Gone

THERE AREN'T MANY secrets in the game. This year Royal doesn't have a halfback who can strike as swiftly as Saxton, or a quarterback as capable as Cotten, or a clutch blocker and runner and pass catcher like Collins. What Royal has is a good defense, a superb kicker in Ernie Koy, and straightaway backs who can plug for a few yards but can't explode.

That's what he has, and he's designed what he does to fit those limitations. Two weeks ago it all worked well enough for a late 90-yard drive to beat Arkansas, 7-3, in a game that Texas was lucky to win. Saturday night, it didn't work.

Whether the Longhorn offense would have worked against Rice if Royal had let it try is debatable. But he didn't let it try on a few occasions.

On the first Texas possession Royal punted with third and five from his own 31. The idea was to let Koy kick the ball a long way and play for a Rice mistake. On the next possession Texas again punted with third and five, this time inside its own 20. Both times Royal clearly showed he'd rather trust Koy and the defense than trust the offense to make a first down.

Then, with seven minutes to go and the score tied, Texas had fourth and one at its 47. The Longhorns lined up for the gamble, but Royal ordered them to punt. With five minutes to play, it was fourth and one at the Texas 48 and again the Longhorns punted.

There was, to be sure, enough time for a Rice fumble and a Texas touchdown. But that was the negative approach. As the No. 1 team in the nation, Texas should have been confident enough to think it could make one yard against Rice and drive on to win.

Texas is no longer No. 1 and probably never should have been this season. The Longhorns deserved to win it last year when they had a better team and failed by inches against TCU. Arkansas ought to be the Southwest candidate this year, but the Razorbacks missed by inches against Texas. Which at least evens things up.

What should have been said is Royal lost his Guts — It should apologize to team & Alumni

Fr

By R[...]
As coach [...] ference's su[...] of the year, [...] is on a big [...] plied by a 6-6[...] omore.

The 41-ya[...] Thomas has [...] tor in the M[...] surge to the M[...]

Against Tex[...] day. Thomas [...] ball 268 yards[...] average, and [...]

Quarterback [...] in college foo[...] heading for [...]

North
Spot In

By the Associated [...]
Northwestern, a Big[...] erhouse which has s[...] ter than 30 points [...] sweeping past five [...] nents, forged int[...] place Tuesday in [...] lege football rank[...]
The Wildcats [...], who handed [...] crushing 35-6 d[...] day, took a res[...] their chief ri[...] Southern C[...] ly poll by [...]

Note left on our garbage can by our collector 11/2/62

Coach:
Before you came to U.T. these folks would have thought they had won a game if they tied one because seldom they came that close to winning a game. I think you have spoiled them by winning so much (smile) I still think you are the best Coach in the business! Trash Collector

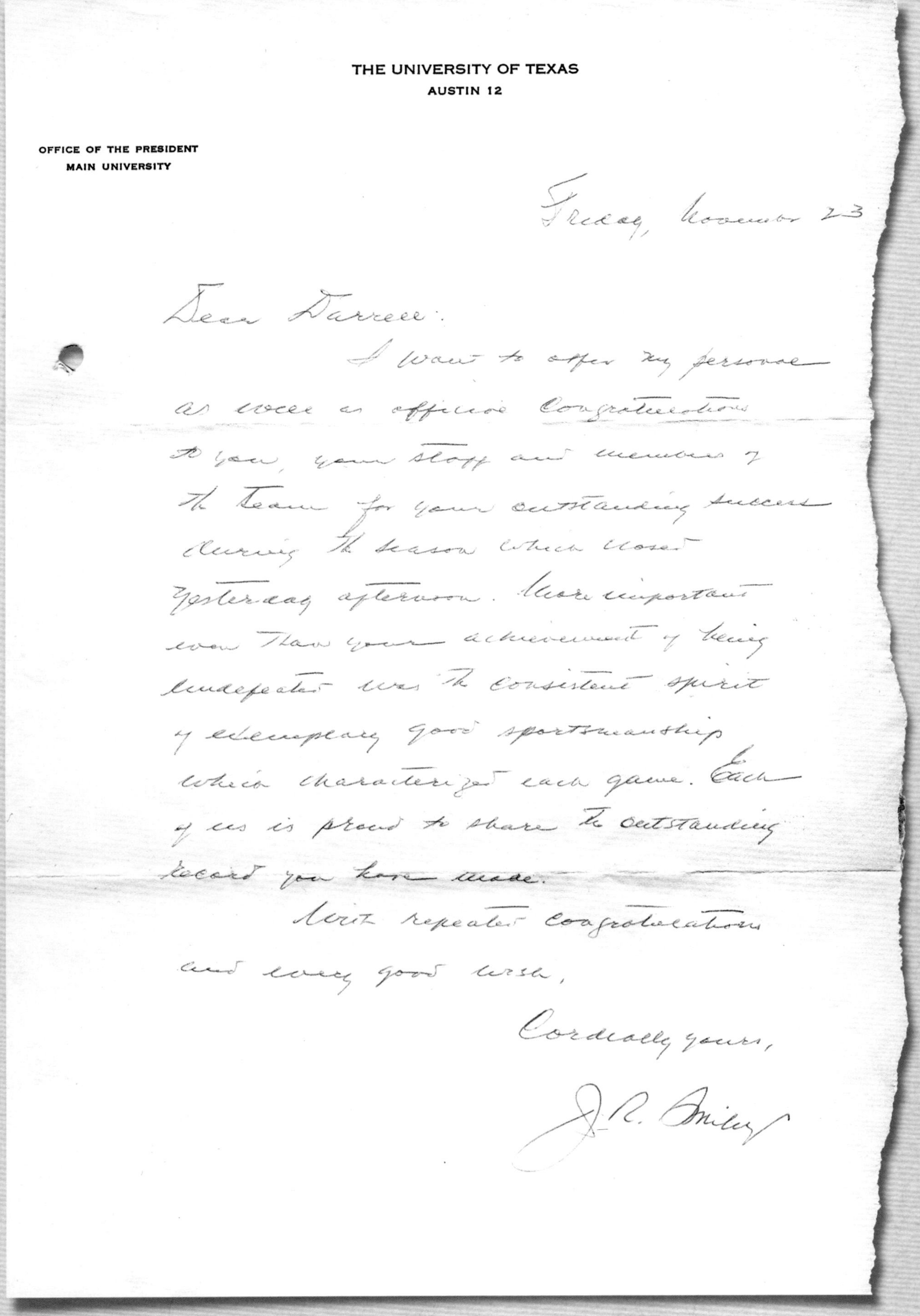

THE UNIVERSITY OF TEXAS
AUSTIN 12

OFFICE OF THE PRESIDENT
MAIN UNIVERSITY

Friday, November 23

Dear Darrell:

I want to offer my personal as well as official Congratulations to you, your staff and members of the team for your outstanding success during the season which closed yesterday afternoon. More important even than your achievement of being undefeated was the consistent spirit of exemplary good sportsmanship which characterized each game. Each of us is proud to share the outstanding record you have made.

With repeated congratulations and every good wish,

Cordially yours,

J. R. Smiley

Darrell had addressed the issue months before when he was holding forth on the topic of "percentage football":

Sure, the people in the stands want you to be bold and aggressive with your offensive thinking. The average fan wants you to play for the win at all times. But there's a small difference. The average fan has nothing to lose. If your team isn't successful in a gamble to win a game, the defeat doesn't hurt the spectators. They'll shrug . . . and go back to their respective businesses on Monday. But you're left sitting there in the stadium with a big hole in your stomach.

Royal's note to the ex-students' association in his weekly football newsletter read:

The Texas people have mixed feelings about the ball game. We have a solid core that is still behind us. For these people I am thankful. We have another group that wants to criticize. I have no time for these people, and it would be a lot better if they did not waste their time trying to help me.

At the end of the 1962 season, the Longhorns won their fourth SWC championship in five seasons. They had logged the school's first undefeated season in thirty-nine years. Dan Cook summed up their winning, though unglamorous, ways in the *San Antonio Express-News*: "They may not pass. And they may not thrill you. But brother, they block and tackle you and in the long run, they usually beat you."

The president of The University, Joseph Royall Smiley, hosted a reception in honor of Darrell and Edith that December. In a personal note to the coach, Smiley made clear the administration's regard for Royal: "More important even than your achievement of being undefeated was the consistent spirit of exemplary good sportsmanship which characterized each game. Each of us is proud to share the outstanding record you have made."

Edith's copies of the invitation and the guest list to the reception given in their honor by President and Mrs. Smiley. (Royal Family Archives)

Mr. and Mrs. Joseph Royall Smiley

request the pleasure of your company

at a reception
honoring
Director and Mrs. Darrell Royal

on

Tuesday, the eleventh of December

at

six until eight-thirty o'clock

2101 Meadowbrook Drive

Reply if declining

INVITATION LIST
Party for Director and Mrs. Darrell Royal, Tuesday, Dec. 11

✓ All members of the Board of Regents and their wives

✓ Mr. & Mrs. Russell Coffee, 1702 Northwood Road
✓ Mr & Mrs. Bill Ellington, 3006 Harris Blvd.
✓ Mr. & Mrs. James "T" Jones, 2503 Cedar View
✓ Mr. & Mrs. James Pittman, 1420 Yorkshire
✓ Mr. & Mrs. Robert Schulze, Route 1, Leander, Texas
✓ Mr. & Mrs. Charles Shira, 1704 Rogge Lane
✓ Mr. & Mrs. Mike Campbell, 1605 Ridgemont
✓ Mr. & Mrs. Frank Denius, 2521 Tanglewood
✓ Mr. & Mrs. Wallace Scott, Jr., 3303 Mt. Bonnell Drive
✓ Mr. & Mrs. Ras Redwine, 2530 Pecos
✓ Mr. & Mrs. O. H. Cummins, 3305 River Road
✓ Mr. & Mrs. Billy "Rooster" Andrews, 2903 Oakhurst
✓ Mr. & Mrs. Harry Whittington, 2004 West 9th Street
✓ Mr. & Mrs. Frank Erwin, 2307 Woodlawn
✓ Mr. & Mrs. Warren Woodward, 1901-B Dillman
✓ Mr. & Mrs. Donald Thomas, 3901 Balcones Drive
✓ Mr. & Mrs. J. C. Kellam, 1409 Westover
✓ Mr. & Mrs. Charles Green, 2705 Verde Vista
✓ Mr. & Mrs. Gary Morrison, 1400 Lorrain
✓ Mr. & Mrs. Allan Shivers, 6 Niles Road
✓ Governor and Mrs. Price Daniel, Governor's Mansion
✓ Mr. & Mrs. Noble Doss, 4207 Bradwood
✓ Mr. & Mrs. Nelson Puett, 3709 Eastledge Drive
✓ Mr. & Mrs. Ed Clark, 2300 Woodlawn
✓ The Honorable and Mrs. Lyndon B. Johnson, Washington, D. C. — *Room P-38 U.S. Capitol Bldg.*
✓ The Honorable and Mrs. John Connally, 53 Westover Road
✓ Mr. & Mrs. Don Weedon, 1309 Meriden Lane

✓ Mr. and Mrs. Jack Perry, 2232 Troon, Houston
✓ Mr. and Mrs. Bedford Wynne, 4421 Normandy, Dallas
✓ Mr. and Mrs. John B. Holmes, 3230 Del Monte, Houston
✓ Mr. and Mrs. John P. Thompson, 4266 Bordeaux, Dallas

Athletic Council:
✓ Mr. and Mrs. Myron Begeman
✓ Mr. and Mrs. Edwin W. Olle
✓ Mr. and Mrs. Lynn W. McCraw
✓ Mr. and Mrs. Joe B. Frantz
✓ Mr. and Mrs. Joe K. Bailey
✓ Mr. R. Gommel Roessner

✓ Mr. and Mrs. Harry H. Ransom
✓ Mr. and Mrs. Norman Hackerman
✓ Mr. and Mrs. Glenn E. Barnett
✓ Mr. and Mrs. Arno Nowotny
✓ Mr. and Mrs. J. C. Dolley
✓ Mr. and Mrs. L. D. Haskew
✓ Mr. and Mrs. F. Lanier Cox

TRYING TO LOUSE UP HIS ACT

FOR FIVE
STRAIGHT
YEARS THE
LONGHORNS
HAVE NOT
FUMBLED
THE BALL

1960
24-0

1961
28-7

1963

1959
19-12

1962
9-6

1958
15-14

BUD
WILKINSON

DARRELL
ROYAL

OKLAHOMA

TEXAS

COTTON BOWL

NEA

MURRAY
OLDERMAN

*"The wins and losses were like grapes... They
always seemed to come in bunches": Darrell Royal
on the Texas-OU series. (Royal Family Archives;
reproduced courtesy of Murray Olderman)*

MCCLANAHAN

Green Socks, and . . .
They've become psychological bludgeon.

*The Baylor game, the eighth of the 1963 season,
pitted Baylor coach John Bridgers's passing offense
against Royal's conservative "percentage football"—
and of course, there were the dreaded green socks.
(Royal Family Archives; © Dallas Morning News)*

Chapter 10

"WE'RE READY"

Ernie Koy was the punter for the 1963 Horns, and he was a good one. He was, in fact, UT's only experienced punter. After Koy was injured before the OU game, Royal told sportswriters that he would use Kim Gaynor, a punter with only high school experience. One writer asked Royal whether it was dangerous to play OU with an inexperienced punter. Royal responded with the story of the boy who had to defend himself when his friends made fun of his date's looks. Bringing an unattractive date was better than bringing no date at all, he explained: "Ole ugly is better than ole nothin'." Within days, Royal got letters from mothers all over the state, chiding Royal for "calling that nice young man ugly." From that moment on, Gaynor became known around the athletic offices as "pretty ole Kim."

As Texas was whipping Oklahoma 28–7 in the Cotton Bowl, Longhorn fans roared "We're number one," forgetting, according to *Sports Illustrated*, "that previous first-ranked Texas teams have always been beaten." In 1961, TCU spoiled the run for the national championship; in 1962, the tie with Rice had done it.

In an interview with Dan Jenkins of *Sports Illustrated*, Royal had spoken of the pride he felt in coaching at The University of Texas: "You hear guys who went to another school in our conference—A&M, Baylor or somewhere—talk for twenty minutes about why they didn't want to go to Texas. But you'll never hear a Longhorn explaining why he didn't go to another school. Put me in a room with 50 people and tell me that half of them went to Texas. I'll sort 'em out. The guy with the blue serge suit with his green socks rolled down didn't go to Texas." As soon as the words

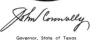

TEXAS WELCOME DINNER

NOVEMBER 22, 1963, MUNICIPAL AUDITORIUM, AUSTIN, TEXAS

PROGRAM

Eugene M. Locke, Master of Ceremonies, Chairman, State Democratic Executive Committee

Music by Volunteers from the University of Texas Longhorn Band, Vincent R. DiNino, Director.

Entrance of Official Guests at Head Tables

Invocation by Dr. ... Methodist Church of Austin

Introduction of M... ... M. Locke

Introduction of ... Byron Tunnell

Introduction ... ...eston Smith

Introduction ...

Entrance of Gove...

Entrance of Vice President and ... ...nson

Entrance of President and Mrs. John F. ... ...edy

Welcome by Governor Connally

Remarks by Vice President Johnson

Address by President Kennedy

Benediction by the Very Reverend Edward C. Matocha, Chancellor of the Diocese of Texas

3:15 Landing For Kennedy

Royal, Ransom Will Pass Longhorn Football to JFK

Mr. and Mrs. Kennedy Arrive in San Antonio
... the White House couple begin three-day Texas speaking tour.

Program and Royal's name tag for the Texas Welcome Dinner in honor of President and Mrs. John Kennedy, to be held the evening of November 22, 1963. (Royal Family Archives)

Photo of President and Mrs. Kennedy on the front page of the Austin newspaper, November 22, 1963. (DKR Papers, DBCAH, di_07382)

left his mouth, Royal worried that the comment might get him in hot water. "Don't worry, Darrell," Jenkins assured him, "the only people who'll be offended will be Baylor and the Aggies." "I made the remark casually," Royal later told Bud Shrake. "Now I read that John Bridgers [the Baylor coach] is going to wear green socks and a blue suit to the game Saturday. Man, those guys must be hip-deep in complexes."

Undefeated Texas took the field against Baylor and its celebrated quarterback, Don Trull. As Royal would remark after the game, "He had us blinking like bullfrogs in a hailstorm with all those passes." With 1:53 left and Texas leading 7–0, Trull had passed Baylor down to UT's nineteen-yard line and was threatening to score. Royal and his defensive coordinator, Mike Campbell, had displayed an uncanny knack for successfully playing their hunches. Royal's ability to analyze and see the heart of a problem was legendary; he had a way of sizing up a situation that was unmatched, except by his friend Campbell. Acting on one of those hunches, Royal and Campbell sent Duke Carlisle, the Longhorns' quarterback, in at safety. Although Carlisle had started at

safety the previous two years, in '63 he had played strictly on the offense. The very next play, Trull lofted the ball to his receiver. Carlisle came across the field from out of nowhere and intercepted the ball to save the game. It was the biggest defensive play of the year.

After beating TCU the following week, all Texas needed was a victory against Texas A&M at Kyle Field to become the first Southwest Conference team to win a national championship since 1939, when the Aggies had won it. As if that weren't electricity enough, President John F. Kennedy and his dazzling wife, Jacqueline, were coming to Austin just six days before the A&M game.

Royal later recounted the events of that day for John Wheat of the Center for American History.

We'd had an early practice, and I'd gone home . . . to dress and put on a suit. . . . I was to be the first one to greet him when he stepped off of Air Force One, and I was to present him with an autographed football. . . . I was home . . . putting on my tie when it came over the television that the president had been shot. I sat down on the edge of the bed and listened as they were giving the report. And I remember I moved into the living room and sat down . . . and stayed there until the conclusion. We ended up sending that autographed football to John Kennedy, Jr.

With the country in mourning, the two schools came close to canceling the game, but eventually decided to play it. Gary Cartwright of the *Dallas Morning News* rode the team bus to College Station. The air on the bus was thick with tension. "I feel I'm 'it' in a game of hide-and-seek," Royal told him. "I'm yelling, 'Here I come, ready or not, and all that's not hid are caught because I'm coming with both eyes open.'"

"This is for all the marbles, the whole bag," Royal told Cartwright. Win this game, and Royal would bring home UT's first-ever football national championship. Lose—well, to lose was unthinkable. Kyle Field was a mud pit, and the Aggie defense was savage, but the Longhorns and backup quarterback Tommy Wade managed to slip and slide past A&M in the last two minutes of the game, 15–13. The University of Texas Longhorns were national champions.

Seventy years after UT had begun playing football, these players who had suffered the loss of their teammate and the loss of their president had won it all. Over the previous thirty-three games, they had gone 30-2-1.

The Longhorns had scaled the mountain and stood at the peak. But there was no time to celebrate, and just barely time to catch their breaths. While Longhorn fans everywhere were ecstatically shouting "We're No. 1!," their coach was already stressing over the Cotton Bowl game. When a sportswriter asked which game that season had been the toughest, Royal snapped, "The next one is the toughest. We've got momentum, but that won't do it. We've got to prepare as though the last game never happened."

Horns Hook It: No. 1!
Texas Is Crowned National Champ

After a couple of near misses, the Horns finally win it all, 1963. (Royal Family Archives)

Royal hugs quarterback Tommy Wade after a narrow win over A&M ensured that the Horns would be national champs. (1964 Cactus, *Texas Student Media)*

Coach Darrell Royal congratulates Tommy Wade (17) after his greatest performance for U.T.

The Austin

FAIR

✿ ✿ ✿

CENTRAL TEXAS: F a i r weather through Saturday. Windy Friday. Thursday temperatures, 51-63. Expected Friday, 41-60. A little warmer Saturday. More US Weather Bureau data Page 19.

A Good Newspa

Vol. 88, No. 146

Austin, Texas, Friday

Jo
T

Picture of a Pooped but Happy Coach

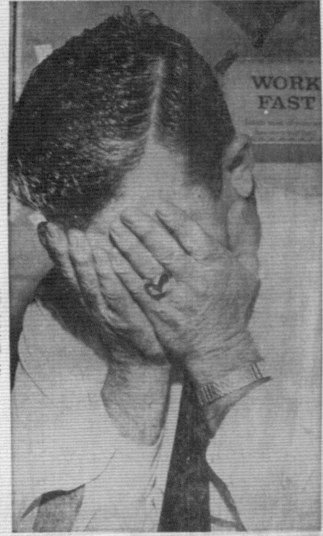

American-Statesman/Frank Johnston

Coach Darrell Royal smiles as he talks over the telephone to Mrs. John Connally when she called him Thursday from Dallas moments after The University of Texas Longhorns defeated Texas A&M University, 15-13, in a thrilling football drama at College Station. Mrs. Connally called in behalf of the governor, who is recovering in Parkland Hospital from gunshot wounds suffered when President John F. Kennedy was assassinated in Dallas. The Longhorns reportedly dedicated the game to Gov. Connally. After talking to Mrs. Connally, coach Royal then put his face in his hands and said emotionally, "I can't get my breath." (See story, Page 31.)

American

r Every Day

ovember 29, 1963   44 Pages   10 Cents

Final Star Home

hnson Counsels US

Count Its Blessings

Captains Tommy Ford,
David McWilliams, and Scott
Appleton, along with Coach
Royal, accepting the 1963 UPI
National Championship Trophy.
(Royal Family Archives)

Everyone was happy for Royal, even his supporters north of the Red River. In the wake of UT's first national championship, the Oklahoma City Sunday Oklahoman named him Sportsman of the Month, December 1963. (DKR Papers, DBCAH, di_07381; © Daily Oklahoman)

8E December 1, 1963 THE SUNDAY OKLAHOMAN

Royal's No. 1 in Oklahoma, Too

By Volney Meece

Darrell Royal . . . Oklahoma Sportsman of the Month

NOMINEES

DISTRICT 1

Large — Small

JOHN YOVICSIN
Harvard University

JOSEPH ZABILSKI
Northeastern University

DISTRICT 2

Large — Small

JOHN MICHELOSEN
University of Pittsburgh

WILLIAM EDWARDS
Wittenberg University

DISTRICT 3

Large — Small

WAYNE HARDIN
United States Naval Academy

CLARENCE STASAVICH
East Carolina College

DISTRICT 4

Large — Small

PAUL DAVIS
Mississippi State University

SHIRLEY MAJORS
The University of the South

DISTRICT 5

Large — Small

PETE ELLIOTT
University of Illinois

HOWARD FLETCHER
Northern Illinois University

DISTRICT 6

Large — Small

ROBERT DEVANEY
University of Nebraska

RALPH GINN
South Dakota State College

DISTRICT 7

Large — Small

DARRELL ROYAL
University of Texas

LES WHEELER
Abilene Christian College

DISTRICT 8

Large — Small

JIM OWENS
University of Washington

DON CORYELL
San Diego State College

(signatures: Johnny Yovicsin, Joe Zabilski, John Michelosen, Bill Edwards, Jess McLaughly, Paul Bryant, Len Casanova, Duffy Daugherty, Wayne Hardin, John McKay, Warren Woodson, Clarence Stasavich, Paul Davis, Shirley Majors, Pete Elliott, Howard Fletcher, Bob Devaney, Ralph Ginn, Darrell Royal, Les Wheeler, Jim Owens, Don Coryell)

DKR

Royal was named the 1963 American Football Coaches Association Coach of the Year. Despite his success and celebrity, he was wide-eyed at meeting his boyhood heroes. Royal collected the autographs of all the nominees on his banquet program, along with those of Paul Bryant, Len Casanova, Duffy Daugherty, John McKay, and Warren Woodson. (DKR Papers, DBCAH, di_07377)

Press conference at the 1963 AFCA Coach of the Year banquet, which was, according to Edith's caption, "The biggest press conference he'd ever seen!" (Royal Family Archives)

Standing at the summit in 1963, Royal looked across at a neighboring peak and saw Navy, with its Heisman Trophy–winning quarterback, Roger Staubach. Texas claimed the winner of the Outland Trophy (awarded to the best interior lineman) in Scott Appleton. Navy had averaged twenty-five points a game, and the Texas defense had allowed an average of only sixty-five yards an outing. It was shaping up to be a headbanger, that was for sure.

The eastern press did its usual bashing of teams outside its geographic area. Myron Cope of the *Pittsburgh Post-Gazette* wrote: "Texas is the biggest fraud ever perpetrated on the football public. . . . Carlisle executes a handoff like a construction foreman passing a plank to a carpenter. . . . Navy will expose Texas as the biggest hoax in modern football history." But while such writers were laughing themselves silly at the idea of Texas beating Navy, Mike Campbell was formulating a defensive plan to shut down Staubach's scrambling. The Horns worked on the "Staubach chase drill" every day in the three weeks leading up to the bowl game.

Until the early '70s, the national champion was chosen before the major bowl games were played. And in 1963, the UPI crowned Texas champ after its Thanksgiving victory over A&M. Yet leading up to the Cotton Bowl, Wayne Hardin, the coach of Navy, started campaigning for voters to reconsider their choice after Navy beat Texas, which it was sure to do. Hardin's in-your-face style allegedly landed him in the doghouse with Navy administrators. He put motivational messages on Navy's helmets and uniforms to inspire the Midshipmen and to intimidate their opponents, a practice that raised eyebrows at the U.S. Naval Academy

and with other coaches. At breakfast on the day before Texas faced Navy, Edith wondered aloud what special slogan Hardin would put on Navy's jerseys for the game against Texas. Royal's response: "I don't care what's *on* the jerseys, Edith. I worry about what's *in* them."

As part of the pregame festivities, the two coaches were interviewed on live television on the playing field of the Cotton Bowl. Hardin launched into his plea. The national-television viewing audience, the fans sitting in the Cotton Bowl, and the Texas Longhorn football team heard Hardin say, "When the challenger meets the champion and the challenger defeats the champion, there is a new champion." Royal's response was short but fiery: "We're ready." David McWilliams, a captain of the 1963 team, called it the best pep talk Coach Royal ever gave. Royal was livid at the moment, but after the game he said, "I should have thanked [Hardin]. That was more effective than any locker room speech I could have given."

The Longhorn coaches' game plan was brilliant. Duke Carlisle's passing attack surprised and then squelched Navy's defense. Texas set a Cotton Bowl record with 267 yards of total offense, 213 of which came through the air. Their defensive scheme was pure genius. Roger Staubach could do nothing against Scott Appleton and Mike Campbell's defensive plan, and the Horns trounced the Midshipmen, 28–6.

Royal sharing a laugh with General Douglas MacArthur at the 1963 AFCA Coach of the Year banquet, New York, 1964. (Royal Family Archives)

"They beat the hell out of us, I'd say."

—Rear Admiral Charles Kirkpatrick, U.S. Naval Academy superintendent, New Year's Day 1964.

Royal's success brought him a constant stream of attention and requests for his time. He was the guest of honor at a brunch given by the Ex-Students' Association and the Texas State Society in Washington, D.C., March 2, 1964. Among the dignitaries present were President Johnson (not pictured), U.S. Attorney General Ramsey Clark (left), and U. S. Representative Frank Ikard, of Texas (right). (Royal Family Archives)

When Bud Wilkinson retired after the 1963 season, Texas and Royal had beaten the Sooners eight years in a row. (Royal Family Archives)

> "The only thing that disturbs me about my profession is the fact that people give you too much credit when you win and too much criticism when you lose. I'll be the same person and do the same things and say the same things when we lose. But people won't believe me then. I won't change, but the people will."
>
> —Darrell K Royal

Chapter 11

WAKE-UP CALL

In the wake of the national championship, life became hectic indeed for the Royals. Everyone, it seemed, clamored for interviews, banquet appearances, golf games, luncheons, their time, and their friendship. It was a whirlwind for the Royal family, and Edith talked about the toll taken by the fame: "We were off, running around the country making speeches and accepting awards, instead of taking care of things at home." For her, "things at home" meant Marian, Mack, and David. It meant PTA meetings, bills to be paid, baseball games, kids, and carpools.

For Darrell, "things at home" meant football. A lot of things suffered as a result of his absence, but one area of neglect didn't become evident for a couple of years: recruiting. He simply wasn't on campus during the spring of 1964. Recruits and their parents wanted to meet with the head guy, but UT's head guy was likely to be addressing the U.S. Congress on Texas Independence Day or accepting a coach of the year award or playing golf in a celebrity pro-am.

But their lives were about to get even more hectic. Royal's friend and mentor Bud Wilkinson retired from coaching the

Sooners after the 1963 season. Royal had beaten his former coach eight years straight, a feat still unmatched by a coach on either side of the rivalry. The University of Oklahoma decided it wanted its hero back, so in early 1964, the Sooners said to their favorite son, "That is enough. Come home."

In the weeks following OU's offer, the Royals discovered that their unlisted phone number "must not be too much of a secret," as Royal said. The Royal household had two phones, each with an unlisted number. While Royal considered OU's offer, their part-time housekeeper did little except run back and forth,

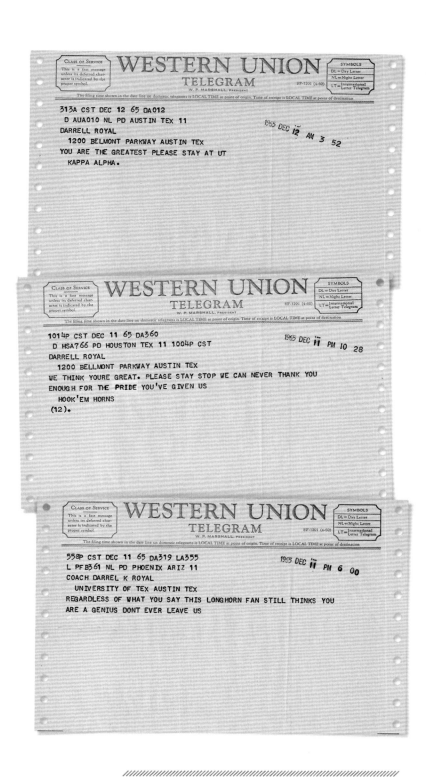

Darrell and Edith served as honorary grand marshals for the Fiesta Flambeau Parade in San Antonio, Texas. (Royal Family Archives)

WESTERN UNION
TELEGRAM

313A CST DEC 12 65 DA012
D AUA010 NL PD AUSTIN TEX 11
DARRELL ROYAL
    1200 BELMONT PARKWAY AUSTIN TEX
YOU ARE THE GREATEST PLEASE STAY AT UT
    KAPPA ALPHA.

1965 DEC 12 AM 3 52

WESTERN UNION
TELEGRAM

1014P CST DEC 11 65 DA360
D HSA766 PD HOUSTON TEX 11 1004P CST
DARRELL ROYAL
    1200 BELLMONT PARKWAY AUSTIN TEX
WE THINK YOURE GREAT. PLEASE STAY STOP WE CAN NEVER THANK YOU
ENOUGH FOR THE PRIDE YOU'VE GIVEN US
    HOOK'EM HORNS
    (12).

1965 DEC 11 PM 10 28

WESTERN UNION
TELEGRAM

558P CST DEC 11 65 DA319 LA355
L PFB361 NL PD PHOENIX ARIZ 11
COACH DARREL K ROYAL
    UNIVERSITY OF TEX AUSTIN TEX
REGARDLESS OF WHAT YOU SAY THIS LONGHORN FAN STILL THINKS YOU
ARE A GENIUS DONT EVER LEAVE US

1965 DEC 11 PM 6 00

When word got out about OU's offer to Royal, Texas alumni went crazy. Royal and Edith were inundated with letters and panicked phone calls and pleading telegrams from sororities, fraternities, campus groups, former players, and alumni, all begging him not to leave. (DKR Papers, DBCAH, di_07364, di_07360, and di_07359)

answering both telephones. Edith told Volney Meece of the *Oklahoma City Times*, "One of the phones is completely worn out. You can't even dial on it." Darrell's response: "You don't realize how many times it's been drop-kicked." The pressure on the Royals was powerful. Darrell considered the offer, mulled it over. OU was his alma mater. Norman had been their home. Sooner fans wanted desperately to get him back, and at OU he wouldn't have to contend with the strict academic standards in place at Texas.

On the other hand, Wilkinson was much loved in Oklahoma, and it would be risky to try to follow behind him. Texas fans knew Royal only as a coach, a grown man, but Oklahoma fans saw him as one of their own, a celebrated former player. "We knew he'd end up a prophet without honor in his own hometown," Edith recalled recently. "Plus, we already loved Texas. It was our home." Or, as Royal himself put it, by that time he was a Longhorn, "dipped and vaccinated."

Texas alumni scurried to set up a slush fund to supplement Royal's income of $24,000. But he was adamant that he would not accept a salary grossly out of line with that of a top professor. So Harry Ransom, the chancellor of The University of Texas System, did the only logical thing: he made Darrell K Royal a full professor and granted him tenure, a guarantee of future employment for life.

The school was in an immediate uproar. Most of the population was relieved that The University had taken this bold move, but the *Daily Texan*, the student newspaper of The University, and some professors vehemently protested Ransom's action. Nevertheless, the plan went through as proposed. From

> "It doesn't matter how much football knowledge a coach has, it's how much he is able to impart to his players that matters."
>
> —Darrell K Royal

the beginning, Royal had extended a hand to UT's faculty, hoping to forge a partnership with them. Each week he invited three faculty members to join the Longhorns as guest coaches. Their access wasn't limited in any way, and Royal didn't pander to them. He just went about his routine of preparing for a game. As he put it: "They saw me when I was pissed off, when I was pleased . . . they just saw me." Many of those guest coaches came away with the realization that Royal was, indeed, a professor.

Shortly after Ransom's action, a sportswriter walked into Royal's office and found him at his desk, reading glasses perched on the tip of his nose and a puzzled look on his face. "I've been sitting here for 30 minutes trying to figure out if 'professor' has one *f* or two."

Royal didn't say so for many years, but he was proud of that designation. He believed it was deserved. "Teaching? Damn right we were teachers," he told John Wheat in *Coach Royal*.

> I gave a test in front of 70,000 people every Saturday. We were teaching the game of football. I would like to think that we taught it in an ethical way . . . in a sportsmanlike manner. I would like to think we taught it to win. . . .
>
> . . . Yeah, we taught a subject. I think I taught it well, so I don't apologize for that professorship. . . .
>
> . . . It was an honor. It was a privilege that I was singled out for a distinct honor, and I consider it that.

In response to the brouhaha, Mickey Herskowitz, a sportswriter for the *Houston Post*, proposed that any University of Texas

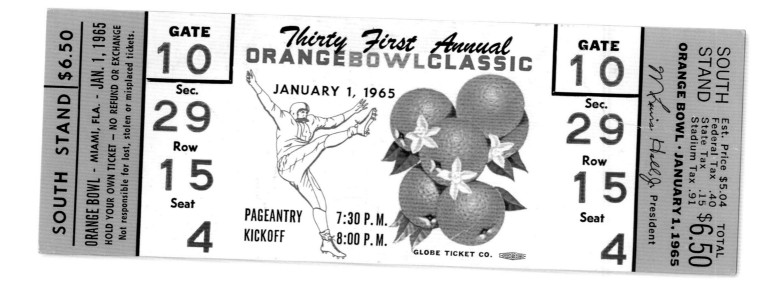

The 1965 Orange Bowl saw Royal and the Horns outlast Bear Bryant and the Crimson Tide, 21–17. (DKR Papers, DBCAH, di_07375)

Texas needed to beat the Aggies in 1965 to salvage a winning season, but the Horns were losing 17–0 at the half. Coach Royal told the team, "I can stand here and draw all kinds of diagrams, but I don't think that will help. It's just a matter of whether you want to win." He turned around and wrote "21–17" on the blackboard. Then he turned back to the team and said, "That's what you can do." That's all he said, and that's exactly what they did. Final score: Texas-21, A&M-17. Here Royal relaxes with Bob Park after the game. (Royal Family Archives)

faculty member who earned a national championship in his or her field should be awarded the honorary title of "coach."

The 1964 season almost matched the previous year's excitement and record. Texas came within one point of winning another national championship, losing only to Arkansas, 13–14. Fifth-ranked Texas finished the season by beating Joe Namath and the top-ranked Crimson Tide 21–17 in the 1965 Orange Bowl, the first college bowl game to be played at night.

The Longhorns and Royal had captured the imagination of the entire country. In a span of four seasons, Royal's Horns had lost only three games and tied one. It was great to be a Texas Longhorn, and Texas fans never doubted that the wins would keep on coming.

In spite of the "Saint Darrell" nickname that Dan Jenkins had hung on him, Royal made mistakes—and plenty of them. He doesn't shy away from talking about those times, and he doesn't try to deflect blame. The 1965 season was a wake-up call for the Longhorn fans and their coach. The effect of the recruiting letdown following the national championship was beginning to show. A win over Texas A&M in the final game was the only way the Horns managed to pull out a winning season.

After that game, Royal still found something to salvage from

the trial of losing to Arkansas, Rice, SMU, and TCU. In his weekly newsletter, he wrote:

> As disappointing as our football season was, still some good things have come out of it. For one thing, it proved the caliber of the Texas fans and supporters. I had always thought it was solid, and that the people would not be easily shaken off the bandwagon. Nothing could be more true. I have received more letters of encouragement and more pledges of support than at any other time since I have been at The University of Texas. I had always thought this support would be there, but it is warming to learn that it actually is.

He will tell you right out that the recruiting letdown he suffered—was responsible for—would haunt him for the next three years. Enduring three years of 6-4 regular-season football was a bitter pill for the Horns to swallow after their successes of the early 1960s.

Although Texas struggled during this period, the eyes of the nation were still on Texas and on Royal. Myron Cope, who had mocked the Texas players before the 1964 Navy game, changed his tune and joined the band. In the September 1966 edition of the *Saturday Evening Post*, he called Darrell the "patron saint of clean-cut coaches," adding, "For every scholarship he doles out, he expects a savage effort." Royal's response: "Well, I don't believe in paying folks to *not* grow cotton."

By the end of the 1965 season, after one season of going 6-5, Royal declared him-

self sick of mediocrity. He blamed no one but himself, and he set out to fix things. He was dogged in his pursuit of the best athletes, and the 1966 and 1967 recruiting classes were among the best in the nation. In 1968, he announced to his players, "We will *never* be 6-4 again," then put that team through a hellish spring training.

The conditioning sessions were overseen by Frank Medina, the most feared man on campus. A full-blooded Cherokee who stood all of four-ten and dressed like the milkman, he served as the trainer at The University for thirty-two years. It was Frank's job to get the players in shape, to get more out of them than they thought they could give. His players today speak of him with love, but back then his workouts were legendarily brutal. Everyone ran the stadium steps wearing weight vests and carrying fifty-pound tackling dummies. He was known for locking his "fat boys" in the steam room for hours at a time. Those he ordained "leaders" were frequently made to do two workouts a day in order to set an example for the team.

Ted Koy called the practices "rock 'em-sock 'em." How hard were things? "The survivors were the ones who made the team. We were 'Medina-ized.'" Bob McKay, an all-American tackle, remembered, "The spring of '68 was a hard time. We were just hoping we'd live through one more day . . . It was full speed. The day I tore my shoulder up was the happiest day of my life. I had to go to the hospital, but I had lived through one more day of practice. I'd lay there in the dorm at night and listen to kids leave. Some just quit, some went to the hospital. But it worked."

"Royal was responsible for developing more people over the years than anyone I know."

—Bobby Gurwitz, *What It Means to Be a Longhorn*

Frank Medina, longtime UT trainer, on the sidelines with Royal. When asked recently to reminisce about Medina, Royal said seriously, "One thing you can say about Frank, he treated all the players alike." Then with a sideways glance and a grin, he said, "He treated 'em all bad." (Royal Family Archives)

Coach Royal encouraging his team. He summed up a
coach's task this way: "A head coach is guided by this
main objective: dig, claw, wheedle, coax that fanatical
effort out of the players. You want them to play every
Saturday as if they were planting the flag at Iwo Jima."
(University of Texas Sports Photography)

Royal's early doodles of the wishbone.
(DKR Papers, DBCAH, di_07369)

—Royal's instruction to offensive backs running the wishbone. The ball carrier was to
follow the outside hip of his lead blocker and resist the temptation to cut inside.

Chapter 12

THE WISHBONE

A disgusted and determined Royal was a force to be reckoned with, and when he set out to make changes, changes were made. He and the offensive backs coach, Emory Bellard, surveyed their stable of running backs—all-American senior Chris Gilbert, junior Ted Koy, and sophomore Steve Worster—and knew they would be foolish to bench any of them. So Bellard took a little of OU's split-T offense and a bit of the Houston veer and came up with an offense that would make good use of a split end while allowing all four weapons in the backfield to be effective. It was a triple option based on reading defenses. It required the right instincts from a quarterback who was brave enough to try it.

Denny Aldridge (Secondary, 1966–1968) recalls when the wishbone was in its infancy:

One clear memory is during the summer of '68 when you [Royal] called me at Rooster's [Rooster Andrews Sporting Goods] requesting that I show up at Gregory Gym. The memory of being the wishbone fullback, Coach Bellard the quarterback, and you being the defensive tackle . . . Watching you and Coach Bellard going over the intricate details, i.e., alignment, stance, footwork, reads, and the pitch, is still a vivid memory some forty-one years later. Done—the wishbone was born!

In the era before the NCAA instituted scholarship limits, Royal recruited dozens of quarterbacks; they were usually intelligent and were often the best athletes on their high school teams. Bill Bradley, from Palestine, Texas, had been one of the brightest prospects in 1965. His dazzling high school exploits had earned him the nickname "Super Bill." He was recruited by schools across the country, and when he chose Texas, one writer suggested that Bradley might revolutionize Texas' offense. Jones Ramsey, the UT sports information director, bristled at the suggestion: "No. Darrell will mold *him*. He'll conform or not play."

In 1968, James Street was Bradley's backup. He recalled both of them having trouble with the new offense: "After the first day of working on the wishbone, Bill [Bradley] and I agreed that it was impossible to run." The fullback was too tight, too close to the quarterback. Royal diagnosed the problem: the fullback needed to be backed up a few yards. He picked up the telephone to call Bellard, who was about to call Royal with the same diagnosis. "It was amazing how we agreed on offensive strategy," Royal said.

Texas unveiled its new offense in the 1968 Houston game, which ended in a tie. Next up was Texas Tech, and with Texas trailing midway through the third quarter, Royal again diagnosed the problem correctly. Bradley was a great athlete, easily the most talented player on the team. But two games into his third season as starting quarterback, it was evident that he and the wishbone weren't jelling. Bradley simply wasn't a wishbone quarterback. Later that year, he turned out to be an amazing defensive back and went on to play for the Philadelphia Eagles, where he was a two-time All-Pro selection.

In the 1968 Tech game, Royal grabbed Street, looked at him for a minute "as if he were having second thoughts," Street recalls. "Then he looked me straight in the eye and said, 'Hell, you can't do any worse. Get in there.'" The game could not be salvaged. Tech upset Texas 31–22. But with Street starting at quarterback, UT won the next one. And the next, and the next, and the next. The Horns never lost a game that Street started. Texas and its new offense dazzled fans and confused opponents for thirty straight games.

After home games, Royal, Jones Ramsey, Bill Little (the assistant sports information director), and various coaches, wives, sportswriters, and hangers-on gathered for postgame interviews, drinks, and snacks in suite 2001 at the Villa Capri Hotel near the UT campus. This allowed writers to get the postgame picture from Royal himself, and in a more casual sort of interaction than the usual interviews or press conferences. It was in that venue that the wishbone got its name. In what is now part of Texas Longhorn lore, Mickey Herskowitz asked Royal what

> "I think we're close to being a good football team. But the big difference is the '63 team has its record on film and it's in the can. This group hasn't even had its picture took."
>
> —Darrell K Royal, when asked to compare the 1968 team with the '63 team

he called his new offense. When he didn't have an answer, Herskowitz remarked that the formation looked like a pulley bone. "That's it, then," said Royal. "Call it the wishbone."

The offense would go on to revolutionize and then dominate college football. Royal started using the wishbone in 1968, and one year later, he won a national championship. In 1970, he won another. Between 1969 and 1979, seven wishbone teams won or shared the national championship title. To the end of his days, Bear Bryant insisted that Darrell Royal and the wishbone saved his career when, in 1971, Bryant asked his longtime friend for advice on how to install the offense. Bryant came to Austin, and Royal set aside time to go over the nuances of the offense with him. Two years later, in 1973, the Bear and Alabama won a share of the national championship using the wishbone. They won again in 1978 and 1979. After Royal helped Chuck Fairbanks at Oklahoma learn the offense, Barry Switzer and the Sooners won back-to-back national championships with it in 1974 and 1975.

The first year of the wishbone, 1968, the Longhorns finished with a 9-1-1 record, tied for the conference championship, and beat Tennessee 36-13 in the Cotton Bowl. They carried a nine-game winning streak into the 1969 season. That year, the 100th year of college football, has been documented and dissected so often that many of the stories from that season have become folklore, even clichés. But in what proved to be the matchup everyone hoped for, the top-ranked Longhorns met second-ranked Arkansas (AP) in one of the most dramatic games in college football history.

At the beginning of the '69 season, Beano Cook of ABC Sports had an end-of-the-season television slot to fill. Cook asked Frank Broyles of Arkansas and Royal if they would be willing to move their annual clash to the end of the year. The coaches were willing, and the game was rescheduled for December 6, 1969. Before the Horns' Thanksgiving Day meeting with the Aggies, sportswriters wanted to talk about UT's game with the Razorbacks instead. Royal would not take the bait. He did concede, however, that if both Texas and Arkansas won their games that week, their matchup would be a big shootout indeed. The press jumped on it, and the "Big Shootout" became the name that would be forever identified with the "Game of the Century." Both teams did win their games that week. Both teams brought undefeated records to that last game.

The buildup to the "Big Shootout" was excruciating. President Richard M. Nixon announced that he would attend the game and present a presidential plaque to the winner. The famed evangelist Billy Graham would also be there. Businesses and long-distance operators in Arkansas

> "This makes them look wiser than a tree full of owls."
>
> —Darrell K Royal, referring to ABC executives who decided to move the Texas-Arkansas game to the end of the season.

In 1969, college teams across the nation wore the number "100" on their helmets to commemorate the 100th year of college football. (Royal Family Archives)

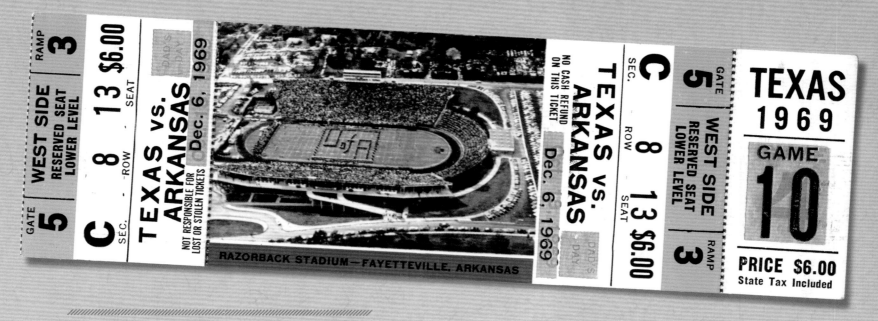

Coveted ticket to the Game of the Century, 1969. The originally scheduled date of the game, October 19, is barely visible underneath the new date. (DKR Papers, DBCAH, di_07373)

greeted callers with, "Beat Texas. How may I help you?" Sophisticated and historically blasé Longhorn fans showed up 35,000 strong to a pep rally in Memorial Stadium. Royal didn't sleep a wink the night before that game. He spent all night calling his coaches for more planning and strategy. En route to the game, he called James Street to the front of the bus and gave him the play to run if they needed two points. Although Seneca is supposed to have said it first, Royal made it famous: "Luck is what happens when preparation meets opportunity." Royal made sure that Street was prepared.

Arkansas shut down Texas for most of the game, aided by several Longhorn fumbles. The Razorbacks led 14–0 until the first play of the fourth quarter. Street, looking for tight end Randy Peschel but finding him covered, rolled to his left and scrambled forty-two yards for a Texas touchdown. He knew what to do next; run the two-point-conversion play Royal had discussed on the bus before the game. It was successful: Arkansas-14, Texas-8.

"Every now and then you have to suck it up and pick a number. You don't use logic or reasons. You play a hunch."

—Darrell K Royal, on his gutsy fourth-and-three call of right 53 veer pass.

Texas was running out of time. Royal had to try something different, something big. In the locker room at halftime, Randy Peschel had told his coach that if he needed to, he thought he could get behind his blocker. Royal remembered that, and facing fourth-and-three with 4:47 left in the game, he knew it was time to gamble. With Street and his defensive coordinator, Mike Campbell, listening, Royal called for right 53 veer pass. Campbell jumped back, then hollered, "Defense, get ready." Up in the press box, the offensive coordinator, Willie Zapalac, went crazy trying to talk Royal out of that call. Royal had twenty-five seconds to make up his mind, but he wasn't rattled. As he put it later: "My whole life was spent on those twenty-five-second decisions. You get used to it." So with his offensive coordinator frantically trying to get the boss to come to his senses, and with his quarterback staring at him in disbelief, Royal pulled his headphones off and made the call. In the award-winning documentary *The Story of Darrell Royal*, James Street said, "This is the difference between somebody being 'good' and [somebody being] 'great.' He had to shut us out totally because we were jabbering about the play *we* wanted to run." History shows that it was a perfect throw, a perfect catch. Although Peschel was covered and there were about six hands going up for the ball, he caught it for a gain of 4.4 yards. Royal confesses, "People say it was a brave call, but if it had failed, it'd been the most criticized call of the century."

President Richard Nixon visited the dressing room and presented Royal, tri-captain Ted Koy, and the Longhorns with a national championship plaque that he had had made, December 6, 1969. The plaque had been left blank pending the outcome of the game, so Nixon took it back to the White House to be engraved with the name of the Texas Longhorns. Edith says that no one has seen that plaque since. (University of Texas Sports Photography)

Then it was Ted Koy for eleven yards and Jim Bertelsen for a two-yard touchdown run. The Arkansas bench watched in stunned disbelief as Happy Feller kicked the extra point that put the Longhorns ahead. When Tom Campbell made an interception, it broke Arkansas's back, and Campbell told the intended receiver as he ran off the field, "That beats y'all." Later, after the game had ended and the locker rooms had cleared, Royal acknowledged that his good friend Frank Broyles had out-coached him that afternoon.

After the victory, national news cameras caught the Texas Longhorns and their coaches saying the Lord's Prayer in the locker room. Much was made of this, and of Royal's comment that he never had his team pray before a game because "he might be tempted to pray for something he shouldn't pray for." Believing that the Lord had more important things to attend to than deciding the outcome of football games, Royal and his team kneeled to express gratitude after a game rather than asking for favors beforehand.

Until the 1970s, national championships were chosen after the regular season but before bowl games were played. And at the end of the 1969 regular season, the Texas Longhorns were named—by Nixon, the AP, UPI, and just about every other polling group—national champions.

Royal and the 1969 team captains—Ted Koy, James Street, and Glen Halsell—were in New York to receive the MacArthur Bowl, the national championship trophy. Royal exclaimed, "I got to be the happiest guy in America."

In addition, the Horns' trip to the 1970 Cotton Bowl was shaping up to be another legendary encounter. For the first time in forty-four years, Notre Dame, the long-idealized and independent football program, voted to lift its self-imposed ban on participation in bowl games. The Fighting Irish wanted to challenge the Longhorns. It's hard to imagine a matchup with more hype or story lines. People were buzzing about Notre Dame's quarterback, Joe Theismann, who had recently changed the pronunciation of his name to rhyme with "Heisman." In a sideshow to the game, Joe Paterno, the coach of Penn State, was still grousing loudly because undefeated Texas was number one and undefeated Penn State was not; although, according to some reports, the Nittany Lions had voted to sidestep playing Texas in the Cotton Bowl so they could return to the Orange Bowl.

The Horns' meteoric season seemed to be burning ever brighter until Royal received the telephone call.

The UT chancellor, Dr. Charles "Mickey" LeMaistre, was on the other end of the line, telling Royal that Freddie Steinmark, their starting safety, had finally gotten his sore leg checked by the trainer, Frank Medina. The leg had been bothering Steinmark all season, and the coaches saw that he had "lost a step" in the second half of the season. Finally, after the Arkansas game, he could stand it no longer. An X-ray of Freddie's leg exposed a suspicious

> "I'm a believer. I wouldn't classify myself as religious, if that means going to church . . . I think it's important to treat people right and to be fair with people. I think there will be a reward for that. I don't necessarily think going in the church house will get you brownie points. It will encourage you and make you a better person; make you more sensitive and aware of being kind to your fellow man . . . but I don't think going in the church house is gonna get you there."
>
> —Darrell K Royal to Bill Little, *Longhorn Album*

spot. He was sent straight to M. D. Anderson Cancer and Tumor Institute. LeMaistre did not gloss over things for Royal. If it were cancer, doctors would surely have to amputate his leg. The prognosis in 1970 was a life span of about two years. (This proved to be prophetic; Steinmark died almost exactly two years after receiving his diagnosis.)

One week after Steinmark played in the Big Shootout, his leg was amputated at the hip because of bone cancer. Freddie declined offers to sit in the Cotton Bowl press box and refused the offer of a wheelchair. He was a player, he said, and he would stand on the sidelines, just as any injured player would.

The game gave rise to several memorable moments even before it began. The field in Dallas had been battered into a

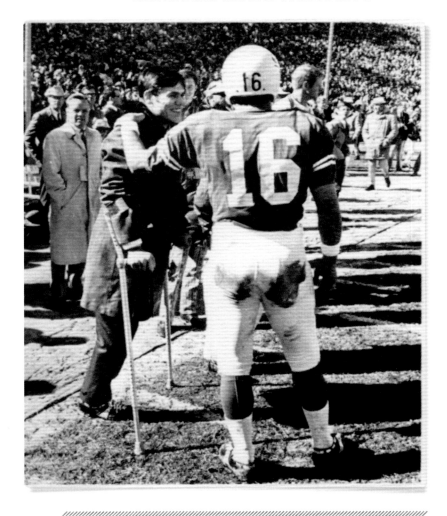

Quarterback James Street greets teammate Freddie Steinmark at the 1970 Cotton Bowl game against Notre Dame. Steinmark had been diagnosed with cancer three weeks earlier. (1970 Cactus, Texas Student Media*)*

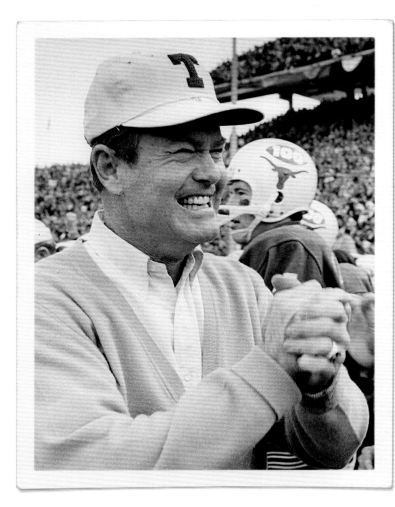

"I'm not one to toy with happiness. It's hard to come by."

—Darrell K Royal

muddy, swampy mess, and there was speculation that Texas would have to alter its offense from one so dependent on the running game. When asked about the possibility of changing, Royal replied, "We're gonna dance with the one who brung us." He borrowed the phrase from a popular 1920s song, but it soon spread like wildfire and became attributed to him.

As the Longhorns came down the tunnel onto the field, when every thought should have been focused on the upcoming game against the Irish, Royal walked in front of the end zone toward the Texas bench, then stopped. He turned, walked to the rail, and asked Cliff Bennett, an eleven-year-old with bright orange hair, whether he had a good seat. Cliff's mother replied that he did not. Royal grinned and handed Cliff a bench pass, then warned, "But don't get in my way."

No coach had figured out yet how to stop the wishbone machine, but Notre Dame outweighed the Longhorns almost twenty pounds a man. The Irish held the lead for most of the game, and with just over two minutes left, the Horns were trailing 14–17 with seventy-six yards between them and victory. Once more, a Street pass—this time to all-American receiver Charles "Cotton" Speyrer—took Texas to within scoring distance. Billy

Dale's touchdown and Happy Feller's extra point with just 1:18 remaining put Texas ahead 21–17. Another dramatic last-minute interception by Tom Campbell sealed a Texas win over the Irish. Campbell hung on to the ball and refused to hand it over to the referee. He ran toward the Texas bench and placed the ball in Royal's hands for safekeeping. Later, in an emotional locker-room presentation, Royal gave the game ball to Freddie Steinmark.

Royal was determined to avoid the mistake he had made after the 1963 national championship. Royal had been so tied up after beating Navy in the Cotton Bowl that, as he later admitted, he "wasn't involved with recruiting almost until spring training started." He promised himself and his staff that he would stay focused on Texas football, but there was plenty to draw his attention elsewhere.

On Thursday, January 2, 1970, the day after the Horns beat Notre Dame, Royal flew to Tampa to coach the Lions Club All-American Bowl on January 3 with Bear Bryant. After a short trip home to Austin, Royal flew to Washington, D.C., on January 10 to receive the Washington Touchdown Club's Coach of the Year and Team of the Year awards, but was back in Austin by the 12th for the Longhorns' annual football banquet. Monday, January 13, found the coach flying back to D.C. to receive the Coach of the Year award from the American Football Coaches Association. In between engagements, he was recruiting.

The 1970 season brought more of the same—victories. Texas had a streak of twenty wins behind it, but the question on everyone's mind was "Can Eddie Phillips be as successful as James Street was?" Phillips answered that question early when Texas beat Cal 56–15 in the season opener. Royal called Phillips's performance "remarkable."

The Horns stormed through the regular season unscathed, prompting Royal to proclaim, "You can talk about your drop-back passers and your pro prospects . . . You take the guys with the stats—I'll take Eddie."

Television tried desperately to hype another Big Shootout. The contest was moved to the last week of the regular season, and both teams were undefeated going into the game. Texas was ranked first, Arkansas fourth. But the night before the game, Royal uncharacteristically issued a warning: "We're ready. We're gonna get body on body and be angry. We're gonna get folks on folks and it's gonna be Worster *and* Bertelsen." That was as close to trash-talking as Coach Royal ever came. The second shootout was almost a shutout as Texas annihilated the Hogs, 42–7. After being voted national champions for the second year in a row by the UPI (the AP choice was Nebraska), Texas again met Notre Dame in the Cotton Bowl. That year, however, Notre Dame exacted its revenge, and the Horns' win streak ended at thirty games. It was time to reload.

AUSTIN, TEXAS

Dear Coach Royal:

As a rancher I am well aware of the hog and cattle market. I think it is significant that steers are up and hogs are down.

I have no doubt that this will be the case Saturday afternoon.

I have not missed a University of Texas football game this season. And while I do not associate this with your current winning streak, I am not going to change my routine tomorrow afternoon. I don't expect the Longhorns to change their routine, either.

I understand that Presidents are now somewhat reluctant to name teams Number One -- especially since Pennsylvania went Democratic last month. But I will go on record as saying that Darrell Royal's Texas Longhorns are Number One in my book and will still be Number One tomorrow night. Despite what you may have heard, Number One does try harder, especially when it's Texas.

Sincerely,

(The husband of a Texas Ex)

Coach Darrell Royal
c/o University Pep Rally
Memorial Stadium
Austin, Texas 78712

December 4, 1970

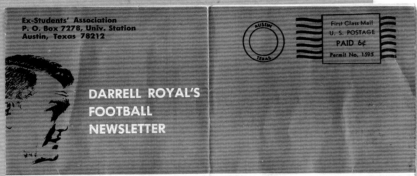

Ex-Students' Association
P. O. Box 7278, Univ. Station
Austin, Texas 78212

First Class Mail
U. S. POSTAGE
PAID 6¢
Permit No. 1595

DARRELL ROYAL'S FOOTBALL NEWSLETTER

TEXAS 56   CALIFORNIA 15

Our opener against California was the sharpest first game since I have been at Texas. Last year we received stubborn resistance from California defenders, and I anticipated the same this year. In contrast to that, our first offensive unit had the ball six times and scored five. The direction and execution of Eddie Phillips was truly remarkable.

Now comes the big question. Can we continue at this pace? I doubt it. Our opposition is going to have a lot to say about that. I honestly believe that in our next nine games there will be three or four in which the margin between victory and defeat will be very thin. It's how well we execute and perform in these tight situations that will count.

But back to our game with California. We thought our starting defense and offense both exceptionally solid. Our offensive line had very few busted assignments, and both graded high when our coaching staff looked at the film.

All of our backs blocked well. Some people came away from the stadium feeling that our halfbacks, Bertelsen and Dale, did not play all that well because they did not see them as ball-carriers, but they were turning in valuable contributions as blockers and fakers. This, of course, opened up excellent running opportunities for Phillips.

Our defense was equally as solid over all, but you would have to single out Bill Atessis, Danny Lester, and Scott Henderson. We especially were pleased with Atessis, since we did not know whether or not he would be in good enough physical condition to go all out. We were pleased!

Our coaching staff has developed a real respect for the operation going on at Texas Tech. Their new staff have done a truly magnificent job of getting their program off to a good start. Every football fan knows they have won their two opening ball games, but the coaching staff of The University of Texas knows _why_ this has happened. We have looked at the films, and they are well coached. It is apparent they have a pattern in mind, and they are not going to deviate from it. They are going to do the same thing game after game, and they are going to get better and better. The worst position you can possibly be in is to be changing from week to week, never really deciding what you want to do. The Red Raiders are not suffering from indecision.

Darrell Royal

for members of **THE EX-STUDENTS' ASSOCIATION**

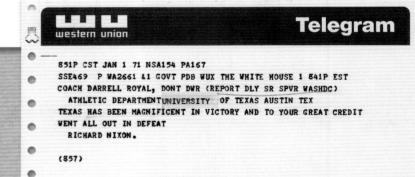

western union   **Telegram**

851P CST JAN 1 71 NSA154 PA167
SSE469 P WA2661 &1 GOVT PDB WUX THE WHITE HOUSE 1 841P EST
COACH DARRELL ROYAL, DONT DWR (REPORT DLY SR SPVR WASHDC)
ATHLETIC DEPARTMENT UNIVERSITY OF TEXAS AUSTIN TEX
TEXAS HAS BEEN MAGNIFICENT IN VICTORY AND TO YOUR GREAT CREDIT
WENT ALL OUT IN DEFEAT
    RICHARD NIXON.

(857)

SF-1201 (R8-69)

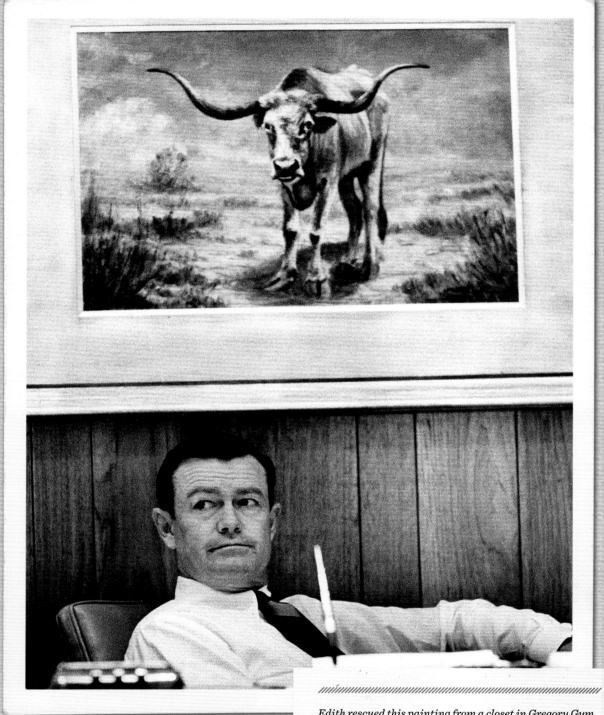

Edith rescued this painting from a closet in Gregory Gym and had it reframed for her husband's office. Royal admires this scrawny, wild steer: *"This one is out on the range. He rustles for what he eats, for water. He'll take you. He'll get after you."* The painting hung behind Royal's desk; players stared it as they waited on their coach or as they were getting a piece of his mind. (Royal Family Archives)

Chapter 13
PHILOSOPHY

By the time he sat in front of Darrell Royal on his 1967 recruiting trip to Texas, Freddie Steinmark carried a sizable chip on his shoulder. The high school senior had received just about every honor that a Colorado high school football player could receive, yet when the time came for colleges to recruit him, he heard nothing. Even the folks in his own backyard, the University of Colorado, passed on him. He was too small. Yet about his meeting with Royal, Freddie wrote years later, "Not once did Coach Royal mention my size."

Royal never let a player's lack of size influence him. He himself had been labeled "too small to play" all his life. He liked his Longhorns lean and mean and hungry, like the one in the painting that hung behind his desk. He recruited the type of player he had been: undersized, mobile, smart, totally dedicated—and with a burning hatred of losing. Steinmark, who weighed 150 pounds when Royal offered him a scholarship, wound up starting at safety and returning punts for the 1969 national champions. Royal says, "I never brought it up to him, never. We either wanted him or we didn't. . . . Hey, he weighed as much as I did when I was at OU."

Every phase of the game was important to Royal, and he emphasized the kicking game, something many coaches treated as an afterthought. "Press the kicking game, for it's here the breaks are made" was a mantra for him, understandable for a guy who was once considered the best punter and punt returner in the nation. He knew firsthand that dramatic plays on special teams could swing the momentum of a game. He employed the quick kick,

> "Punt returns will kill you quicker than a minnow can swim a dipper."
>
> —Darrell K Royal

OKLAHOMA COACH Bud Wilkinson (right) is exponent of the Split-T formation. Handling the QB role this season is the Sooners' All-America candidate, Darrell Royal.

A CONSISTENT runner, Royal bucks the line with authority. He's Oklahoma's top runback star, averaging 32.8 yards (a team record) each time he takes an enemy punt.

Small
SOONER
M·E·N·A·C·E·S
Big
Seven

8

As a 148-pound quarterback at OU, Royal reminded one sportswriter of "a skinny little fellow who looked like an appetite in search of a good meal." (Norris Anderson, writing in the Miami News, 1949; DKR Papers, DBCAH, di_07347)

Opposite page: Royal, considered the premier punter in the nation, 1946. He learned firsthand how effective special-teams play can swing the momentum of a game. (Royal Family Archives)

MDRT

K

1946 - O.U.

One of Royal's pregame checklists: Press the Kicking Game. The coach's philosophy: "Most teams, I'd guess, work on their kicking game at the end of practice when everyone is tired. We work on it first." (DKR Papers, DBCAH, di_07384)

him!'" The 1964 Horns had a powerful running attack and were leading the nation in scoring, but still people asked, "When are you gonna throw the ball?" In response to fans and writers who labeled him too conservative, Royal once remarked—half in jest— "Three things can happen when you throw the football and two of them are bad." The quip took on a life of its own and added to his conservative image. The coach might have been kidding when he said it, but the proof is in the numbers. In 1972, senior tight end Julius Whittier led the team in touchdown receptions. As a matter of fact, Whittier caught every single touchdown pass thrown that year. And he caught *it* against the Aggies.

Jones Ramsey, the longtime sports information director at Texas, told the story of the team doctor, Paul Trickett, attending to two players who had collided in practice. Both players had fallen to the ground, but one boy was having trouble breathing; his tongue was blocking his airway. Trickett ran onto the field and knelt beside the player, working furiously over him. Coach Royal ran onto the practice field behind the doctor, studied the situation, then started barking questions into Trickett's ear: "Why don't you do this? Have you tried . . .? Don't you think you should . . .?" Without a hint of a glance in Royal's direction, Trickett snapped, "Why don't you pass more?" Point taken. Royal turned and left the trusted doctor to his work.

kicking on third instead of fourth down, a maneuver many people thought silly or too conservative.

Not everyone shared Royal's enthusiasm for the quick kick. Bud Shrake was one of Royal's biggest needlers among the press corps, and Dan Jenkins shared this story from the 1962 college all-star game in Chicago. Royal arrived at a cocktail party wearing a tiny tie clasp in the shape of a punter. When he walked over to greet Shrake, the writer pointed to the tie clasp and said, "What is it, Darrell, second and two?" It cracked Royal up, and he moved around the room, repeating the joke. Another time, Shrake joked: "If you want to see somebody nervous, look at Darrell Royal when he suddenly realizes it's third down and his team still has the ball."

Royal was also tagged early on as being "anti-pass." Walt Fondren, Royal's first quarterback at Texas, said in *What It Means to Be a Longhorn*, "Coach Royal hated incomplete or dropped passes. He'd say, 'If a guy's open, run down there and hand it to

Royal wasn't opposed to passing when it served his purposes, especially when throwing the ball would surprise an opponent. In 1958, in his first win over Oklahoma, he launched a late-game passing attack with a seldom-used quarterback, Vince Matthews, then put his regular starter, Bobby Lackey, back in to seal the 15–14 win. In 1963, the Longhorns' perfect season was in jeopardy when Texas was trailing A&M 13–9 late in the fourth quarter. A flurry of passes by the backup quarterback, Tommy Wade, set up the winning score with just 1:19 left. And in the 1964 Cotton Bowl game, people were stunned when Duke Carlisle passed his way

> **"I'm not married to any one philosophy or any one idea. You have to break the pattern enough that people don't have you completely zeroed in."**
>
> —Darrell K Royal, after surprising fans by starting Tommy Wade, a pass-oriented quarterback, against Baylor in 1962

to a victory over Navy and into the Cotton Bowl Hall of Fame with 213 yards passing.

In 1969, Royal shocked his players and his offensive coordinator when he called 53 veer—a pass play that the team hadn't even practiced that week—in the Big Shootout versus Arkansas. The resulting win solidified the Horns' number one ranking. Texas followed that act by beating Notre Dame in the Cotton Bowl on a fourth-and-two sprint-out pass. Royal commented ruefully, "Now I'm pictured as a man who takes chances. Two stinkin' plays, and I'm a helluva gambler."

Royal was a mastermind when it came to motivating his teams. He didn't give rah-rah pep talks; he didn't believe in them. He issued challenges instead. Marvin Kubin, who played guard for Royal, described it this way: "When he talked to us before a game, he talked to us like a man who was going to play himself. He's so sincere about what has to be done." In 1967, when the Horns were losing to Oklahoma in a lackluster effort, Royal asked his team, "There's a heckuva fight going on out there, by one team. Why don't you join it?" Final score: Texas 9, OU 7. Following that game, Bill Van Fleet, a sportswriter for the *Fort Worth Star-Telegram*, said: "I don't have any idea what Darrell Royal told his team at halftime today. But some Monday morning when I've got a hangover and don't want to get up and go to work, when I'd just as soon lie there and maybe die, I just wish he'd walk into my bedroom and tell me the same thing he told them." Dan Cook of the *San Antonio Express-News* was awed at the coach's ability to motivate his team: "Just how Royal manages to touch his boys so deeply and keep them fired so high week after week . . . only he can say. But he does it better than any other man in the honorable coaching profession."

> **"The foremost rule is: be natural. If you're not completely natural, you couldn't convince your players Doris Day is a girl."**
>
> —Darrell K Royal

> **"You can't kid a kid. If you're not honest with your players, you're kidding yourself."**
>
> —Darrell K Royal

When Royal was recruiting James Street, he knew that other schools were discouraging James to come to Texas. After all, "Super Bill" Bradley was already situated there, and the press accounts had Bradley walking on water. Coach Royal presented Street with this challenge: "If you go somewhere else, you will *never* know whether you could have played with the best." That struck a chord with Street, and the rest is history.

Charley Shira, who coached with Royal for years, called him "an excellent psychologist . . . the boys can tell whether a coach is concerned with how they're doing. He treated the boys like adults."

The flip-flop. The wishbone. Upgraded facilities. A return to burnt orange. Beating the Aggies and winning the Southwest Conference almost every year. Of all the changes Royal made for good at Texas, the innovation he was proudest of came in his first season. Royal had been hired under trying circumstances. The football program was at an all-time low, compiling a 1-9 record in 1956. University president Logan Wilson had raised the academic standards at The University the season before Royal was hired. Texas was the first state university in the nation to require entrance exams for all freshmen. There was a heavier scholastic burden on Texas' upper-division athletes than on players at any other Southwest Conference school, including Rice. Many boosters believed that besides emphasizing academics, Wilson intended these measures to deemphasize football on campus. None of this scared Royal. Instead of railing against the toughened academic standards or trying to skirt them, Royal embraced them.

Royal claims he was never a strong student. He spent two years in the first grade, and he still winces at the shame of it. All kinds of factors were at play, but the bottom line was that no one at home was interested in his grades. No one looked at his report cards; there were more important things to worry about. As he got older, he realized there was only one way to realize his dream of coaching: he had to make it through college.

Gene Greyston, a sportswriter for the *Fort Worth Star-Telegram* who attended OU with Darrell, told the *Saturday Evening Post*, "He was quietly studious and was an avid reader. . . . He thought himself along into all-America quarterback acclaim and the coaching profession. . . . He was self-driven to study in the classroom and applied that to football, too." In every facet of his life—athletics, academics, public speaking, coaching, communications, and public relations—he embarked on a purposeful mission to improve himself and his skills. Years after Bud Wilkinson coached Darrell on the field and coached against him each October, Wilkinson said, "Royal's ambition inspired him to perfect himself in so many different phases. . . . He hated to be mediocre at anything." Just as he did as a boy, "he continued working constantly to better himself in every related area of football."

Where his own players were concerned, he saw that it was going to be difficult to keep them in school, yet he agreed that rigid classroom requirements would result in his acquiring more intelligent and "higher-type" athletes at Texas. He knew that he and his staff would have to recruit harder, smarter, and in large quantity to offset those competitive hardships and to account for attrition. He believed that the increased discipline and self-control required of the players in practice would be reflected in classroom performance. He made the connection plain: "We must have discipline. When we have it, you'll see the classroom grades go up."

UT's Athletics Council urged Royal to hire a full-time recruiting coordinator, but he insisted, "We don't need another 'get 'em here' coach; we need a 'keep 'em here' coach." Royal looked down the road and found Lan Hewlett, a former teacher from Lockhart, Texas, to oversee the players' scheduling, class attendance, grades, and progress toward their degrees. Today, colleges spend millions of dollars each year on tutors, academic counselors, and plush study halls for their athletes. But in 1957, with no pressure from the NCAA, Royal became the first coach in NCAA history to hire a full-time academic counselor, or "brain coach." The coaches' reaction to players skipping classes was swift and cut across all lines, from starters to the "bluebirds." Jack Collins, a starting running back in 1959–1961, cut class the week of the OU game. "And I remember having to run stadium steps with Frank Medina at 5:30 in the morning. I don't care if you were a starter or what. You didn't get by with that." Any player on scholastic probation or in danger of making that

"The pros are entertainment for private gain; the colleges are entertainment for educational gain."

—Darrell K Royal

list was sentenced to mandatory study hall for two hours a night, four nights a week.

One big incentive for persevering was the gift of a "T" ring, which Royal gave to any player who graduated. The gold ring, designed by Royal himself, has a raised orange stone topped with a white block *T*. In the beginning, Royal paid for the rings out of his own pocket so that "nobody could bitch about it." The Athletics Department eventually took over the responsibility, but for many years, Royal footed the bill. "The players needed to know it was important to me. I want those men to graduate, even if the only reason they do is to make the old SOB pay for that ring." Royal still sees those rings today, and if he spots one, he will likely "bump T rings" with the wearer. To the players, earning a "T" ring is a matter of immeasurable pride, and the ring itself is considered a treasure. Tom Loeffler, a former presidential aide and U.S. congressman, put it to Royal this way: "Most importantly, you have personally been by my side throughout each of my triumphs and defeats. I hold your faith in me on the football field, in the classroom, in the public and private sector as a true blessing in my life. One of my most prized

The proud tradition Royal started continues today; the "T" ring is offered to letter winners in all sports, but only if they graduate. Photography by Rick Henson.

possessions is the 'T' ring you gifted me upon graduation. I have worn this ring proudly every day since, not only because you gave it to me, but because it embodies who you are and who we should all strive to become."

Under Royal's terms, there was only one way a man could receive a "T" ring: he had to be on the team and he had to graduate. Larry Stephens, a defensive lineman under Royal in 1957–1959, played several years of pro football but had not graduated. Every off-season, Royal visited Larry at his home to try to convince him to finish school. Finally, after his pro career came to an end, Stephens did return to The University for his degree—more than ten years after playing for Royal. "You do what Coach wants you to do or never get any peace," he said. "He's tougher on you after you quit playing than when you're playing for him, and that was tough enough."

A sampling of tributes from other players makes clear the importance of earning a "T" ring. From Fred Bednarski (kicker, 1957–1958):

Thank you for emphasizing the importance of education and graduation. This was a tremendous motivation for me to be diligent in my studies and to earn my degree. Each day I wear proudly the "T" ring that you bought for me when I lettered and graduated. Through the years you have always been available to me and to your former players who will never forget the pride that you had in each and every one of us. We will always remember you as the greatest coach and friend who inspired us to live with integrity and strive for excellence.

From Olen Underwood (lineman, 1962–1964):

Coach, I have received many awards since I left The University.

Every recognition I have received can be laid at the feet of two men: my father, and you. . . . I can say with comfort no award I have received means more to me than the orange and white "T" ring given to me by my head coach upon graduation. Every Saturday in the fall, you stood before a group of young men and told them, "Great Teams Make Goal Line Stands." You taught all of us that that principle applies in all walks of life.

From Randy McEachern (quarterback, 1977–1978):

You influenced your players in so many ways, but my favorite tradition of yours is the "T" ring. Not much needed to be said. . . . We knew what it meant, and we knew what it took to get it. There was no easy way to get this prize. Not even an all-American player could get a "T" ring unless he graduated. . . . This was just what was expected. I wear mine everyday with pride. It's a great reminder of your influence in my life. Here's to you!

And from Keith Moreland (defensive back, 1973–1974):

You can't imagine what it meant to me to get my "T" ring at age 38. That's an integral part of the experience, knowing that you played football for Darrell Royal, graduated, and have that ring. I've got a national championship ring for baseball and a World Series ring, and that "T" ring is just as important to me as those other rings.

During the Royal years, 80 percent of football lettermen earned their degrees, a fact in which Royal takes tremendous pride. Knowing how easy it is for football to take over players' lives, he saw support for academics as part of his legacy: "The tail should never wag the dog, but as long as football is in its proper place on the campus, then it is good."

The team that Royal had called "average as everyday's wash" carried him off the field in triumph after the 1973 Cotton Bowl game. (1973 Cactus, Texas Student Media)

> *"Football is hard enough when you **want** to be out there."*
>
> —Darrell K Royal on former player Gary Shaw's admission that he had never wanted to play college football

▼

Chapter 14

BEGINNING OF THE END

Despite devastating personnel losses—the offense had only three returning starters—the 1971 Longhorns kept the streak going by winning a fourth consecutive SWC championship. Just twelve days before Texas was to face Penn State in the Cotton Bowl, Texas A&M hired Royal's offensive backfield coach, Emory Bellard, to be the head coach. His presence in the press box was missed, and in what Royal called "one of our most embarrassing games," the Nittany Lions spanked the Horns, 30–6.

Royal called his 1972 team "average as everyday's wash" before the season started, but leading that team was one of the most rewarding experiences he would ever have as a coach. Texas started off well enough with three wins, then got shut out by OU, 27–0. After that whipping, Royal's "average" team went on to win Texas's fifth SWC title in a row. They beat Bama and the Bear, 17–13, in the Cotton Bowl in a defensive triumph. The 1973 *Cactus* reported that Royal showed "more emotion than usual, skipping off the field like a youngster on his way home with a straight 'A' report card." The team that their coach had called "average" may not have been the best Longhorn squad ever, but they came the farthest, finishing third in the nation.

* * * * *

The bowl victory provided a satisfying end to a year that had been soured by the harshest, most sustained public criticism of Royal and the Longhorns to date. On the Royals' living-room bookshelf sits a hardbound copy of *Meat on the Hoof*, written in early 1972 by Gary Shaw, a disgruntled former Longhorn football player. The book hit the stores about a year after Texas won its second national championship, and in a firestorm of destructive publicity, it sold more than 350,000 copies. It was intended to be an exposé of the abuses of UT football and its coaches. Shaw depicted Royal as tyrannical and unfeeling, trying to run off players who weren't playing well enough so that he could redistribute their scholarships.

The criticism was searing, and it scorched Royal. Still, he spoke candidly to his players about it. Shortly after the book's release, Royal interrupted practice and gathered the team at the middle of Memorial Stadium's field. He got right to the point.

> We all know about this book, *Meat on the Hoof*. I'm not here to indict the book or to defend myself. But I regret to tell you that one part is true: Gary wrote that several years after he quit the team, he walked up to me, and I didn't recognize him.

This was a serious accusation against the coach. Royal's memory for faces and names and his players' physiques was exceptional, and it was a matter of pride that he could remember all his former players and call them by name. Royal continued:

> Gary had grown his hair down to his shoulders, had lost about 30 pounds, and had grown a full beard. I did not recognize him. I hate to admit it, but he's telling the truth in that part. Fellas, I don't think the majority of that book is true, but y'all are going to have to read it and judge for yourselves. We're not going to change the way we do anything; I just wanted to get this out in the open.

A few teammates saw Shaw as a hero who dared dig up the skeletons of the most successful program—and coach—in the country. Other players claimed they didn't recognize the program Shaw had described. Regardless of which version was correct, Shaw's version of the truth tarnished the sterling image of Darrell Royal and The University.

Another controversy that dogged him for the rest of his career was the glacial speed with which the Southwest Conference and The University moved to integrate athletics.

"Let's face it," Royal told the *Boca Raton News* in 1973:

> It's a fact that when I first came here, Texas wasn't integrated. Then . . . the regents said we could start integrating, but they meant that we didn't have to push it or worry about it. After a few years, they were, "All right, we really meant it." Then they progressed to "Gawl-dog, let's really go out and make the effort to totally integrate the school, totally integrate athletics."

When Royal was hired, in 1956, the UT regents declared that "they just weren't ready yet" to integrate. Finally, in 1963, Texas became the first Southwest Conference school to permit the integration of athletics, but there was no mandate; the regents were simply giving their permission. The action, said Lou Maysel of the *Austin American-Statesman*, "was like handing Royal an anchor and telling him to swim with it."

The dorms were still segregated. The dining halls were too. Although the regents had said, "Go ahead," they made no provisions for any black team members to eat or sleep on campus.

Royal later took part of the blame. He regretted his foot-dragging:

> I'm sorry I didn't integrate sooner. There was no question but what it was just and right. . . . Part of it was legislated, part of it was people stopping, analyzing the situation, and facing up to what is right and wrong. . . . Any fair-minded person who looked at it, who did some thinking about it, wanted to do what was right.

Royal began recruiting black players in the mid-1960s, and a couple of them enrolled in The University in 1968, but left after one year. Royal finally snagged Julius Whittier, a talented and personable player from San Antonio, who became the first African American football letterman in UT history. Other African Americans followed; by 1972, there were six black players on the team.

Royal was still stinging from the slap of *Meat on the Hoof*, when the Associated Press ran a five-part series on integration—or the lack of it—and the treatment of black UT football players. Royal himself cooperated and gave his time to the project. He was eager to have the issue aired, and he hoped to quiet opposing coaches' claims that he was a racist. He felt confident in authorizing his six black players to cooperate with the AP.

Robert Heard and Jack Keever cowrote the series. They painted Royal as a racist, and he was blindsided by the damaging comments his players made. Coaches who had lost many a recruit to Royal rubbed their hands in glee at having more ammo to use against Texas. The second installment of the series opened with this statement: "Darrell Royal's image is so bad among some blacks that they suspect he even taunts and mistreats his maid." In actuality, his "maid" in Starkville, Mississippi, thought so highly of him that she named her son Darrell Royal Reese.

> **"You know something? I'm not sure I would have been happy either as a second-stringer, a dummy holder."**
>
> —Darrell K Royal, discussing former player Gary Shaw

Thursday – Nov 16, 1972

Dear Coach Royal

I'm writing this note with a lump in my throat and a prayer in my heart. I am so sorry that a few Blacks have such feelings for you, as was expressed in the News papers.

For eleven years I have known you as a fair and wonderful person! Don't let talk and such things get next to you. Please continue to express and do things as you have been doing. As a Black person I feel you are doing a wonderful job. You and your Family are in my prayers.

May God Bless you

//

Left to right: *Paul "Bear" Bryant, Harold Stinson, president of Stillman College, and Darrell Royal, 1970. Royal quietly served for years on the board of trustees of Stillman College, a historically African American liberal arts college in Tuscaloosa, Alabama, and helped forge a relationship between Stillman and UT. (Royal Family Archives)*

///

Despite the AP series accusing Royal of racial insensitivity, he received support from much of Austin's African American community, including this letter from a black housekeeper. (DKR Papers, DBCAH, di_07357)

Most of the players were mortified when they saw their words in print; although none claimed to have been misquoted, most felt they'd been put on the spot, taken advantage of. Each of the six made their way to Royal's office to apologize, and in each case, Royal was willing to let bygones be bygones. But the lasting damage to Royal's reputation and The University's was done.

Royal was hurt, and he was confounded by the accusations. He had coached and befriended black players in Edmonton, and when white players on the team made racist remarks, Royal was quick to chew them out. At Washington, Royal had inherited a team full of dissension and racial division in 1956. Observers doubted whether Royal, coming from Mississippi, was equipped to solve the program's problems. But he surprised many onlookers. Royal Brougham of the *Seattle Post-Intelligencer*, wrote, "Firmly, skillfully, quietly, the coaches licked the problems. There are no favorites, no discrimination; a fair deal for all." That year, Royal's backfield consisted of Credell Green, Luther Carr, Bobby Herring, and Jim Jones, all African Americans.

In 1976, the Stillman College choir presented a concert at the First Southern Presbyterian Church in Austin. Among the performers was Bill Caldwell, a senior baritone who had auditioned with and been accepted to both Southern Methodist University and to The University of Texas. Darrell and Edith attended the concert that night, and afterward, they ate dinner with Caldwell and James Arthur Williams, Stillman's choir director. "I can't remember the restaurant," Caldwell recalled, "but I'll never forget this: as soon as we were seated, a waiter placed an enormous tray of appetizers on our table and said, 'Coach Royal, compliments of the house.' It occurred to me then that I was eating dinner with someone special."

During the course of the meal, the director explained that after graduation, his star pupil would be attending either UT or SMU, and that the young man was leaning toward SMU.

"Darrell and Edith looked at one another," Caldwell said. "I could see there was unspoken communication between them. Then Darrell said, 'Bill, if you do decide to come to The University of Texas, Edith and I would like to help with your housing and

tuition and such.'" At this point, Caldwell's mouth was hanging open. "We could get you a scholarship; there's the Earl Campbell Chevrolet Award. It's only a thousand dollars, but that would help." Caldwell stammered, "Well, sure I'll come."

At summer's end—in the middle of two-a-day practices—Edith and Darrell met Bill at Austin's Mueller Airport. Again he noticed the parting of the crowds and the stares as Coach Royal moved among the masses.

Caldwell became a part of the Royals' lives: "They didn't just help me financially. Oh, I babysat their grandchildren, and Darrell would hand me some money as he dropped me off at Jester Dorm. But he and Edith made me part of their family. When the dorms closed, I stayed at their home. I worked in the athletes' dining hall, and I ate there, too. I once drove their car to Jones Hall in Houston to hear the opera. . . . Their generosity was boundless.

"They didn't demand it or even seem to want it, but people in Austin treated them like royalty." Caldwell laughed, "When Darrell Royal walked in to attend my master's recital, you'd have thought Pavarotti had arrived. Everyone backstage was excited and whispering, 'Oh, my God! He's here! He's here!' That's probably the only time a UT football coach attended anything in the Music Department."

Today, Bill Caldwell is the chair of the Department of Fine Arts and Music at Central State University in Dayton, Ohio. He has nothing but admiration for the Royals:

Everyone up here in Buckeye Country knows about what the Royals did for me. This was his way of reaching out to a student at an historically black college. And people called him a racist? Judging by the way his players talked about him to me, and based on what he did for me, I call him ideal and trustworthy. People will always try to tarnish a man's good name. . . . People like to believe negative gossip. But I tell you, I have performed all over this world and that man deserves a lot of credit for what I've been able to achieve in my life. I am proud to be a friend of Darrell Royal's. And I'm not talking about his football team, I'm talking about the man.

Bill Caldwell. He was one of dozens of UT students—nonathletes—whom Darrell and Edith sponsored through their years at Texas. As Edith puts it: "Darrell and I enjoyed sponsoring different students, students who had nothing to do with athletics. We 'adopted' an international student each year, and that was always such fun for us. 'Course, we didn't get as close to most as we did to Bill." (Royal Family Archives)

Your children are not your children.
They are the sons and daughters of Life's longing for itself.
They come through you but not from you,

. . . .

For life goes not backward nor tarries with yesterday.
                                    —Kahlil Gibran, *The Prophet*

In 1973, Edith and Darrell were going through a rough patch with their daughter, Marian. She had divorced her husband, Chic Kazen, an attorney, and moved from Washington, D.C., back to Austin with their two toddlers. Chic opened a law practice in his hometown of Laredo.

Marian was a loving and attentive mother, but her parents didn't understand her affinity for the Armadillo World Headquarters scene, and they didn't approve of some of her friends. Chic and Marian became embroiled in a child-custody battle, and Marian was frustrated by her parents' determination to remain neutral in the fight. One morning in March, Marian Royal Kazen drove to the Episcopal Church of the Good Shepherd in West Austin to pick up her elder son, Christian, from nursery school. Christian's little brother, David, was three and a half, and he begged his mother to let him swing on the school playground. Marian relented, even though it made her late to pick up her former sister-in-law for lunch. She finally got the boys in the car. Christian was coloring in the back floorboard, and David was in the front seat with his mother when a University of Texas shuttle bus slammed into Marian's car. Christian was unharmed, but David's leg was broken just above the knee. He was in a full-body cast for months.

Marian was in a coma. Edith and Darrell reacted to Marian's injury in different ways. The hospital was a few blocks from Memorial Stadium, and Darrell visited often, spending time at her bedside. Edith could hardly force herself to walk into Marian's hospital room. Seeing her beautiful daughter like that

Marian K Royal, an art student at The University of Texas in 1964, studying the progress of a bust she was sculpting of her mother. (Royal Family Archives)

Marian and Christian Kazen, exhausted mother and son, c. 1969. (Royal Family Archives)

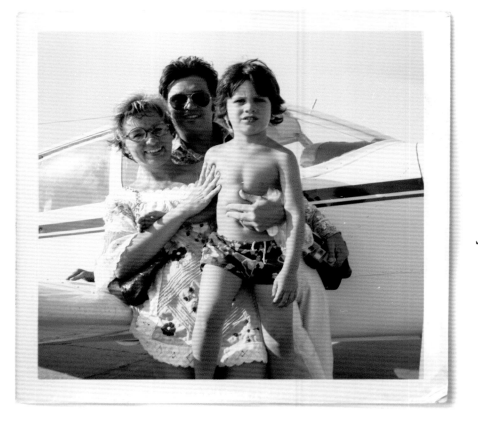

was unbearable. Plus, she had grandbabies to watch after and two other children to comfort.

The parents of Reggie Grob rushed to Austin to stand by the Royals as they had stood by the Grobs' side eleven years earlier in Brackenridge Hospital.

Marian remained unresponsive for twenty days. She died on April 11, 1973. Darrell and Edith reacted in different ways to Marian's death, too. They tried to comfort each other, but they could not. They grieved in such different and separate ways.

Edith remembers:

> I wanted to be with Darrell. I needed his companionship. I needed to cry and to talk about Marian with him. . . . Darrell needed to keep moving. He needed diversions. He needed to be with lots of other people. To me, it seemed he just went to the stadium or the golf course, and that didn't seem like grieving at all. Finally, one of my dearest friends who had lost a child told me that I needed to grieve in my own way, but I had to allow Darrell to grieve in his own way.

Edith's blue eyes pool with tears.

> You just learn how to put one foot in front of the other, to keep breathing. . . . It doesn't come natural, that's for sure. Oh, lots of things helped us through it—the love of all our friends, of course.

One of the first people to knock on their door was Willie Nelson. He offered consolation the best way he knew how: through his music. He arrived at their home, guitar in hand, and played "Healing Hands of Time," a song about a man whose love has left him and who anxiously awaits the healing hands of time to mend his heart.

Edith continues,

> I had a psychiatrist friend who lived near us. Every single day for weeks he stopped in my driveway after work just to check in, to see how I was doing. Sometimes he'd just tap on my kitchen window and smile at me. I never forgot that kindness; it was one thing that helped me survive. . . . Mary Ann Ramsey [the former wife of Jones Ramsey, UT's sports information director] was ahead of her time. She brought over a book called *The Prophet*, by Kahlil Gibran. That's the first time I read the poem about children—

> "Your children are not your own." I had that read at Marian's funeral. . . . In fact, it may have been Mary Ann who read it.

Edith cared for Marian and Chic's sons throughout the ordeal, and it helped her survive those days. But after Marian's death, a representative from the Kazen family came to tell her gently that the boys would be moving to Laredo with their father. Edith admits: "That was so tough; my guts were ripped out all over again. But they were Chic's children. They had to go."

Edith told a friend after Marian's death, "When you lose a child, after the anguish comes a kind of strength. You realize that from here on out, nothing—not the loss of a parent, or a friend or even a spouse—can ever hurt you that badly again."

Then the unthinkable happened. In March 1982, the Royals' telephone rang at two in the morning. It was a call from Brackenridge Hospital, telling them that their thirty-year-old son David, their youngest, had been in a motorcycle accident. The doctor told them gently that there was "no need to hurry."

Edith recounts what people were able to piece together about the accident:

> I don't know that much about David's accident. His friends knew he had bought a motorcycle, but he told them, "Do not tell my mama I have this. She doesn't want me to have one, and she'll have a fit if she finds out." At around one in the morning, he was working on his motorcycle in his garage. He took it for a test drive and rounded the corner from West 6th, heading north on Mopac. No one knows how it happened, but David lost control of his motorcycle, hit a traffic sign, and died.

Edith, David, and Darrell, Cuernavaca, Mexico, 1963.
David Royal was the "baby" of the family, as was Darrell,
and the apple of his family's eye. (Royal Family Archives)

Best friends David Royal and Keith Tanaguchi clown
around with the coach. (Royal Family Archives)

David's death overwhelmed them with renewed grief for Marian as well, as Edith continues:

Yes, the love of your friends is just about *all* that can get you through it. There's no other way. And to have it happen twice is still, even thirty years later, sort of unbelievable. When David died, almost ten years after Marian, it was just like she had died all over again. Darrell and I had to grieve for both of them. Again.

For a long time, I didn't know how to respond when people asked me how many children I had. Was I supposed say, "I have one son?" Was I supposed to say, "Well, I used to have three, but two died?" There's no etiquette book that can tell you how to answer that.

We made some changes around our house. No more phone calls after 10:00 p.m. Darrell's buddies used to call at all hours of the night; they'd be drunk, and they'd call to play him a new song or just to tell jokes and laugh. But after David died, I told Darrell, "Either you tell them or I will. No more calls after 10:00 pm. It's too scary." At least now we can sleep through the night.

I started going to a twelve-step program about a year before David died, and it helped me learn how to give Darrell his space. I learned that just because his grief didn't look like mine, that did not mean that he wasn't dying inside, too. Learning how to be apart may have actually kept us together. But I know we almost did break up after Marian died.

I learned that you don't try to change anybody to fit what you want them to be. It only took me forty years to figure that out. Darrell just loves to control things, but I finally just told him, "I'm not coachable!" And I went back to church. I'd gotten so slack about going. Darrell's television show taped on Sunday mornings, so I went with him to the studio instead of going to church.

The deaths of their children destroyed any privacy they had and put their lives on display. They felt split open, eviscerated, but in the process, their hearts were softened. One result of living through and triumphing over the pain, the threat to their marriage, and their shaken faith is that they have comforted and encouraged thousands of souls. They are among the first to offer

"I think of them every day, yes. But now I think of them
with joy, not sadness. I think of how beautiful Marian was,
or how cute David was as a little boy . . . but not in grief.
Those memories are not colored with grief anymore."

—Edith Royal

comfort to people who are suffering. "It's something I relate to," Royal told Bill Little in *The Longhorn Album*. "All of us have lost family members, but there is nothing quite like losing a child."

His coaching, their response to others' tragedies, and their generosity—already seemingly boundless—evolved. The Royals' marriage, having been tempered twice through unspeakable tragedy, was made stronger and more resilient as a result.

In the weeks following Marian's wreck, Edith cared for her grandsons, ages three and six. Serving them, loving them, comforting them helped save her.

It was another baby that kept Edith clinging to this existence after David's death. On the day of David's funeral, a girl whom Edith had never met handed her a note, saying, "I need to talk to you." Edith called the girl, Beany Trombetta, about two weeks later and invited her to their home in Onion Creek. Beany bravely told the grieving parents that she was pregnant with David's child. Edith talked with David's friends and was convinced that the girl was being truthful. Beany assured the Royals that she wanted nothing from them, only to offer them a relationship with their grandchild. Darrell was suspicious. He was heartsick with grief and insisted that he would not be a part of it, but Edith's strength carried the day: "He did not want to be involved, but he tried to accept whatever I accepted. I told him, 'Well, you can do what you like, but that is David Royal's baby, and that baby is my grandchild.'"

> ## "It is possible to survive great grief by holding a baby."
>
> —Barbara Brown Taylor,
> *An Altar in the World*

When their only granddaughter, Elena, was born, all Darrell's resolve fell away. To look into Elena's eyes was to look into David Royal's, the resemblance was so great. Darrell found that it was, indeed, possible to survive great grief by holding a baby. At a pickin' party about eight months later, a grinning Coach Royal walked through the crowded room, greeting guests with baby Elena on his hip.

After their move to Texas in 1956, the Royals couldn't visit family in Oklahoma for Thanksgiving because of the annual football game against Texas A&M. If Texas went to a bowl game, which it usually did, there was no Christmas travel either. Once Marian and Chic started dating, the Royals began spending holidays with the Kazens, and the two families grew close. Later, throughout the marriage, separation, and divorce, then the custody battle, the Royals and the Kazens worked diligently and faithfully to maintain their friendship. They could not have envisioned what a blessing that would be, for when Marian died, there was nothing to repair. Both families were in the tragedy together.

Today, Chic, his sons, and his daughter from another marriage celebrate with Curley Ferris (the friend who introduced Chic to Marian) and with Beany, Elena, and Elena's half sister and with Mack Royal and his wife, April, and with all the Kazens. Edith laughs, "We never lose a family member. Even if someone gets a divorce, they'll come back and bring their new husband or wife." They may need a roster to keep up with the players, but it makes for a lively and loving holiday.

//

The Royals, Kazens, and other ancillary family members gather for Thanksgiving on the Pedernales, mid-1980s. Holidays are noisy, wild, and full of their close-knit and disparate "patchwork family." (Royal Family Archives)

The proud grandfather shows off his only granddaughter, Elena Royal Trombetta, c. 1986. (Royal Family Archives)

Cartoon showing Darrell Royal being "schooled" by Bud Wilkinson after Texas lost to OU in '57, Royal's first year as the Longhorns' coach. The game was the Horns' sixth loss in a row to the Sooners. (DKR Papers, DBCAH, di_07388)

> **"The only way anybody's going to beat Oklahoma is to go out there and whip 'em jaw to jaw. Texas has to develop a football tradition. It had one once, but it lost it. When we get one, maybe we can stop that bloodletting up at Dallas and turn it into a good show."**
>
> —Darrell K Royal, before Texas' 1958 victory, 15–14, over the Oklahoma Sooners, his first as a coach

Chapter 15
OU REVISITED

Through all the passion and hatred the Texas-OU game evokes, the competitive Royal states with certainty: "I have found that the players who have played in that game really do have respect for their adversaries. And it kind of puts you in a unique group of guys."

If the gladiators who have fought in that arena form "a unique group of guys," Royal belongs to an even more elite fraternity. He is one of only a handful of men to have experienced the combat from both sides.

Royal gets this series, perhaps better than anyone alive. As a player, Royal went 2-2 against the Longhorns and earned all-American honors along the way. He modeled his coaching style after that of Bud Wilkinson, his coach at Oklahoma, and tried to reflect his polite and dignified manner. Royal and Wilkinson both sought to keep the rivalry and the game at a "white competitive heat" without allowing it to slide into thuggery.

In Royal's second year at UT, the underdog Longhorns surprised everyone, especially the Sooners, sneaking by them 15–14. The narrow margin came from a two-point conversion after a touchdown. Royal had opposed the NCAA's adoption of the two-point play, but in a brilliant "if you can't beat 'em, join 'em" moment, turned it to his advantage in what would be the first game in NCAA history to be won using the two-point conversion. The hard-fought defensive battle was an emotional victory for the former Sooner. George Cross, the president of OU, came by the Texas locker room to congratulate Royal on the win, but the coach was nowhere to be found. Cross finally found him outside the locker room, sick at his stomach. Royal apologized and said, "Somehow it just doesn't seem right to beat Mr. Wilkinson."

Royal remains the winningest coach in the history of this series. He is the only coach on either side to win at least ten coveted "Golden Hat" trophies, and he is the only coach to win eight in a row. All told, Royal took part in twenty-four Texas-OU games, and coaching against his alma mater, his record was 12-7-1. It was that "1" that finally got him.

In Sports Illustrated *(October 22, 1962), Royal summed up his feelings about playing in the Red River Shootout. (Royal Family Archives)*

THEY SAID IT

• Darrell Royal, Texas coach, asked what he used to think about before the Texas game when he was an All-America quarterback at Oklahoma: "Self-preservation."

* * * * *

He has seen it at its best.

Royal noted, "The OU game was sold out in 1946, when I was a freshman, and it has been sold out ever since." The game often had national championship implications; Dan Jenkins, writing for *Sports Illustrated* in 1963, captured the spirit of the contest when he wrote: "The University of Texas football season begins with the Oklahoma game. All before it is so much throat-clearing."

And he has seen it at its nastiest.

There was the near riot in 1947 when OU fans, protesting several suspect calls, threw bottles onto the field at the refs. Darrell kept his helmet on and moved to the center of the field for fear of being hit by one of the missiles.

A fight that broke out in 1962 with four seconds left threatened to mar the Horns' 9–6 victory. Royal raced onto the field with the police to help restore order. The coach was finally able to assemble his men at midfield. He hollered at them, "You've got four seconds. One play. This is a football game, not a gang fight. Hold your tempers. Don't spoil winning for us. Win it and get off the field like gentlemen."

In 1972, Texas installed a quick-kick play specifically for the OU game. The Longhorns had not run the play for four years, and the only indication that the quick kick was coming was the substitution of Greg Dahlberg at center. No one would have known this unless they had been watching the Texas practice. But of

Royal, #21, led the Sooners past the Longhorns in 1948 and '49. (University of Texas Sports Photography)

course, those practices were closed to the public. "We really don't have that many secrets," Royal had said at the beginning of the week. "We're just closing our bedroom door, making practice more of a family deal."

The game was a defensive war, and the Horns' 3–0 lead held until late in the third quarter. On third down, from the UT twenty-five, Royal called for the quick kick. When Dahlberg went into the game, the Sooner players started yelling, warning one another, "Quick kick! Quick kick!" They blocked the kick and went on to win the game, 27–0. Afterward in the locker room, a joyous Lucious Selmon told reporters that the Sooners had practiced that play all week. OU's head coach, Chuck Fairbanks, admitted his team knew the kick was coming when they saw Dahlberg enter the game.

For the second year in a row, OU beat Texas with its own offense, the offense that Royal had helped Fairbanks install in 1971. Against the advice of Emory Bellard, the architect of the wishbone, Royal had agreed to help Fairbanks install UT's productive offense. OU wasn't in the Southwest Conference, and Royal had enjoyed a friendly relationship with Bud Wilkinson and Fairbanks, so he saw no reason not to share his expertise. Bellard and the rest of the coaching staff, however, thought Royal was crazy to share anything with the Sooners. Royal spent time with Fairbanks after the '71 season, schooling him on the finer points of the wishbone. It was a generous act that Royal would come to regret.

The 1976 Texas-OU game was one of the nastiest in the series. Royal had been convinced since the '72 game that OU spied on Longhorn practices, but having no concrete evidence, he said nothing. On the Thursday before the '76 Oklahoma game, however, Royal received reliable information from a Texas alumnus that a man named Lonnie Williams allegedly admitted that he had disguised himself as a construction worker, finagled his way onto Memorial Stadium's upper deck, secretly watched the Longhorns practice, then furnished helpful information to the Sooner staff.

Royal was enraged. In the days leading up to the Oklahoma game, he called out OU's coach, Barry Switzer, publicly and offered to donate ten thousand dollars to the alleged spy's favorite charity if he would take and pass a polygraph test. Royal also offered Switzer ten thousand dollars to pass a test proving he had not received confidential information about Texas' practice. Switzer declined.

Royal pressed the issue and upped the ante, offering to quit if Switzer and Larry Lacewell, OU's defensive coordinator, could pass the test. Switzer not only declined, he scoffed at the accusation and painted Royal as a paranoid old fool. He claimed, "Some coaches had rather sit around and listen to guitar pickers than work hard."

Coach Royal granted an interview to Robert Heard, a reporter for the Associated Press, to discuss the shameful situation. Heard was the same reporter who had cowritten the unflattering and incendiary five-part series on UT football, integration, and Royal's alleged racism. After years of dealing with him, Royal knew to guard his comments carefully if Heard were present.

After the interview was finished—or so Royal believed—he commented to Heard, "Why, those sorry bastards. I don't trust 'em on anything." Heard deemed, however, that the interview was *not* over, and when those comments hit print, the combustible situation caught fire.

Royal had not beaten Oklahoma since 1970, and he wanted to win this one badly, perhaps more than any other game of his career. After all of his and Wilkinson's efforts to keep the series intense but respectable, it had disintegrated into a sordid affair—personal, ugly, hate filled.

The outcome for Texas didn't look any more promising in '76 than it had for the last five years. The quarterback was unproven. The hoss, Earl Campbell, was nursing a hamstring injury. Johnny "Lam" Jones, the fastest player in college football, was out; all-American defensive back Johnnie Johnson was out. The injuries were so numerous that it was hard to keep track.

Sixteenth-ranked Texas was the underdog going into the game—Oklahoma was ranked third—but Mike Campbell's defensive scheme was brilliant. Texas' defense shut down OU's version of the wishbone, while punter Russell Erxleben did his usual job of keeping OU pinned in its own territory. OU linebacker Daryl Hunt was thrown out of the game for violently clotheslining Johnny "Ham" Jones, who was lost for the remainder of the game.

Texas led 6–0 until late in the fourth quarter. The Horns were confident of their ability to hold the Sooners, but after OU stripped the ball from the arms of a UT running back, the Sooners recovered and moved the ball thirty-seven yards in ten plays to score. "It was like having bleacher seats at the siege of the Alamo; you knew how it was gonna turn out, but you couldn't avert your eyes," Steve Ross wrote for

> **"I regret that Switzer wouldn't answer the tough questions. . . . We wound up providing him a forum for a non-denial denial. But your commitment to ethics and morality came through strongly . . . This is one Texas-Oklahoma battle you won easily."**
>
> —A representative of ABC Sports in a letter to Darrell and Edith, October 1976 (Royal Family Archives)

Barry Switzer
Gerald Ford
+
DK

Barking Carnival, a website devoted to Longhorn sports, more than thirty years after witnessing the game.

OU missed the extra point, and that was how the game ended, 6–6. Players, coaches, fans on both sides—everyone was disgusted with the outcome. This one had been about more than football; this one had pitted—in the minds of Texas fans—cheaters against those with integrity, evil against good. But this time, the good guys took it on the chin. The game seemed to rip out any heart that was left in Royal. Trudging up the tunnel, he looked ten years older than he had looked at kickoff.

In March 1978, Larry Lacewell admitted the spying took place and expressed sincere regret both publicly and in a telephone call to Royal. Lonnie Williams, who was later accused of spying on closed practices by Nebraska, Michigan, and California, has kept quiet about it. In his 1991 autobiography, *Bootlegger's Boy*, Switzer admitted that Oklahoma had indeed, spied on UT's practice and had used that information against the Longhorns.

Years later, however, Switzer recanted, claiming that he had admitted to cheating only to make Darrell happy. Royal's friends and Texas fans have never forgotten this ugly chapter in college football, but the coach let it go years ago, saying, "There's no sense picking old scabs or digging up bones."

The season didn't get much better after that. It had been three years since Marian's death, and not only had the tragedy taken a substantial toll on the Royals' marriage, but some of his intensity, his drive, had gone missing as well. Losing seemed more painful, and winning wasn't quite as important anymore. Once he had been fueled by a pure love for his job, for the adrenaline and the competition and the intellect required to outsmart the opponent, for the immense pleasure of leading and developing young men. But now he was tired. He was tired of trying to force his own sense of honor onto college football, tired of a game that was changing for the worst before his eyes. He was tired of the demeaning work of courting eighteen-year-old prima donnas who had no sense of honor themselves. He was tired of the cheating, the coaches who went along with it, and an NCAA that was not moving swiftly or thoroughly enough to suit him. After twenty-five years, he was tired of teaching the same subject and giving the same interviews. And he was tired of living every minute under constant pressure and scrutiny.

He and Edith agreed that it was, indeed, time to "set his bucket down."

> **"I didn't want to stay until I'd used up all the enjoyment, because that's too long to stay anywhere."**
>
> —Darrell K Royal, looking back on his retirement after the 1976 season

Ann Campbell, the mother of Earl Campbell, sent Royal a letter of support after the 1976 Texas-OU game. (Royal Family Archives)

I hope by this time you have gotten to yourself and [are] feeling some better. I was in Dallas Saturday. . . . Coach Royal, I want you to hold your head up. . . .

As long as the world stands there is going to be some body that's going [to] want to be out front without paying the price. . . . You have friends and lots of them. One is Ann Campbell. . . . Every time I waked up last night after looking at Sun. paper with your head down, it [did] something to me.

I am writing because I want you to know someone else love[s] you and cares . . . and that is the Lord Savior and Jesus Christ. Always remember you are not out there alone. . . .

Love,
Mrs. Ann Campbell

Ann Campbell and Coach Royal celebrate Earl's award at the 1977 Heisman Trophy Award banquet in New York City. The Royals enjoyed a close friendship with Mrs. Campbell, and she was one of Coach Royal's most vocal supporters. (Royal Family Archives)

"Darrell Royal was the greatest coach of the last fifty years. He was not only a great coach, he was a complete coach."

—Frank Broyles, who retired as Arkansas's coach on the same day that Royal retired

Coach Royal with James Street, late 1970s. According to Bill Little: "The minute they [players] got that 'T' ring that Darrell gave them with such pride, they began to see, 'This guy really did care about me and really did think I mattered.'" (Royal Family Archives)

Chapter 16

LESSONS FROM THE COACH

"When you get in that end zone, act like you've been there before." This Royal-ism, an admonition to his players to conduct themselves with class, has become standard advice given by coaches at all levels, all over the country.

Darrell Royal believed that his job involved much more than winning football games. His mission was to shape his players into first-rate men. By example and instruction, he imparted to them the importance of class, integrity, punctuality, hard work, and fairness.

Class

Darrell Royal had confidence in his players to do what they were asked to do, told to do, coached to do. No one wanted to disappoint him, but on the rare occasion when they did, he did not let it slide. He had a lesson to teach, even at the end of their football careers.

Loyd Wainscott, all-American defensive tackle from 1966 to 1968, told this story on himself: In the 1968 A&M game, his last home game as a Longhorn, Wainscott plowed over the Aggie quarterback, and he let his excitement get the better of him.

Loyd jumped up, with the Aggie still on the ground, and flashed the "Hook 'em" sign in his face. Before the next snap, Loyd found himself on the sidelines, his face mask firmly in Royal's grasp. Royal was all over him. "We *never* do that at Texas. You know better than that—that's low class. Now get back in there, make a play, and let me substitute for you the right way." It was Loyd's last game, but Royal was still teaching him. The journalist Holland McCombs mused on the class displayed by Royal's 1964 Longhorns: "They may kill you, but they'll be polite about it."

During the 1973 Texas Tech game, played in Memorial Stadium, Texas' student section expressed displeasure with a ref's call by erupting in a chorus of boos. The booing lasted longer than usual, and it caught Royal's attention. When he looked across the field, he watched one of the Texas cheerleaders waving his arms from side to side, egging on the students. Before the other squad members could get the rogue cheerleader under control, an overweight team trainer, dressed in burnt orange with a face to match, came running around the track from across the stadium. He was huffing and puffing and gasping for breath, but he finally managed to cough out, "Coach . . . Royal . . . said to make the . . . booing stop. And he means . . . now!"

Integrity

Royal believed that a coach was obligated to his players and to the game of football itself to run a program based on honor and integrity. He told Bill Little in 2007:

> I have a pretty strict code as far as athletics is concerned. If you're playing under the real rules of golf, for instance, there is something weak in a person who moves his ball from behind a tree, who nudges or mis-marks his ball.
>
> Adherence to the rules, sportsmanship and ethics . . . those are the things we *have* to stand for. Athletics is a whole lot like life. You will always be tempted to "cut across." If you do that in college athletics, you are doing it with those who are the future citizens who will be leading our cities, our states, and our country. You are sending them the wrong message.

Chris Gilbert, an all-American running back from 1966 to 1968, recalls: "Other coaches made promises, offered money. Darrell offered a four-year scholarship and nothing else. . . . He promised he'd give me a hard look and a chance to start. He's one of the most honest coaches I'd ever met." Bill Hamilton, who played linebacker for the Horns during Royal's last years (1973–1976), is equally emphatic:

> Your integrity is and was always unquestioned. I still feel a sense of pride that you did things the right way and shunned the practices of so many schools back then. I have never met a player from UT that was recruited with illegal inducements. Your examples of integrity and honesty still inspire me to do the right thing when doing the wrong thing is so much easier.

Steve Collier was a running back, linebacker, and safety from 1974 to 1977. He wrote Coach Royal on his eighty-fifth birthday:

> I define a man of integrity as someone whose life is "integrated"; he is the same good person on and off the field, by himself, or in a stadium of observers. This kind of man inspires selfless teamwork. He inspires excellence without having to demand it. He brings the best out of his men because of their admiration and . . . love for their leader. . . . You were a surrogate father to the many teenagers who came under your leadership. You have hundreds of sons who will carry your imprint of integrity and pass it on for generations.

Opportunity

Royal elevated the stature of the UT program to such a level of national recognition and quality that almost every boy in Texas wanted to play for him. Johnny Lam Jones said, "You felt so honored that Coach Royal would even consider you to play at his school; when you found out UT wanted you, it was a done deal."

Royal was known also for taking a chance on players that others schools overlooked. Glenn Blackwood was an undersized, underrecruited defensive back from San Antonio.

> I can still vividly recall standing at the equipment room window where the depth chart was posted my first day of football at UT. As I looked for my name, I felt someone staring over my shoulder. I looked back, and it was Coach Royal standing there! He asked where I was on the chart. I pointed to my name at left corner, sixth or seventh string. He said, "Don't worry, son, the cream always rises to the top. If you are good enough, you will move up the chart." I never forgot those words and they served me well through my years at UT (1976–1977) and in the NFL (1979–1987, Miami).

"A lot of coaches feel that a boy doesn't have to like you as long as he respects you. But if I had all the rest—respect and discipline— . . . and a boy left school without a personal feeling for me, it would be an empty profession."

—Darrell K Royal

Players given the opportunity to be one of Royal's Longhorns realized just how blessed they were. Richard Kimbrough, who played linebacker for Royal put it this way:

> Coach Royal, you changed my life. You opened doors of opportunity for me even though I was not an important cog in the wheel. I am grateful for the life-changing events you provided for me. I am very proud to be a small part of your legacy and proud to "dance with the one that brung me."

Keith Moreland had long dreamed of playing football for Coach Royal and the Longhorns. He lettered as a sophomore defensive back and was slated to start in the 1974 season. Moreland was also on the Texas baseball team, and it quickly became evident that baseball was where he would make his living. In a gut-wrenching, life-changing decision, he decided to give up his football scholarship to concentrate on baseball. He was confident in the correctness of the decision, yet he was still sick at his stomach.

He had to tell Coach Royal. He found the coach jogging around the track at Memorial Stadium. Royal's response to the news that he was losing one of starting defensive backs surprised Moreland. "He told me, 'Son, I don't agree with your decision, but I respect you for making it.' I still remember . . . that," Moreland told the *Austin American-Statesman*. "It was one of the hardest days of my life and . . . he made it easier on me."

One day in the early 1970s, a female student called Royal and said she wanted to try out for wide receiver. She had speed, she said, and good hands, and she knew the game of football. She really believed she could cut it. He tried to dissuade her, but instead of laughing at her or mocking her—even in the retelling of the story—he invited her to practice to stand on the sidelines with him. They stood watching drills for about thirty minutes, and the longer they watched, the quieter she got. Practice was hard hitting and violent, made more so by the crash of helmets colliding with shoulder pads, and players grunting as they were tackled and groaning as they pulled themselves up. Finally, she turned to him, offered her hand, and said, "Thank you. You were right; it's a lot different down here than it is up there in the stands." Royal treated her respectfully, holding to his credo: "You can tell a lot about a person by watching how they treat people who can't do anything for 'em."

Punctuality

Royal was unfailingly punctual—and he demanded that his players be as well. "Royal was a stickler for punctuality, especially when it involved practice or team meetings," Jones Ramsey wrote in his memoirs. "One day in the late '60s, guard Mike Dean was fifteen minutes late for practice. He arrived in the middle of Royal's talk to the squad at the middle of the field. After Dean arrived, Royal told the pre-med major: 'Dr. Dean, if I ever decide to have you operate on me after you finish medical school, I hope you won't be fifteen minutes late for my operation.'"

Dean, now a dentist, never forgot the lesson. He wrote his coach after the twenty-year reunion of the 1969 national championship team:

> Thanks . . . we were #1 because you are #1, not only as a coach, but as a human being. Your attitudes toward competition and people will be passed from generation to generation. P.S. I even try to be on time now.

Edith weighs in on the subject: "You know, he *still* drives me crazy about being on time. Even now, when he's eighty-six years old, I can tell him a time that something's supposed to happen. . . . I'll say, 'So-and-so's going to be here about 7:00 to pick you up.' But 'about' never satisfies him. It's got to be a precise time with him. Sometimes just to make him happy, I'll say, 'They'll pick you up at 9:07.' Of course, it doesn't matter. He gets everywhere ten minutes early anyway."

Hard Work

Royal knew that building a winning football team, like building strong character, required intensely hard work, yet most of the players went home to work summer jobs, so they were responsible for their own conditioning. Each week, Royal wrote his players, encouraging them to keep in shape, maintain a good attitude, and stay out of trouble.

June 15, 1966

Dear Longhorn:
It is a simple formula—men who want to win the most pay the biggest price and wear the Champion's crown. Put this question to yourself: Are you willing to sacrifice this summer in order to be in top physical condition September 1?

We stand a chance to hold our heads high with pride—or ashamed and bowed—after the season's conclusion. What you do this summer, to a large degree, will dictate which of these conditions we will find ourselves come Thanksgiving Day against the Aggies.

"Potential means you ain't done it yet."
—Darrell K Royal

* * * * *

June 17, 1966

Dear Longhorn:

No one can be proud of being a Longhorn unless you are proud of the personal conduct of the squad as a whole. Your personal conduct wherever you go this summer casts a reflection for good or bad on your team. If you do not have the courage to make the Longhorn image one of which we can all be proud, then *please* be man enough to drop off of the squad.

Each time you do stop-think-then refuse to do the wrong thing, you are building pride. Each time you are weak and give in, you are tearing down pride. This pride is something that is vital to our winning as a team but it is also vital to your winning as a man.

* * * * *

July 26, 1966

Dear Longhorn:

If winning is not important, why the hell keep score?

* * * * *

August 5, 1966

Dear Longhorn:

Defeat comes from within. There is no such thing as defeat, except in no longer trying. . . . It is when an individual admits down deep in his heart that he has had all he wants that he becomes defeated. As long as he is still fighting and has not given up, there is still a chance.

Defeat truly comes from within. I am far more concerned with what is inside of your heart than the figures that show on the scoreboard. You can be behind on the scoreboard but if you have not give up from within we will always have a chance.

Don Talbert, who played tackle for the Horns (1959–1961) and then eight years in the NFL, recalls: "In the pros, guys said, 'Man, I'd have liked to play for ole Darrell.' I told 'em, 'You might have wished you'd played for him, but your ass would have had to get in high gear to do that.' . . . You didn't just waddle around out there. . . . You came to hit, to run, to win games."

Fairness

In Royal's universe, the same rules applied to everyone, and players who assumed otherwise did so at their peril. Royal did not play favorites. He never placed a player on first team simply because he was supposed to be good. As Jim Bob Moffett, who played tackle for Royal (1958–1961), remembered: "He couldn't let his personal relationships keep him from putting the best player on the field. He was my coach . . . *then* he became my friend."

His staff continually graded players, posting a new depth chart every day. If a player wasn't performing up to expectations, he was demoted, simple as that. The locker room was split into two smaller rooms, and for anyone demoted from second to third team, it meant cleaning out his locker and making that long, sad journey to the other locker room.

Scott Appleton, one of the best defensive men ever to play at Texas, confirmed Royal's objectivity: he "has one set of rules. They're the same for the No. 1 fullback and a No. 6 guard, and they don't bend." Jerry Sisemore agreed, "Nobody's a superstar in Coach Royal's program. He demanded that everyone was on the same level; you weren't gonna act like you did it yourself." You do it right, or you won't be afforded the opportunity to do it at all.

Developing Young Men

Royal truly believed that coaching football was all about developing young men. It mattered to him that they had pride in themselves, that they conducted themselves with honor, that they went through life with shoes polished and fingernails trimmed, that they didn't "get too chesty when you win, or too despondent when you lose." James Street put it this way: "He taught us far more than just football. Our hair had to be cut right, our shoes shined, our fingernails clipped. For a head coach of his stature, it was still important to him that we learned that we were 'representing ourselves, our families, our schools.'"

It might have been the poverty, wearing hand-me-down overalls so big that they had to be safety-pinned on each side so no one could see down his pants legs. Or having to make do with shoes two sizes too small and held together with string. It might have been the red Oklahoma dust covering everything that left him never feeling clean. Or it might have just been his personality, but Edith says, "Darrell is so particular about his dress and appearance; especially his hair. He's even obsessed with *my* hair. I can't walk out the door without him saying, 'Edith, you need to fix your hair before you leave this house.'" The coach washes his hands compulsively, dozens of times a day. And he will never be caught wearing scuffed shoes. For as long as he coached, he kept a spare pair of polished shoes under his desk—just in case.

Royal's training sometimes began even before a new recruit showed up for his first practice. When Johnnie Johnson, a four-sport star from La Grange, Texas, met Coach Royal at a Longhorn alumni banquet, he was a nervous wreck. "Coach Royal was bigger than life." Johnnie was shy, unable to look Royal in the eye, and offered a "dead fish" handshake. Instead of scolding Johnson or writing him off, Royal walked Johnson to a corner of the room where they could speak in private. He reminded Johnnie of his rare talent and that he had every right to be proud of himself and of his accomplishments. "He showed me how to shake hands firmly, how to look folks in the eyes. Then he took me back to the crowd as if nothing had ever happened."

Johnson's teammate Alfred Jackson added, "I appreciate Coach Royal; he instilled so much more in us than just football. We didn't realize we were learning discipline and life lessons."

No one was more competitive than Royal, and no one hated to lose more than he did. Yet he managed to keep sight of the goal, the focus: "This game is all about developing young men." In 1961, when lowly TCU beat Texas 6–0, that sole blemish on the season kept the Horns from winning the national championship. It was a bitter, bitter loss, but Bob Moses remembers the coach's reaction, adding, "That's when you appreciated Coach Royal. Because as hard as this loss was, he showed us how to hold our heads up and go on. 'That's football,' he said."

Glenn Blackwood expressed a sense of heartfelt gratitude shared by many of Royal's players:

> Thank you for pushing us to be men. Thank you for expecting us, as the champions we should be, to be ready to play on Saturday and not thinking a big speech before the game was necessary. Thank you for having Mike Campbell as defensive coordinator. Thank you for not coddling players. Thank you for bringing Willie in for pickin' sessions. Thank you for appreciating the value of a player who can think on the field. Thank you for valuing men of character. Thank you for being a great coach, a coach that was one of a kind, a coach that took boys and turned them into men, a coach I will always be proud to say was my coach. You are a great man.

> **"When I played pro ball, I'd always have my playbook and two fingernail files in my bag. Coach Royal taught us to do that."**
>
> —Roosevelt Leaks, fullback, 1972–1974

What It Was Really Like to Play for Royal

Edith's albums are full of letters from Royal's players, and to a man, those players acknowledge just how blessed they were to have been coached by her husband, the rarest of men. Lessons learned from their coach unite his first Texas team in 1957 with those last boys he coached in 1976. Fortunately, many players have been willing to share some of the things that defined their time as one of Royal's Longhorns.

Royal claimed he had an open-door policy for his players, and that was true. But few players went by his office just to shoot the bull. Bob McKay, an all-American offensive tackle (1968–1969), said, "If you went by his office, you went at a high rate of speed. At practice, if he came off that tower, you hoped he went the other way. If not, you were fixing to get your ass chewed. I went in his office five times and four weren't worth a damn."

When it became evident in 1968 that for all his talent, Bill Bradley just was not a wishbone quarterback, Coach Royal sent word that he wanted to visit with Bradley in his office. Years later, riffing on a well-known Royalism, Bradley said, "Now, when you go to a coach's office, three things can happen and *all* of them are bad."

Besides sharing common triumphs and common miseries, the men who played for Royal share a common language, references of just a few words that tell an entire story. Anyone who played for him knew the following:

- *"Let's give 'im three."* Three short claps. At the end of practice, with the team huddled around him listening for last-minute instructions and waiting to be dismissed, Coach Royal recognized players who had done something noteworthy by saying, "Let's give him three." Everyone—players and coaches alike—would give three short claps. Nothing earth shattering, but those players knew it was the highest of praise to be recognized by Royal and "given three" by your teammates and coaches.
- *"Press the kicking game, for it's here the breaks are made."* There's not a Royal player alive who, when he witnesses a blocked punt or watches a kickoff returned for a touchdown, doesn't either mutter to himself or holler at the television, "Press the kicking game!"
- *"Don't bitch; transfer."* In a reminiscence to the coach, C. F. "Babe" Drymala, who played guard for Texas in Royal's first years there (1956–1959), recalls: "In 1959 I was on a committee to complain to you about the declining food preparation at Moore-Hill Hall. We made an appointment with you in your

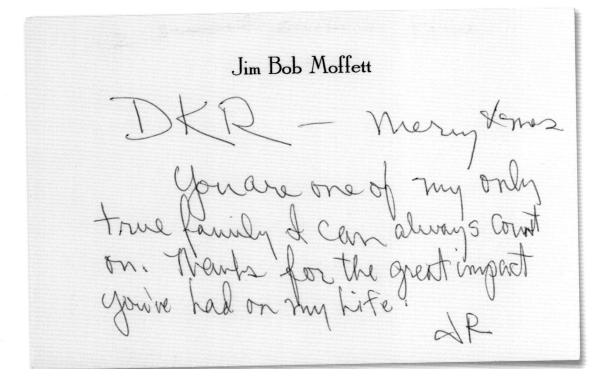

Jim Bob Moffett

DKR — Merry Xmas

You are one of my only true family I can always count on. Thanks for the great impact you've had on my life!

DR

A Christmas note from Jim Bob Moffett (tackle, 1958–1961). (DKR Papers, DBCAH, di_07356; reprinted by permission of Jim Bob Moffett)

office. You listened to our complaints and asked, 'Are you finished?' We said, 'Yes sir.' You stood up and said, 'Boys, don't bitch. Transfer.' And that was the end of that. However, we did notice that the food improved."

- *"Don't bitch at the officials."* Pat Culpepper, cocaptain of the 1962 team, said in the introduction to *Coach Royal: Conversations with a Texas Football Legend,* "If you played football for Darrell Royal, you knew the kicking rules; you knew better than to draw stupid penalties."

Relations with Players

Royal was such an intimidating figure on the field that most players avoided eye contact with him, much less a full conversation. He was not a buddy to his players. Few got close to him while they were on the squad, but as soon as their football careers were finished, that relationship changed.

The players came to know that his feeling for them and his service to them did not end when they left school. He was available for counsel or golf or Mexican food and beer. He never forgot their names or their contributions to the program. He helped them get jobs. He visited them when they were ill. He attended their parents' funerals. His concern for his players never ended.

Bob Lenz, an offensive guard on the 1973 team, expressed how much Royal's continued involvement in his life had meant:

Most people who have not played for you only know you from the pictures they see, the statistics they look at, or maybe a video they have seen of your life. What most people don't know, however, is what you have become to most of your players after they leave The University. You have become a father to some, mentor to others, lifetime friend to all.

I was not an all-American, nor did I come from a family that had given money to The University for years and years. Yet after I was out of school for about 15 years you took the time to meet me and write a letter of recommendation to my law school admissions committee. Among the hundreds of applications the committee received, that letter from you stood out and was a major factor for my acceptance into law school.

Coach Royal had a unique relationship with his quarterbacks. Several times a week during the season, Royal invited his starting quarterback to his home to play checkers—not your conventional game of checkers, but offensive and defensive checkers. On the Royals' kitchen table, the quarterback would line up his checkers in UT's offensive set, then Royal would quickly set his checkers up in the opponent's defense. The coach would move his defensive players around, then quiz the quarterback on what play he would check off to, what defensive players they would read if they ran the option to one side or the other. Marty Akins, an all-American quarterback for Royal, recalls, "Edith would bring cookies and drinks, and—you know how competitive he is—we'd always start our sessions with a real game of checkers first."

A four-year starter for Royal, Akins counts the time spent one-on-one with his coach as a life-changing blessing: "The first couple of years, I was in awe of him and probably a little scared of him, in spite of how much time we spent together. I started relaxing a little and opening up a little my junior year, but by my senior year, he was like my dad. We were best friends. I could say anything to him. It's no wonder that I love him and think of him as a father."

Coach Royal, surrounded by his devoted players on the thirty-fifth
anniversary of the 1963 National Championship, November 1998. Left
to right: Tommy Ford, halfback, captain; Tommy Nobis, offensive guard,
linebacker; Tom Stockton, fullback; Lee Hensley, tackle; Coach Royal;
Clarence Bray, center; Clayton Lacy, tackle; Joe Dixon, halfback; David
McWilliams, center; Frank Bedrick, guard. (Royal Family Archives)

Edith and Joe Jamail cut up at the Waldorf Astoria in New York City. (Royal Family Archives)

Tex Ritter (left), Jimmie Riddle (back to camera), and Darrell at a party before the first-ever Willie Nelson Picnic, July 3, 1973. (Royal Family Archives)

The Hollis Boys: from left, Bill Covin, Darrell Royal, Leon Manley, Leon Heath, and J. W. Cole of the Sooners' 1949 squad. (Royal Family Archives)

**"I sometimes wonder if anyone has ever had more fun
in their lives than we have had with our friends."**

—Edith Royal

**"You can have differences of opinions and still get along or, heck, let a
guy slide. He makes a mistake—let him slide . . . that's what friends do.
They let each other make mistakes and still care about you."**

—Darrell K Royal

Chapter 17
FRIENDS AND OTHER DIVERSIONS

It is easy to see why the Royals' friends revere them. They take the attitude of the prodigal son's father: no matter how long you have been away or how long it has been since you called, there is no recrimination. They greet you as if they saw you yesterday, as if they had been waiting all day just to see you. They collect friends as they do family members—making new ones while keeping the old.

Longtime Friends

Darrell's Oklahoma teammates and their wives are still among the Royals' closest friends. Leon Manley and Darrell Royal were teammates since they played sandlot football in Hollis. They played together as Sooners, and Royal even coached Manley in the Canadian Football League. When a spot came open on the Texas staff in 1966, Royal wanted to hire him; he had great respect and affection for his lovable and rumpled friend. As he told Edith: "I sure do love Leon, but Edith, I've never hired anyone who couldn't keep his shirttail tucked in." Darrell hired him anyway, and they teamed up for two national championships and six straight Southwest Conference championships.

There are no qualifications for belonging to this wide but enviable circle. From the wealthy and influential to people who have nothing to offer except love and loyalty, their friendships reach from the White House to the roadhouse and the poorhouse. They have befriended countless college students, United States presidents, Texas governors, up-and-coming musicians, prominent Longhorn boosters, and astronauts. Then there are the strays, those who were lost but now are found, thanks to the Royals' direction and support. They neither expect nor do they want anything from their friends except a habit of honesty, a sense of humor, and friendship returned.

You can't talk about Darrell Royal's friends without talking about Louie Murillo. Here is how Edith explains it:

Louie Murillo and the coach.
(Royal Family Archives)

"I don't think this country ever produced a better coach. . . . I *know* it never produced a better man."

—Joe Jamail, in *The Story of Darrell Royal*

We just inherited him, I think. He grew up on the east side [of Austin], so as a kid, he always hung out at Memorial Stadium, helping wherever he could. When we moved to Texas, he was just there. He's helped us and we've helped him. I'm not real sure how old he is . . . he's not, either. But he served in Korea and Vietnam as a mechanic on tanks. He still comes over and watches John Wayne movies with Darrell or eats lunch with him. I suppose we're family by now.

One of the Royal's closest friends is Joe Jamail, legendary Houston litigator. Jamail tells a story on himself about a time when his reaction to an exciting play on the field could have cost Texas a victory:

We were in the Cotton Bowl, 1973, playing against Alabama. Our quarterback [Alan Lowry] was running for the winning touchdown. I was not aware that the previous week, the officials ruled that if anyone stepped onto the field, it would nullify the play. After Texas scored the winning score, I was so excited I jumped on Willie Nelson's back, and we ran into the end zone. I thought Coach Royal was going to have a total collapse—he yelled at us, "What are you doing?" I told Willie to just keep running.

On Sunday evenings during football season, families across Texas settled on the sofa to watch *The Darrell Royal Show*, cohosted by the late Cactus Pryor. The two showed highlights and rehashed the outcome of the previous day's game. They rehearsed very little, and it wouldn't have helped anyway. Pryor and Royal were both irreverent, off-the-cuff kind of guys, and that was the fun of it. "We'd decide what topics to discuss . . . I'd throw 'em and the coach would hit 'em," Cactus recalled. Cactus also hosted the weekly Longhorn Booster meetings and emceed the Headliners Club luncheons, using Darrell as fodder for laughs. Their lasting friendship was based on love of the burnt orange, mutual respect, and the fact that they always laughed at each other's jokes.

The press made much of the Royals' friendship with President and Mrs. Johnson, but it was a real and a rare friendship. It was simpler for the Johnsons to see the Royals after the president left office, and their friendship blossomed. Darrell recalled just how close the two were:

The President jumped on me one day about not calling him often enough. I said, "Mr. President, I called you last week." I mean, you just don't wear out the ex-president of the United States! He said to me, "Darrell, I want you to call me like you'd call your mama."

Cactus Pryor and Darrell Royal preparing to tape The Darrell Royal Show at the KTBC studios. (Royal Family Archives)

If Cactus and Darrell were together, you could bet they would be laughing. They shared a love of The University of Texas and love of a good joke. Photo by Russ C. Smith, ChocolateMedia.com.

"You are the finest example of an inspiring young leader that I know."

—President Lyndon Baines Johnson

Darrell and Edith were honored guests at Lyndon Johnson's inauguration, January 20, 1965. (DKR Papers, DBCAH, di_07314 and di_07313)

Darrell Royal and President Johnson at the 1962 Cotton Bowl festivities. (Royal Family Archives; photo by James Langhead)

The Johnsons began attending Longhorn football games and encouraged the coach to bring his players to the ranch to break bread with them. Darrell and Edith enjoyed visiting the LBJ Ranch in Stonewall, and the two couples vacationed together in Acapulco. Luci Johnson Turpin, the President's daughter, wrote Darrell: "After a lifetime of public service, I don't think my parents knew what vacation was all about . . . but you helped him discover the rejuvenating power of playing with loved ones."

Rivals

Royal counted many coaches among his friends, some of whom were his biggest rivals during the season. Bud Wilkinson, who coached and mentored Royal in college, then coached against him for close to a decade, wrote Edith and Darrell, "Let's keep in touch. You are among the best people I have ever known."

> **"I am not a football fan, but I am a fan of people and I am a Darrell Royal fan because he is the rarest of people."**
>
> —Lyndon Baines Johnson

The Broyleses traveled often with Edith and Darrell, and whenever the two men were together, a golf course wasn't far away. "Speed golf" was their hallmark. Playing fifty-four holes in a day was not uncommon for them, but once they played eighty-one. "We had the perfect wives to foster our friendship, because Edith and Barbara loved our vacations together," Broyles wrote to Royal.

We were lucky that they both loved to go shopping and sightseeing and that allowed us to play as much golf as we wanted to. I like to say that they were "scratch shoppers." One thing that kept our golf game pure was that, in all those years, we *never* talked about our football games on the golf course. . . .

Please know that I feel blessed to have had you as my dear friend for more than 50 years.

Wishing you all the best,

Frank

Sooners' coach Bud Wilkinson honoring his former player at a party sponsored by Look *magazine for the Football Writers Association of America Coach of the Year award, 1963. (Royal Family Archives)*

From left: Frank Broyles, Bill Solms (an executive with Coca-Cola), and Darrell relax after one of their golf marathons, 1964. (Royal Family Archives)

On the surface, Royal's friendship with Paul "Bear" Bryant seemed an unlikely one. Bryant was the head coach at Texas A&M when Royal was hired at Texas. Royal recalls, "He was the first Southwest Conference coach I heard from, and Edith still has that telegram somewhere." Darrell first met Bryant at Oklahoma. Coach Wilkinson had assigned Royal to explain to Bryant what OU was doing with the split-T and what drills they ran in practice. Bryant treated Royal well, even though he was a whippersnapper and a senior in college.

Jones Ramsey, who served as sports information director for both men, agreed that they were a lot alike, but that Royal was "a sweet Bear Bryant." Through the years, they shared laughs and drinks, football, fierce competition, and friendship. That friendship would serve them both well. In 1969 and 1970, as the Longhorns were overpowering teams with their wishbone offense, the Crimson Tide was finishing seventh and eighth in the Southeast Conference. Before the 1971 season, Alabama had not won the conference in five years.

Bryant secretly visited Austin in the summer of 1971. He and Darrell holed up in the Royals' apartment in the Cambridge Towers—their West Austin home was being renovated—and Bryant picked Royal's brain. Some of Royal's assistants thought he was making a mistake, but Royal and Bryant were friends and their teams were not in the same conference, so Royal opened his playbook and his game films to Bryant. They talked after every game that season—sometimes two to three times a week—comparing how opponents were defending against the wishbone.

The next year, however, pitted Royal—"the innovator"—against Bryant—"the embellisher"—in the Cotton Bowl on January 1, 1973. Seventh-ranked Texas beat fourth-ranked

Alabama 17–13. Bryant never did beat a Darrell Royal–coached team, but he was a darned good student. Bama won the SEC championship eight times in the 1970s, and won three national championships—in 1973, '78, and '79—running the wishbone. Bryant publicly credited his friend Darrell Royal with saving his coaching career.

Pickin' Friends

As a boy, Darrell was lonesome for a mother's love, and he worked harder than a little boy should have to work. But he took solace in the radio, and when he got a chance to choose the station, he listened to Bob Wills, the Chuck Wagon Gang, Jimmie Rodgers, and the Lucky Strike Hit Parade. He loved the lyrics of those ol' sad songs.

He came to admire the talent of songwriters, and he clung to the lessons and the truths of those words like a life preserver in stormy seas. Along with athletes, these songwriters were his heroes.

His appreciation for country music was well known. Mickey Herskowitz wrote in 1964: "Nothing cleanses Royal's mind of cares like guitar pickin'." And as the Royals' celebrity grew, they met and formed friendships with some of the biggest names in country music: Charley Pride, Merle Haggard, Larry Gatlin, Willie Nelson, Floyd Tillman, Jimmy Dean. He befriended and promoted songwriters—both successful and aspiring—whose talent and wit he appreciated. Darrell and

LARRY GATLIN

MY JEFE,
IF YOU HADN'T BEEN
THERE, I WOULDN'T BE
HERE. LOVE YA!!
HOOK 'EM,
            [signature]
P.S. LOVE YOU TOO,
RACK 'EM!!
            [signature]

Left to right: *Mickey Newbury, Darrell Royal* (standing), *Larry Gatlin, Willie Nelson, Rudy Gatlin, and Steve Gatlin at one of the Royals' pickin' parties. Photography by Rick Henson.*

Edith lent respectability to country music, the songwriters, and what would become the outlaw country movement in the anti-establishment era of the late 1960s and early 1970s. He *was* the establishment; his reputation of demanding discipline, straight behavior, and good grooming from his teams was widespread. But after Marian died, and then after he retired, he worried less about his image and about how things looked to others. He traded his starched shirt and tie for jogging suits and tennis shoes.

Royal wanted to share the pleasure he derived from his friends' music. Plus, a little exposure wouldn't hurt them at all, so he and Edith hosted "pickin' parties," at which the only rule was "listen or leave." These "guitar pulls," which sometimes lasted all night, were an opportunity for friends to hear the music and experience new sounds. If guests were chatting and laughing it up, they couldn't appreciate the songwriters' craft and they were keeping others from enjoying it. It never bothered Darrell

to emit a shrill whistle, formerly witnessed only by his players at practice. When coach whistled and then hollered, "Red light," it meant that the show was about to begin and all who weren't holding guitars needed to shut up.

On those magical nights, you might find yourself sitting on the floor next to Mickey Mantle or Lady Bird Johnson, the astronaut Gene Cernan or the author James Michener, as Willie Nelson, Merle Haggard, Kris Kristofferson, and Rita Coolidge sang "Will the Circle be Unbroken" in the Royals' living room. The guest list was eclectic, and Edith kept a pot of chili or black-eyed peas simmering on the stove. There was always lots of cold beer.

"Oh, those parties were fun for a good, long while," Edith said. "And we're still friends with those musicians. But the parties were overdone, and our guests took far too many privileges. We loved opening our home and having friends over, but some just did *not* know how to behave or when to leave!"

Willie

At first glance, it would appear that Willie Nelson and Darrell Royal don't have much in common. Royal is known for his neat, meticulous style of dress. Nelson, much less concerned about appearances, "dresses the same if he's got millions, or if he's broke," Royal says. Royal is disciplined, conservative, a straight arrow, while Nelson makes no apologies for his politics, his lifestyle, or his affinity for marijuana.

They first met in the late 1950s, at a "package show" held in the old City Coliseum, a cavernous Quonset hut that also housed the Austin Rodeo. Both men were relatively unknown then, but Royal had begun to rebuild the Longhorn football program. Nelson was sporting short hair, wearing a suit and tie, and playing way down the bill of the show. They developed a friendly relationship and saw each other from time to time, but when Royal gave a close listen to an album Nelson gave him, he was struck by Willie's talent. As Royal's star was ascending, Nelson's was burning out. Although well known

as a songwriter, he was getting nowhere as an entertainer in Nashville. After he divorced for the second time and his house burned to the ground, he packed up and headed home to Texas. He settled in Austin, and Royal set out to help him. He tried to get people to listen to Nelson's music, believing that if people really heard his talent as a singer, he could make converts out of them.

Coach Royal invited his players and their dates to hear Willie play private concerts for them in Dallas before the Cotton Bowl or in the "T" Room in Memorial Stadium. It was Royal's gift to both his friend and his players, who got a kick out of seeing this relaxed side of Royal. Edith remembers,

> **"The coach has done an awful lot for me. . . . He's always there. . . . He's a big part of my life. We think of each other a lot."**
>
> —Willie Nelson to
> Brad Buchholz,
> *Third Coast Magazine*

Once when Willie couldn't pay his band, in the late '60s, I think, Darrell staged and promoted a private show at the Back Door [an east Austin beer joint located behind Cisco's Bakery]. He invited the Athletic Department and his friends to pay twenty-five dollars a couple to listen to Willie play. Willie was embarrassed; he didn't believe people would pay that much to hear him. They did. It was a big success, and he was able to make payroll for his band.

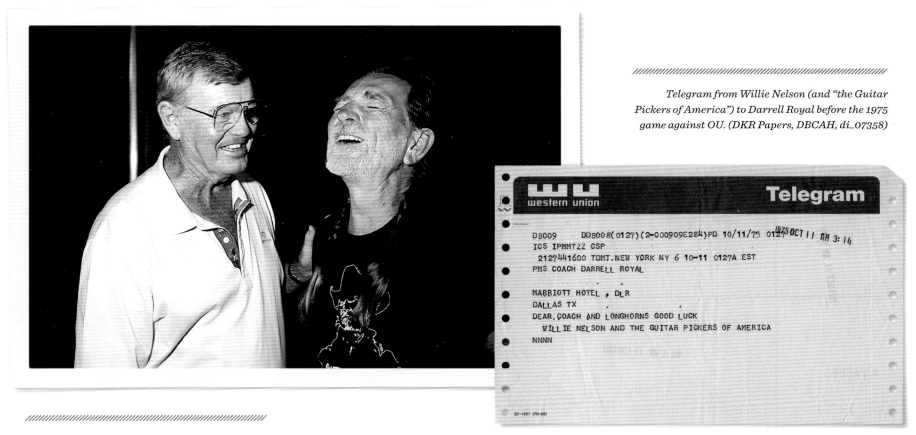

Willie Nelson on Darrell Royal: "He's one of the best friends I have." Photography by Rick Henson.

Telegram from Willie Nelson (and "the Guitar Pickers of America") to Darrell Royal before the 1975 game against OU. (DKR Papers, DBCAH, di_07358)

> **"One of the reasons I like Willie is he forgives me of all my faults. And still likes me."**
>
> —Darrell K Royal, in *Coach Royal: Conversations with a Texas Football Legend*

It is no wonder they were drawn to each other. Neither has any artifice about him; neither tolerates artifice in others. Royal has had a lifelong passion for country music. And Willie's secret passion was sports. At tiny Abbott High, Nelson played four years of football, baseball, and basketball and ran track for four years. Both men lived their adult lives in the public eye, yoked to impossibly high expectations. Both have seen spectacular success and fame; both have suffered embarrassing failure and criticism.

And both have suffered the unmatched pain of losing a child. Willie's career changed, and so did his appearance. Willie helped launch the outlaw country movement in Austin, and as his celebrity grew, he wore his long hair in braids, grew a beard, and spoke openly of smoking marijuana.

After retirement, Royal's life changed, too. Players, peers, and politicos saw a different side of him. Many thought it unsavory for Royal to associate with Nelson and other scruffy songwriters.

In 1975, even the OU coach Barry Switzer chided Royal for spending too much time with "those guitar pickers."

Yet in 1982, Switzer found a picker friend of his own. He sent a letter, written on Oklahoma Football letterhead, to radio stations all over the country, promoting a country-and-western singer named John Kelly. Switzer had signed Kelly to a nine-year contract in the hopes that "John can do for me what Willie did for Coach Royal."

The letter, not surprisingly, found its way into the Royals' hands, and it tickled Willie and Darrell on so many levels. Royal had promoted Nelson's career—had helped him become "Willie"—not for money, but out of friendship and in the certainty that others would appreciate the poetry of Nelson as Royal did.

The men laughed over the letter and decided that the time had come to execute an official contract between them. They drew up the contract by hand (on "A&M Athletic Department" letterhead) and mailed copies to Barry Switzer. The two swear that cold beer was not involved.

///

Willie Nelson and Darrell Royal's "contract," copies of which were sent to Barry Switzer in 1982. (Royal Family Archives)

In 1975, as Royal was preparing to step down from his coaching pedestal, Willie's "Blue Eyes Crying in the Rain" was the number one country-and-western single in the country. No one was happier about it than Darrell Royal. It was Willie's turn to be the star while Royal took a few steps back from the limelight.

After Darrell's retirement, Edith built a small house out in the country in Spicewood, overlooking a cove on the Pedernales River near Willie Nelson's Cut-N-Putt Pedernales Country Club. She remembers how happy they were to live out there. "The men would play a round of golf, then go sit at Willie's in their golf carts, put on Mickey Newbury's 'An American Trilogy' and watch the sun go down while they drank their beer."

The Press

Early in his career, Royal was thin skinned, and he bristled under any criticism. When an influential Texas Ex offered to take him to lunch, "just to offer some constructive criticism," Royal brusquely declined the invitation, saying, "I work better under friendship, support, and compliments."

He had his run-ins with reporters and could get testy when questioned, but thin skin doesn't wear well on a man whose job invites millions of critics. Most coaches detest being second-guessed—whether by their wives or by the press—but Royal eventually learned to laugh when writers poked fun, or to ignore them when they criticized his decisions. In this area, as in most, Royal was adaptable. Mickey Herskowitz, the longtime Houston sports columnist, remembered a day when Bud Shrake of the *Dallas Morning News* called Royal about 4 p.m., when the coach was in meetings. As Herskowitz tells it: "Darrell called Shrake back about 7:30, and Shrake snapped, 'I don't need you now. I needed you at 4, when I had a column to write,'" and slammed the phone down." It was abrupt, but Darrell got the message: Bud's time was valuable, too. "Darrell told his secretary that if any writer on deadline called, to let him know. He didn't go into a tirade. He understood, and he responded. It was pretty remarkable." Edith was not surprised. "You know, Darrell is sensitive to others because he's so easily hurt himself. It might not be evident right at first, but he is tenderhearted."

He came to understand that writers had a job to do, so he tried to work with them and give thoughtful and different answers to

> **"Many coaches have claimed to have been misquoted, but I have never been misquoted by the press. Now, there were many times I wished I had spoken differently."**
>
> —Darrell K Royal

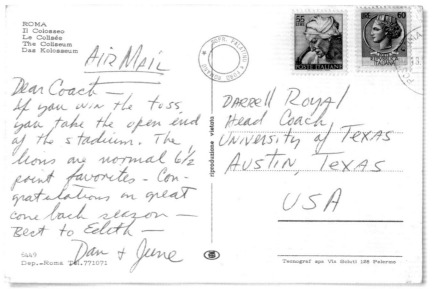

After visiting the Colosseum in Rome, Dan Jenkins of Sports Illustrated *offered his good friend Darrell Royal some helpful advice. (DKR Papers, DBCAH, di_7457 and di_07370; reprinted by permission of Dan Jenkins)*

reporters. Just as he appreciated the craft of songwriting and a well-turned phrase, he appreciated humor and an intelligent sports piece. He became close friends with many sportswriters: Blackie Sherrod, Bud Shrake, Gary Cartwright, Jim Trinkle, Burle Pettit, and, of course, Dan Jenkins, longtime writer for *Sports Illustrated* and *Golf Digest* and author of the classic football novel *Semi-Tough*. As the years passed and Royal and Jenkins became more comfortable with each other, they did more laughing and partying than interviewing. Jenkins was the first to call him "Saint Darrell," poking fun at fans and writers who believed he could do no wrong.

Charity golf tournaments make for strange bedfellows. Former rivals Barry Switzer and Darrell Royal were paired at the Ben Willie Darrell golf tournament, which was held in Oklahoma City one year. Photography by Rick Henson.

Ben Crenshaw, Willie Nelson, and Darrell Royal laugh as Willie delivers the punch line to one of his infamously dirty jokes. Photography by Rick Henson.

Diversions

Edith was worried sick when Darrell decided to retire altogether. "He was so young; I was sure he'd get sick of just playing golf every day. He sure proved me wrong."

Golf has been more than just a game to Royal. Some of his finest memories are of playing rounds with friends, laughing and feeling the pressure of life sail with each swing of the club. It became his refuge when he was trying so hard to escape his grief that he couldn't bear to go home in the evening. Golf filled a vacuum in his life after he retired, and as arthritis settled in and he could no longer jog, golf became his last means of competing. He swears, however, "I do not let a bad score ruin my enjoyment for golf."

Over the years Royal turned his love of golf and of country music into a gift, the gift of charity. The annual Darrell Royal Tournament benefited the Boys Clubs of America and brought the best of country music entertainers to The Woodlands, Texas. Later, he teamed up with Ben Crenshaw, the professional golfer, and Willie Nelson to host the Ben Willie Darrell East Austin Youth Classic, an annual celebrity golf tournament and country music showcase. The tournament raised more than four million dollars for underprivileged boys and girls in east Austin.

Another favorite pastime was "movin' 'em around," or playing chess. The coach sought out challenging games, and he was, not surprisingly, a highly competitive player who could "see" several plays in advance and who could usually predict his opponent's moves. Timmy Doerr, who both played (1961–1965) and coached (1969–1976) for Royal, can vouch for his mentor's tenacity: "Just because you got his queen, you think the game is over. Not so fast, partner. You can and will lose if you don't bring your complete A game. I know. On a vacation in Mexico, I don't remember winning. He defines the word 'competitor.'"

Royal appreciated the similarities between chess and football, since achieving victory in both required controlling key areas of space through strategy. Take away the opponent's main threats, contain them, and try to better your field position with each move or series. It was the perfect "relaxation" for this man whose mind never slowed down.

Like golf and country music, chess is something else Royal and Willie Nelson share. Both are competitive, serious players. Royal once explained the pleasure of playing Nelson: "It's hard to find people you're evenly matched with. It's no fun to lose all the time, but it's not fun to win all the time, either."

Curley Ferris was one of Marian's closest friends. A frequent visitor at the Royals' Belmont Parkway house, he was also a frequent challenger at chess. He never could beat Royal, though, and once after Curley went home dejected and frustrated after yet another defeat, Darrell told Edith, "I feel so bad. I know he wants to win and I feel terrible about beating him every time." Edith pleaded with her husband, "Couldn't you let him win just one time?" Darrell was stunned. He looked at Edith as if she were a complete stranger. "Edith. You just don't *do* that!"

> "You learn a lot about people—the good and the bad—by playing golf with them."
>
> —Darrell K Royal

Royal, Willie Nelson, and Larry Gatlin wear "team uniforms" furnished by their friend Earnest Owen, far right. Photography by Rick Henson.

Willie and Darrell "movin' 'em around." (Royal Family Archives)

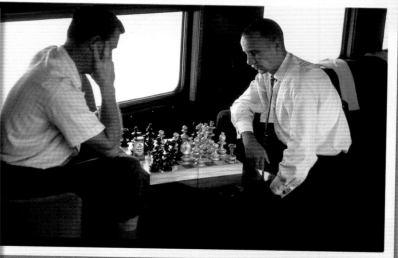

Royal looked for pickup chess games wherever he traveled. He scared up a game with a fellow passenger on a train headed for Cuernavaca, Mexico. (Royal Family Archives)

Royal faces the press after announcing his retirement to his players in a closed locker room after the victory over Arkansas, December 4, 1976. (1977 Cactus, Texas Student Media)

Royal and the Longhorns on the field at the last game Royal coached in Memorial Stadium, December 4, 1976. (University of Texas Sports Photography)

> "Climbing is a thrill. Maintaining is a bitch."
> —Darrell K Royal

Chapter 18
SETTIN' HIS BUCKET DOWN

All he had ever wanted to do was coach. He had done that and done it better than almost anyone before, during, or since that night. And there, on that turf, where so many of his dreams and so much of his life had played out, that is where it would end.

Memorial Stadium had been his children's playground and their second home, and it could be argued that he had spent more time there in the previous twenty years than he had at their home on Belmont Parkway. The Royals' conversations, their interests, their lives had revolved around what took place on that field.

He remembered what the place looked like the day he and Edith had circled the stadium for the first time, and he recalled how he had worked to transform it. He had formed unbreakable bonds with fellow coaches and players on that field, in that stadium.

Throughout the 1976 season, Royal had managed to sidestep questions about his retirement, but he and Edith had made up their minds that he would step down as head coach after the '76 season. Frank Broyles had announced three days before the Texas game that he was leaning toward resigning. It was fitting that these two men would end their careers coaching against each other. Rivals on the field, Royal and Broyles were the closest of friends during the offseason.

At their last pregame meeting at midfield on that misty night at Memorial Stadium, the two men hugged, expressed their love for each other, then walked away to fight it out for the nineteenth time.

In spite of a 5-5-1 record for the year, the crowd gave Darrell Royal a standing ovation in honor of his fifteenth win over Arkansas. His players, sensing that this was the end of an era, hoisted their coach onto their shoulders for a final victory ride off the field. There, in the locker room underneath the stadium, the fifty-two-year-old legend told his team that he had just coached his last game for The University of Texas.

> **"I'm just proud as hell to have been coached by him."**
> —Brad Shearer,
> all-American defensive tackle

Royal carried off the field in triumph by his players after beating Arkansas one last time. He retired from Texas with a 167-47-5 record that included three national championships and sixteen bowl appearances. (1977 Cactus, Texas Student Media)

◖●◗ FOOTBALL

DKR: 167-45-5

For the majority of UT students, Darrell Royal is a legend. When the talk is Texas football, Royal ranks with the orange and white, Bevo and "Texas Fight." On Dec. 4, 1976, Darrell Royal not only left the head coaching position, he also left a 20-year record untarnished by a losing season.

Royal is a former All-American quarterback for Oklahoma. He coached Canadian pro football for two seasons where he earned a winning record of 16-3. In 1956, after completing one year of his four-year contract at the University of Washington, Royal resigned to accept the head coaching position at UT. Royal's predecessor was Coach Ed Price who resigned after his sixth season. In the Dec. 6, 1956, issue of The Daily Texan, Price is quoted as saying that he withdrew "in an effort to get everyone unanimously behind the Longhorns." Price left with a losing season, and Royal received an enthusiastic reception at UT. Royal was "picked on the basis of his success in the coaching profession."

Royal leaves his UT coaching career with a 167-45-5 record. During his 20-year term, Royal has led the Longhorns to 16 bowl games. The Southwest Conference title has been won or shared by the Longhorns 11 times under Royal. Coach Royal says that the high point of his career was the 1969 game against Arkansas. Unlike this year's match against the Razorbacks, the '69 game held a great deal of significance since it was a battle for the Southwest Conference Championship.

"We were number one, and Arkansas was number two. It was the last college game of the season because it was put off so it could be televised. At one point we were behind 14-0 and we came up and won 15-14 and went on to win the National Championship," Royal said proudly.

Perhaps Darrell Royal is best known for his Wishbone offense, but he will be remembered for the inner strength and support he has given his teams. Royal will stay on at UT as Director of Athletics, but the 20-year love affair between Longhorn fans and the head coach has come to an end. Royal is optimistic about the future of the Longhorns and says they will be "bigger and better" in 1977.

His resignation hit the public like a seismic shock. Few saw it coming, and it sent aftershocks across the country. Sportswriters wrote adoring columns, lamenting the loss of his wit and his freshness. Tom Murray of the *Murray Go Round Report* reflected on the passing of an era:

Darrell Royal is a rare talent. For 20 years, at least, he has been probably the premier college football coach in America. If one Texas fan has personally called to express a loss akin to death at Royal's retirement, at least another 1000 have duplicated that statement. University of Texas people . . . were content in the knowledge that in Darrell they had a man who would handle the difficult King of the Mountain Longhorn Coaching job as brilliantly, as competently, and with total class, as was humanly possible. And, now he is gone. By *his* choice. . . . We are going to miss you, Darrell. God only knows how we are going to miss you! You have, uniquely, contributed so much to the lore of the great University of Texas, there is no way any of us can repay you.

Few coaches have been more praised or honored during their lifetimes. People across the country, not just Longhorn fans, mourned as if for a death. His resignation represented the premature passing of an era. Royal's unique personality, intensity, and integrity had been perfect for the growing and changing University of Texas. Fans believed, with good reason, that he simply could not be replaced. To date, he has not been.

Some UT administrators and regents had grown disgusted with the looks of Darrell's guests on Memorial Stadium's sidelines. Wearing long hair, sporting T-shirts with foul language, his "pickers" received privileges others would have loved to have. Darrell got an earful about how it appeared to the world when he was hanging out with such unsavory characters, those people he called his friends.

Frank's Erwin's fingers were in every piece of The University pie, but he longed to sink his teeth into football. The

> ## "Ain't a horse that can't be rode and there ain't a man that can't be throwed."
>
> —Darrell K Royal

> ## "You can't win a peeing contest with a skunk."
>
> —Darrell K Royal

BOBBY DODD
ATHLETIC DIRECTOR
GA. TECH AA - 190 THIRD ST., N.W. • ATLANTA, GEORGIA 30332 • PHONE 894-5412

MESSAGE	REPLY
TO	DATE
DATE	

Dear Darrell,
The Tickets came in the mail this morning — I mailed my check back immediately — Darrell I'm very grateful for your help -- I was desperate —

I'm so glad you and Frank dropped out of coaching — Its getting so bad there is no place for an ethical and honest man to be — Sincerely, Bob

BY
Form N-N73 © The Drawing Board, Inc., Box 505, Dallas, Texas 75221
INSTRUCTIONS TO SENDER:
1. KEEP YELLOW COPY. 2. SEND WHITE AND PINK COPIES INTACT.

SIGNED
INSTRUCTIONS TO RECEIVER:
1. WRITE REPLY. 2. DETACH STUB, KEEP PINK COPY, RETURN WHITE COPY TO SENDER.

Bobby Dodd, the former head coach of Georgia Tech, sent Royal a note congratulating him on retiring at the right time. (Royal Family Archives)

longtime UT regent and former chairman of the board was a fanatical friend of The University. He had willed into existence new and improved sports facilities across campus, and he lobbied the legislature for additional funding for his pet projects. But when it came to the football program, he was like a hyena eyeing a lion's kill. He snapped, howled, and dipped in close to the prize, but Royal had had no intention of sharing.

For much of Royal's time at Texas, Erwin wanted to see him gone. Most of the time they tried to stay out of each other's way, but according to sources in a column by Mickey Herskowitz (*Houston Chronicle*, September 15, 1996), after three 6–4 seasons (1965–1967), Frank Erwin stood in front of the board of regents and demanded that Royal be fired. His power play failed. It infuriated him to lose that battle, but the war was not over.

Erwin detested losing to OU. He resented Royal's refusal to bend the rules. Erwin wanted Royal to stop the conservative coaching and open up the offense. In 1996, sixteen years after Erwin's death, Mickey

> **"There were no limits to what Erwin would do to win, to benefit UT. Darrell had limits. He had a higher standard than most coaches . . . than most people."**
>
> —Austin businessman close to both Erwin and Royal, quoted by Mickey Herskowitz, *Houston Chronicle*, September 15, 1996

Herskowitz wrote that Erwin had "wanted Darrell to 'mind' him." And why not? Almost everyone on campus and in the state of Texas did. Erwin "did not admire independent thought in others," said Herskowitz.

They were both proud and stubborn, widely influential men. Both had their loyalists. Royal's charisma and ability to befriend members of wildly varying social groups attracted intense loyalty; he was liked by most everyone and deified by many. Erwin was ever aware of that fact, and the two were cordial with each other. But if they never became close friends, it was because, as one source said, "Kings don't bow to other kings."

With his retirement came rumors that Royal had been forced out, that former governor Allan Shivers or Erwin or Lorene Rogers (UT's president) had conspired to get him to step down.

Most of the people involved in that chapter of the Texas Athletics Department's history are dead. Aside from Darrell, Edith has more knowledge of the goings-on than any other living person, but she's not saying.

Honest as she is about her own life, she is unwilling to skewer others publicly. The rumor that most give credence to is that in early November 1976, Royal told Allan Shivers, then chairman of the board of regents, of his decision to retire. The coach had two requests: that he be allowed to stay on as athletic director, and that he get to name his successor. It was not unheard-of for coaches of Royal's stature to be granted that privilege.

Shivers urged Royal to reconsider, but Royal would not be dissuaded from the decision he and Edith had made. He and Shivers usually got along well, but Shivers was not happy Royal's retirement from coaching.

The usual procedure for choosing a new coach calls for the combined recommendation of the athletic director—Royal—and the Athletics Council to be sent to the president of The University, in this case, Lorene Rogers. But after Royal made his resignation official, Shivers usurped the accepted procedure and appointed a seven-member search committee, to be chaired by Rogers. The committee consisted of Shivers, J. Neils Thompson, the chairman of the Athletics Council, and four members of the Athletics Council—Wales Madden, Professor Robert Jeffrey, Mickey LeMaistre (UT chancellor), and Jim Boone, the president of the Student Bar Association. Lou Maysel, a sports columnist for the *Austin American-Statesman*, wrote, "The group had about as much expertise in picking a coach as Royal has in biochemistry, which is Rogers' academic field."

Darrell Royal, the virtual face of The University, was not named to the committee. Not only would Royal—one of the most successful and most venerated coaches in the history of college football—not be allowed to name his successor, he would not be allowed to cast a vote. It was alleged that someone behind the scenes was fueling the fire. Some believed that Erwin hoped Royal would be so humiliated by the selection process that he would resign as athletic director.

In spite of this public snub, Royal urged the committee to select his friend and coworker of twenty-one years, defensive coordinator Mike Campbell. Before Royal resigned, he felt certain that the job would go to Campbell. Campbell was widely acknowledged as having a brilliant defensive mind, and his loyalty to The University was unquestioned. He had turned down several head coaching job offers over the years to stay at Texas.

When Royal first told his friend of his decision to retire, Campbell was stunned: "Why on earth are you retiring now? We've got Earl [Campbell] coming back! We're gonna win with this bunch."

"Mike, I'm tired. Plus I want to leave a little ham on the bone for you next year. I know you can handle it." The finalists for the job Bear Bryant called "perhaps the best college football job in America," were Mike Campbell; Jerry Claiborne, from Maryland; and the Wyoming head coach, Fred Akers, who had coached on Darrell Royal's staff for eight years.

Those who thought they were in the know expected Campbell to get the nod. But Royal's strong endorsement of Campbell ended up being the kiss of death. The handling of the whole selection process seemed designed to slap Royal in the face, to show him, finally, who had ultimate power around campus. Campbell was treated shabbily; he waited hours for a phone call when it seemed almost everyone else knew the outcome. Royal, the athletic director, was told of the committee's decision just moments before the news was released to the public.

When the committee selected former UT assistant coach Fred Akers to succeed Royal, those in the Campbell camp were angry, bewildered, wounded. Akers immediately asked Campbell to stay on as defensive coordinator, but Campbell declined. As the athletic director and Akers's former boss, Royal said all the right things.

> Naturally, there are some hurt feelings. Mike has a lot of friends, followers, and believers. But so does Fred.... Now it's time we all get back into the same boat and begin to pull for the same color again. We have our coach and he's a good one.
>
> The people who run this great University, after proper investigation, chose Fred. It is a choice I can enthusiastically support. And as UT athletic director, I will support Fred.

Privately, though, he admitted, "I feel like a dog that's been kicked off the porch out into the rain."

Almost four decades later, people who were around during those years still want to know what *really* happened. When asked about those hurtful times and his dealings with Erwin, Shivers, and Rogers, Royal's response is classic and classy: "I don't have a bone to pick with them. Besides, they're not around to defend themselves."

Royal stayed on as athletic director for two more years, and he was miserable. He did not like being an administrator. As he told John Wheat: "I didn't like the paperwork; I didn't like the meetings; I didn't like the rule books; I didn't like the NCAA meetings, Southwest Conference meetings, all the meetings, at the university level."

He had long thought that after he quit coaching, he might finish out his days as athletic director. But Royal was used to the adrenaline rush of making split-second decisions, not to the

"He's got a paddle to fit every ass."

—Darrell Royal, referring to a subversive staff member who sidestepped Royal as athletic director and went straight to Frank Erwin

"Darrell, not only a champion in his field but also a great citizen and warm friend": Alan Shivers and Darrell Royal after the Horns' 1963 national championship. (Royal Family Archives; photo by Bill Malone)

drudgery of sitting behind a desk. He saw changes coming and problems looming.

He was in favor of the thirty-scholarship limit, believing that it would "even out the teams" and "make for a stronger Southwest Conference." But that still represented a challenge, particularly when he could look around, throw a football in any direction, and hit a school that was either actively cheating or turning a blind eye to it.

With the passage of Title IX legislation in 1972, which required that women be given an equal opportunity to participate in college athletics, he foresaw a financial crisis in college athletics. As athletic director, he was responsible for implementing its directives on campus, and in 1975, Royal and The University established and poured money into the Women's Athletics Department as a separate entity, with its own athletic director,

its own athletic council, and its own budget. No school had done more for women's athletics. He was absolutely in favor of women's right to compete, but practically speaking, how would it be paid for? Truth be told, he just didn't want to mess with it. Royal served on President Gerald Ford's Committee on Title IX and was as blunt with the president as he was with anyone: "Who should pay for women's athletics? The University? Men's athletics? I just knew it would be a tremendous financial burden."

The NCAA's refusal to crack down on cheating stuck in his craw, too. He advocated the use of lie detector tests to expose violations, but was shot down by some, not taken seriously by others. "If you're gonna catch people who are cheating, you have to basically catch a liar," Royal said. "I really and truly wanted to clean up intercollegiate athletics and get the people who were buying athletes. It was either that or quit myself, because you can't compete with 'em."

Rough draft of a press release written on December 21, 1979, and initialed by Peter Flawn and Darrell Royal, announcing Royal's resignation as athletic director and his appointment as special assistant to the president for athletic programs. The news was to be announced on December 27, but the press caught wind that something was brewing, so Flawn and Royal released it on December 22, in El Paso, just before Texas kicked off against Washington in the Sun Bowl. (DKR Papers, DBCAH, di_07312)

Mack Brown and Darrell Royal.
Photo by Carrell Grigsby.

> **"I've never had any trouble turning the page in the book of my life."**
> —Darrell K Royal

▼

Chapter 19

THE POPE OF AUSTIN

For a while after he left the athletics department altogether and had no official tie to it any more, he seemed to drop out of sight. Part of it was just Darrell's way; he knew it would be difficult to follow him and his legacy, and he didn't think Fred Akers, or any of the subsequent coaches, for that matter, needed interference from him. Part of it was surely the friction that resulted between Royal and Akers after behind-the-scenes politics had made the hiring process so painful. Whatever the reasons, this legend, the touchstone of all that was good in college athletics, became invisible around UT athletics.

As Royal was contemplating resigning as athletic director, Peter Flawn, the president of The University (1979–1985, 1997–1998), approached him with the idea of becoming special assistant to the president. Royal had assumed he would be quickly forgotten, but Flawn recognized that Royal's talent, influence, and aura were too valuable to squander. The University still needed him.

Royal jokingly explained his job this way: "I've agreed not to give any advice unless I'm asked. And they've agreed not to ask." His duties were varied, but he was basically on call to the University president. He represented The University at functions,

visited with the new athletic director, DeLoss Dodds, raised money for scholarships, and was a goodwill ambassador for The University. Yet for too long he was not welcome around Memorial Stadium.

In 1991, then–head coach John Mackovic made it clear that he was not interested in learning about or observing established Texas traditions. He told well-intentioned boosters and staff members that he "intended to make his own traditions." So for the first time in recent memory, former players were not allowed at closed practices and were shut out of the weight room. Coach Royal was still Big Man on Campus, just not around Memorial Stadium.

Royal had long been one of Mack Brown's coaching heroes. Royal sat on the selection committee that hired Brown in 1998. The two formed an instant bond, and before Brown recruited a single player or coached a down of football, he won over the Longhorn Nation with his public praise of Royal. Suddenly, Darrell was back in the public eye. Brown brought him back to Memorial Stadium, where he belonged. But by this time, Royal's name was on the thing. Brown sought his advice and included him at all football functions. He publicly invoked Royal's name at every opportunity; he wanted his players to know this man who had helped build the tradition they were supposed to continue. For older fans yearning for a return to the glory days, Brown had quenched a thirst. Royal had remained in and around The University, but his public presence had been missed. For Longhorn fans across the country and across the generations, Royal was the standard bearer of all that was right about college athletics, and for a long time they had sensed that had been lost. But now, thanks to Brown, Royal was back on his pedestal.

When The University hired Brown, Royal gave him the secret to success at Texas: "To be the head coach at Texas, you need to smile, you need to like the state of Texas, you need to like the people, you need to stop and talk to them. You need to sign those autographs . . . You need to know what you're doing on the field, you need to recruit well, and you need to win all your games. Other than that, it's an easy job."

No matter how long he has been retired, a coach is always known as "Coach." No matter his age, he will be called "Coach" until the day he dies.

Yet around Austin, Royal is not just "Coach", he is "The Coach." When anyone says, "I'm having lunch with the coach today," no further explanation is necessary. There is only one.

The actor Ed Marinaro said in *The Story of Darrell Royal*, "He's like the pope of Austin." Why is that? Why does a man, retired for three and a half decades still command the reverence usually afforded His Holiness the Dalai Lama?

Doug Looney, a former senior writer for *Sports Illustrated*, described Royal's legacy: "The numbers still generate gasps. Rolled into one brilliant package, Darrell Royal was Picasso and Mozart and Einstein and Rockne and Patton and Churchill and John Wayne and Thomas Jefferson; he was also Willie Nelson and a 35-foot sidehill putt for a birdie and a sunset over Maui." Mickey Herskowitz, a longtime Royal observer, put it this way in the *Houston Chronicle* in 1996: "Like Mickey Mantle, Darrell Royal had a name that rang so pure, you could not imagine anyone else doing the grand things each of them did, in their time, in their games. . . . He was the first football coach I can remember who was referred to in print by his initials—DKR—as though he were in a category with JFK or LBJ or AT&T."

Texas senator Kay Bailey Hutchison hosted a reception in honor of former secretary of state Henry Kissinger in Austin. As the two approached Royal, Hutchison began to introduce Kissinger to the coach, but before she could finish, he blurted out, "Darrell Royal! Of course I know Darrell Royal!" Photo by Rick Henson.

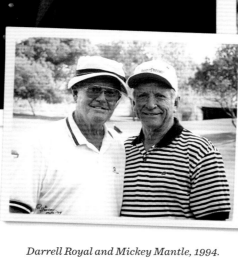

The man himself downplays his continuing celebrity. "A fan will bring his son over to introduce me, and that kid wasn't even born when I quit coaching. He has no idea who I am. That kid's looking at me like a goat looking at a new gate."

During festivities for President Johnson's inauguration, in January 1965, Governor John Connally hosted a reception at the Statler Hilton in Washington, D.C., for the Texas delegation. One lady from Dallas saw guests standing in two lines, one twice as long as the other. She presumed the longer one was the line for the buffet. "No, ma'am," the lady was told, "that's the line to meet Darrell Royal!"

The annual Texas High School Football Hall of Fame banquet held on the Baylor University campus in Waco, Texas, is a special night. The hall is packed with the honorees' families and friends, former teammates, and their high school and college coaches. At the 2008 induction, half of the old Southwest Conference was represented, along with a representative of the Big 8. Barry Switzer of Oklahoma; Darrell Royal, Texas; R. C. Slocum, Texas A&M; Spike Dykes, Texas Tech; Grant Teaff, Baylor; and David McWilliams, a former head coach at Texas, were all there shaking hands and signing autographs before the ceremony began. But for only one of those men did people stand in a line ten-deep to shake his hand, to get an autograph for their child, or to express gratitude for the honor he had brought to the sport of football. Many standing in that line had not been born when he was coaching, yet they knew. They had been told.

It didn't matter who was in Waco, Royal was still the king. Regardless of the occasion, regardless of the other luminaries in attendance, the unassuming Royal "still commands the adoration usually reserved for popes and monarchs. Mere mortals stare slack-jawed, and the legends line up to kiss his ring."

The trajectory of his career was that of a rocket whose ascent thrilled children and adults alike. He did his best work before he reached his fifty-third birthday. Who can imagine what he might have accomplished had he not left the game he loved—the game he changed—so early?

Darrell Royal

85th Birthday Party

Given by his 1957 to 1976 Longhorn teams and Mack Brown

Saturday, July 25th
7:00 p.m. to 10:00 p.m.
Darrell K. Royal Texas Memorial Stadium
North End Zone Club

Dress: Casual

*Invitation to Royal's eighty-fifth birthday
party, hosted by his players and the Texas
coaching staff. (Royal Family Archives)*

"Well, I'm still on the right side of dirt."

—Darrell K Royal

Chapter 20

THE FOURTH QUARTER

Royal's former players had talked for years about throwing a party to honor him. Various teams had held reunions, and Royal had been honored by The University and by the Athletics Department. But there had been no formal "thank you" salute from his players. Finally, Bill Hall, a team manager in the late '60s, set things in motion for an eighty-fifth birthday celebration to honor Coach Royal. With help from Edith, James Street, Randy McEachern, and others, former players, managers, and coaches from across Royal's twenty-year career were contacted.

"The price of coaches has gone up greatly since I quit. I was just born too soon."

—Darrell K Royal

Edith asked Royal's friends and former players to write him a letter recounting touching memories or amusing anecdotes or ways that he had touched their lives. The letters flooded in. Most were full of gratitude, while a few remembered the times his discipline rained down on them. Some contained stories that poked fun at him. There were letters of eloquence and letters of only two lines, but they all exuded the same feeling of love and reverence for this man who had once seemed larger than life but now was recognized as a loyal friend.

Rick Ingraham, offensive guard (1974–1977), wrote:

> Everyday I use the lessons you and your staff taught us. We all profited so immensely because of you. You gave us more than we could ever repay, and your legacy will live forever thru us and our children. My only regret is that we did not win more for you, though I am proud that we won with a clean program. Integrity, Poise, Character, Accountability, Leadership, Citizenship, Honesty. You set a very high standard and I am still striving to achieve the ideals you represented to us. Thank you so much.

Honor Franklin, the wife of Bobby Mitchell (offensive guard, 1968–1970), thanked Royal for his example:

You were a stable, reliable, fair, patient coach and he never ever wanted to disappoint you. You provided a moral compass and inspiring example, and I write to express my deepest appreciation for so profoundly and positively influencing and impacting his life.

Dan Jenkins sent an especially warm letter of gratitude and appreciation.

July 24, 2009

Hey, Coach:

Congratulations on shooting 85 without any mulligans. Once again you're my hero. I often think about all the great days in the past—especially the time we both escaped "the green socks" on that Saturday in 1963. That was a close one.

As you know I've been at this business a long time and you're still my favorite subject who became a friend. Not just the greatest college football coach I ever knew and covered, but the best person to know and best guy to hang out with.

You made my job easier than anybody I ever knew, and I just want you to know on this occasion that I haven't forgotten.

Warm regards from an old friend,

Dan Jenkins

Edith marveled, "When I read those letters from his players, I couldn't get over how many of them remarked that his practices were the most organized and efficient and that the way those practices were run served as a model for their own businesses and their lives."

On a blazing hot, humid July evening, more than 300 players, managers, and coaches representing every Texas team he had coached gathered in the north end zone of Darrell K Royal–Memorial Stadium to tell old stories and to shake Royal's hand, perhaps for the last time. Those now-grown men took the opportunity to truly thank the coach who had helped form them, had cared about them enough to demand that they be well groomed, get their degrees, and conduct themselves with class and confidence.

Now, in Royal's eighty-seventh year, much of what happens in his day is forgotten: who took him to breakfast, whether the Horns won the basketball game, what he and Edith discussed the night before. He bristles at having to use a walker and refuses to use it in public. He is an athlete, after all. His ability to recall people's names was always remarkable; it pains him today to have lost that gift. His memory is a worn and faded map, and the roads he traveled long ago are the ones he remembers best. The Royals live in

Royal on retirement: "I'm not bored. I'm not a guy with nothing to do. I've enjoyed my retirement. . . . As far as I'm concerned, everything's ham and jam." Photo by Rick Henson.

Willie Zapalac (left) served on Royal's staff for twelve years, 1964–1975. Leon Manley (right), Royal's lifelong friend, coached at Texas from 1966 to 1976. The men's last reunion came in 2009 at Royal's eighty-fifth birthday party. Photo by Paulette Hamilton.

Querencia at Barton Creek, a lovely, well-appointed independent-living facility nestled in the hills of Barton Creek Country Club. When the couple first moved there, Darrell told people, "They've got three sections: a go-go, a slow-go, and a no-go. Right now, we're enjoying good health. We're in the go-go section."

He sat at his breakfast table recently, entertaining a visitor. His hair is solid white now, and he was looking natty in a burnt orange windsuit. He studied a black-and-white photo of his 1956 University of Washington coaching staff. He was trying to accommodate his friend, who asked him to identify the men in the picture. He protested at first, claiming that he couldn't remember their names. But he held the photo in his gnarled fingers and slowly began to name the men: "Well, let's see. . . . That's Ray Willsey. . . . And of course, that's Mike [Campbell], and there I am. Hmmm. I'm sorry, but I don't remember any of those others." He stared at the photo for a full minute and finally said, "I believe that's Jack Swarthout on the right. But I'm afraid I can't help you with anyone else." Yet instead of relinquishing the photo, he held onto it while another minute passed. The coach recovered another name and another, and eventually he named everyone on his 1956 Washington coaching staff.

He touched one face on the photograph, glanced sideways with a little grin, and said, "That's John Baker. He didn't make the traveling squad."

Leon Manley, a lifelong friend and one of Royal's assistant coaches (1966–1976), died in 2010, and Edith was asked to speak at the funeral in Coach Royal's stead. She is the spokesman for the couple now. It was a tough task for her; she had known Leon since she was seventeen. Leon and his wife, Johnnie, had been there at almost every phase of the Royal's life: Hollis, the University of Oklahoma, Edmonton, The University of Texas.

Edith sat at her computer and contemplated what she wanted to say at Manley's service. With Darrell looking over her shoulder, she scrolled through pictures of Darrell and Leon's years together at Hollis, OU, and Edmonton, where Royal coached Manley. Edith began telling a story from 1952 that involved Leon and one of Royal's other players. Darrell interrupted her to correct her on several details until finally, exasperated, Edith said, "Well, why don't you tell it, then?" "Well, all right. I believe I will." He slowly and carefully told the story from sixty years ago, and Edith's expression softened as she caught a glimpse of the old Darrell, laughing and vibrant and remembering.

He no longer gives interviews, so Edith was surprised when he agreed, in his eighty-sixth year, to appear on the *Coffee with the Kyle Sisters* radio show. He entertained them at the station

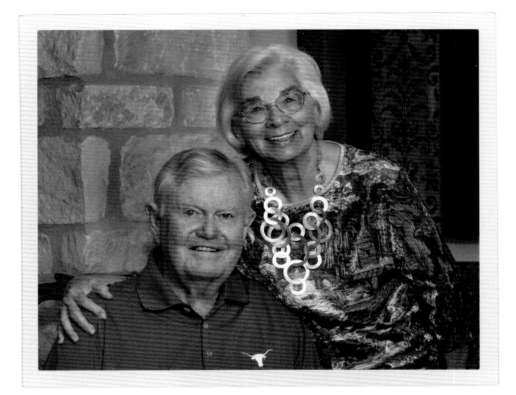

with anecdotes from long ago. Before too long, the Kyle Sisters had him singing "Amazing Grace" and "The Old Rugged Cross," hymns he remembered from his youth in the Church of Christ. It was a sweet moment in the twilight of this great man's life, where he turned back to things he had clung to as a child.

After the show, Edith sat in a friend's car by herself and put the CD recording of the radio show into the deck. The tidal wave of memories and sadness and companionship and inevitability overtook her, and she cried as she listened to her husband recite "The Eyes of Texas" as the Kyle Sisters sang backup. Arthritis and neck problems finally caught up with him, and he had stopped playing golf several years back. He enjoys riding in the cart when friends play as long as it doesn't get too hot. If it does, they will drop him off at the 19th hole of Barton Creek Country Club; he's got no shortage of friends there. He served on the club's board of governors for years.

Their schedules are almost as full today as they were during the UT years, full of get-togethers with friends, award ceremonies, University events, football practices, reunions, and charity commitments. And sadly, they go to more and more funerals. "As I was leaving the house today," Edith said recently, "somebody called him to come sign some photos, and another called to see if he would ride with him for nine holes. Chic is taking him to the stadium for the spring football game this weekend. His players and friends are

> "I've always been too busy with tomorrow to look back at yesterday."
>
> —Darrell K Royal

so faithful about taking him to lunch or giving him a ride over to practice. We have a wonderful assistant, Colleen Kieke, that helps him with his schedule, or I don't know how we'd manage. We stay busy, and that's how he likes it. But a perfect day for me would be to just sit at home and read a book."

Coaches are well known for their reluctance to second-guess themselves, and they resent like heck when anyone else does it. Sixty-seven years of marriage has solidified this attitude in both of them. Learn from your mistakes and go forward. Darrell swears that he has never had concrete goals he planned to reach nor set any future plans: "It's one day at a time. I just try not to make the same mistake today that I made yesterday". Edith admits that she does have regrets, "but something I'd change? No, not like my own actions or anything. I don't think I'd change any of them because the regrets I do have, I've learned a lesson from them."

Sixty-seven years. Things have come full circle, and they've experienced a role reversal of sorts. In the past, Darrell was always busy, never skilled at puttering around or relaxing. If you picture the little boy in Hollis who had so much energy that he tried to race the cars that drove by his house, you will get an idea of Darrell as a grown-up: on the move, on the phone, thinking, planning, running ideas past Edith or his staff. She was planted, anchored, enabling him to have a home and a family. For most of those years, they were a partnership. For most of those years, they were great friends. "We were so devoted to one another," she now says, "that sometimes I wonder if we didn't neglect our kids."

He has always been private with his deepest emotions and is clearly not one to analyze their marriage. But as time has passed and he has become dependent upon her, he is even more appreciative of who she is and what she enabled him to do. In 2004, he told Pat Baldwin of *Private Clubs Magazine*, "I know the odds are against a marriage lasting 60 years. My wife, Edith . . . she's been very tolerant."

Edith has been an equal force in this partnership, although it didn't always appear to be so. She was happy to be a homemaker, a supportive friend who allowed her husband to be in the limelight and who never clamored for the attention herself. But she is no pushover; she has always stood her ground. One friend commented that she was not so much Darrell's wife, but rather he was Edith's husband. Edith remembers:

Some years we were so simpatico; others we were just barely hanging on. We didn't fight about a whole lot, most of the time. I gave my opinions, but I kept my resentments to myself. And I had a lot, but we didn't have much time together anyway, and I didn't want to start a fight.

We used to go to Mexico every year with friends, but one year I arranged for us to go down there together, just the two of us. We never got the chance to be alone, and I was looking forward to it. One day while I was planning the trip, he looked at me and asked, "Well, what am I supposed to do in Mexico all by myself?" I was furious. I stayed mad about that a few months.

She chuckles as she carefully turns the crumbling pages of a scrapbook, reciting the names of people in the photos, marveling at the life she and Darrell have had. It is a respite to look at their young, vibrant images in the newspapers. It brings tears and a smile when she sees the family portrait of five. She tenderly touches the image of David Royal licking chocolate icing from the beaters of the mixer.

It is telling, the things she kept. Most were about her husband's career and accomplishments, but there were photos and letters from friends, dozens of poems and songs written about them by fans, stories she clipped from the newspaper that struck her heart. She pulls a brown leather box, its hinge almost broken, from far in the back of a bottom dresser drawer. Early in their marriage, Darrell had talked her into throwing away letters he'd written while in the service, letters that she had tied up in blue ribbon and saved. But later, without telling

A note from Darrell to Edith, written directly on a package containing a gold lamé Neiman Marcus robe. (Royal Family Archives)

Darrell Royal, overlooking the Pedernales. Reporters have asked Royal through the years how he would like to be remembered. Most often, he responded, "I want to be remembered as an honest and ethical guy who won a few more than he lost." But when faced with that question in his later years, his answer was simple: "He meant well." (Royal Family Archives)

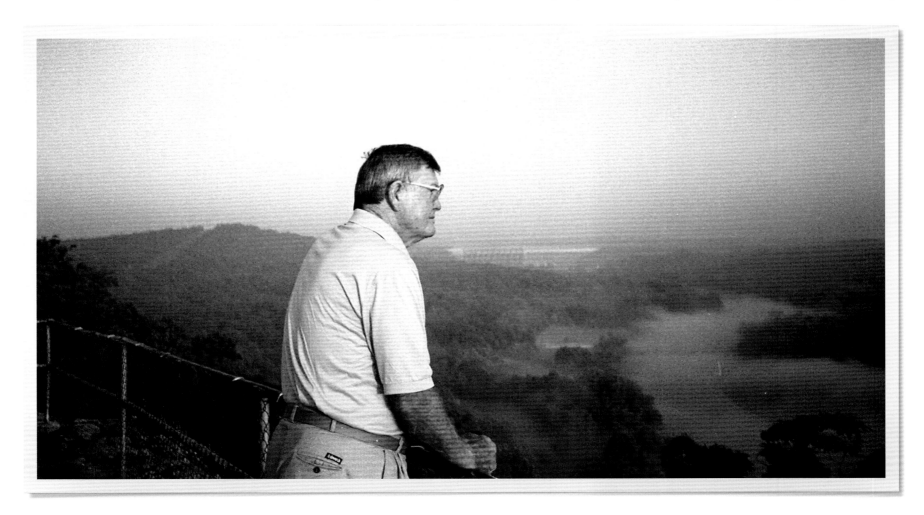

him, she started a new collection. Housed in this worn leather box with a gold embossed cover were cards from gifts and flowers he had sent, amorous anniversary cards, and short but eloquent love notes written in his elegant handwriting. She shared him with the public for most of their sixty-seven years, but these treasures, these pieces of him were hers and hers alone.

Edith offered these notes to show a different side of Darrell, and she offered them with this admonition: "Look at them, then forget about them. I just wanted you to see how sweet he could be." Among them is a note that was written directly on a dress box. Here is why she saved it. Once when Darrell and Edith were at a coaches' convention in Dallas, she and Gene Stallings, Texas A&M's head coach, were standing outside the window of Neiman Marcus. The mannequin inside the window wore a beautiful

gold lamé robe, and Edith couldn't help admiring it. "Gene, look at that robe. Isn't that just the most beautiful thing you've ever seen? I just love that robe."

They walked on, and she forgot about the conversation and the robe, but the next day when Edith returned to their hotel room after a wives' outing, she found a package on their bed with a note written directly on the packaging.

Pat Culpepper summed it up beautifully in *Coach Royal*: "Whatever The University of Texas football program is today is a direct result of Darrell Royal's insistence on doing things the right way. His story is important to understand because it is the very foundation for change at The University of Texas. His legacy became the standard to match for every football coach who followed his twenty-year tenure."

"What I kept, I lost. What I gave, I have."

—Paraphrase of the epitaph of Edward de Courtenay, third Earl of Devon, 1419, painted on a sign that hung in Darrell Royal's locker room for twenty years

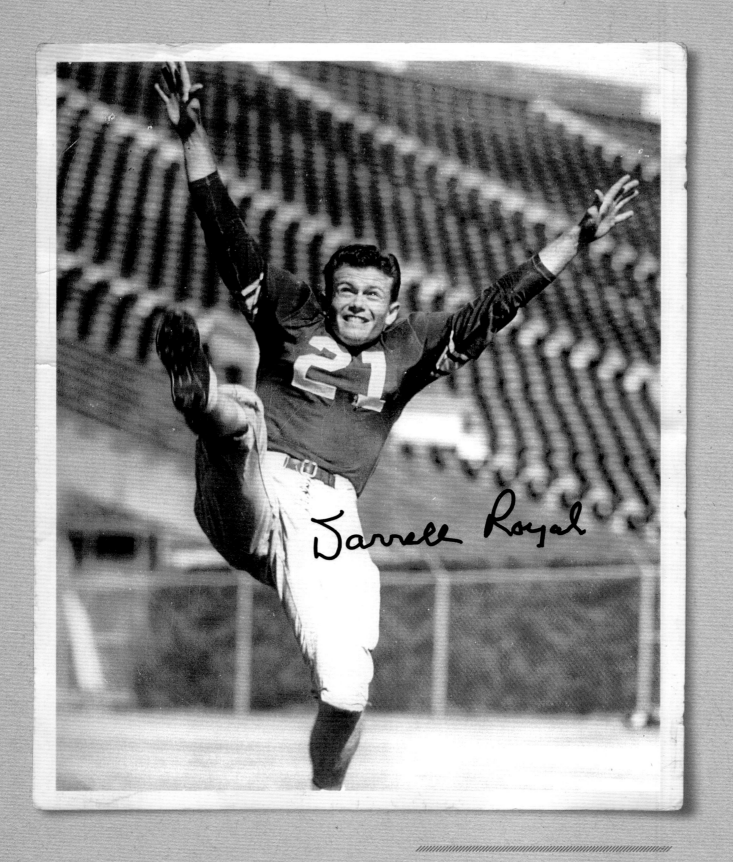

Darrell Royal

Darrell Royal, who played at Oklahoma from 1946 to
1949, is still considered one of the greatest all-around
players in Sooner history. (Royal Family Archives)

> "If everything had already been done, there would be nothing left for young people to accomplish. There are always going to be people who run faster, jump higher, dive deeper, and come up drier."
>
> —Darrell K Royal

Appendix A

ROYAL AS A SOONER, LONGHORN, AND HONOREE

Darrell K Royal at the University of Oklahoma

All-American quarterback, 1949

Third-best career winning percentage, .938, 1946–1949

First Sooner chosen National Back of the Week, November 5, 1949

Seventh in career punt-return average, 15.71 yards, 1946–1949

Tenth-longest play: 96-yard punt return

First in career interceptions: 18, 1946–1949

Tied for most interceptions in a game: 3 against Oklahoma State, 1947

Tied for most interceptions in a season: 7, 1947

Tied for third-longest punt: 81 yards against Oklahoma State, 1948

Tied for fifth-longest punt: 78 yards against Missouri, 1947

Selected for Blue-Gray Football Game, 1949

Selected for first Senior Bowl, 1950

Big Eight Football Hall of Fame

Blue-Gray Football Hall of Fame, 1991

Darrell K Royal at The University of Texas

167-47-5 record

8-7-1 bowl record

National championships: 1963, 1969, 1970

Southwest Conference championships (won or shared): 1959, 1961, 1962, 1963, 1968, 1969, 1970, 1971, 1972, 1973, 1975

8 top five national finishes

11 top ten national finishes

Winning percentage of .788

Winningest football coach in Southwest Conference history

> "Texas' winning tradition will not be entrusted to the timid or to the weak."
>
> —Sign that hung in Royal's Longhorn dressing room for 20 years

Darrell Royal receiving the 1963 AFCA Coach of the Year award. (Royal Family Archives)

Darrell K Royal's Collection of Honors

Honorary Lifetime Member of the Texas Exes (first coach and first non-alumnus to be so honored)

Honorary Texan, awarded by the Texas House of Representatives, 1957

Football Writers Association of America Coach of the Year Award, 1961, 1963

South Texas Hall of Fame, 1963

American Football Coaches Association Coach of the Year Award, 1963, 1970

Headliners Award in recognition of distinguished achievements in athletics and education, 1964, 1969, 1977

Texas Press Association's Distinguished Service Award, 1965

Coach of the Decade (1960s), ABC Sports, 1969

Field Scovell Award for advancement of sports in Dallas, 1969

Coach of the Year, Touchdown Club of Washington, 1970

Coach of the Decade (1960s), nation's sportswriters, 1970

Mr. South Texas Award, 1972

Member, Board of Trustees, American Football Coaches Association, 1971–1975

President, American Football Coaches Association, 1975

Texas Sports Hall of Fame, 1976

Mr. Sportsman Award, Interfaith Charities of Houston, 1980

National Football Foundation College Football Hall of Fame, 1983

Legends of Coaching Award, Downtown Athletic Club, 1991

Oklahoma Sports Hall of Fame, 1992

Austinite of the Year, 1995

Horatio Alger Award for Lifetime Success, 1996

Harvey Penick "Excellence in the Game of Life" Award, Caritas of Austin (awarded to Edith and Darrell Royal), 1999

Cotton Bowl Hall of Fame Inaugural Class, 1998

Legends Award, Dallas All-Sports Association, 1999

Texas Sportswriters Coach of the Year Award

College Football Coach of the Year, Columbus Touchdown Club

Southwesterner of the Year

Southwest Conference Coach of the Year

First recipient of the Bear Bryant Lifetime Achievement Award, 2000

Oklahoma Heritage Society Hall of Fame, 2000

First recipient of Contributions to College Football Award, Home Depot Awards, 2002

Reds Bagnell Award, awarded by the Maxwell Club, for fostering and promoting the integrity of the game of football, 2005

The University of Texas Distinguished Service Award (only the fifth person to receive award), 2006

First recipient of the Darrell K Royal Patron Award, Texas Heritage Songwriters' Association

Amos Alonzo Stagg Award, 2010

Longhorn Hall of Honor, 1976

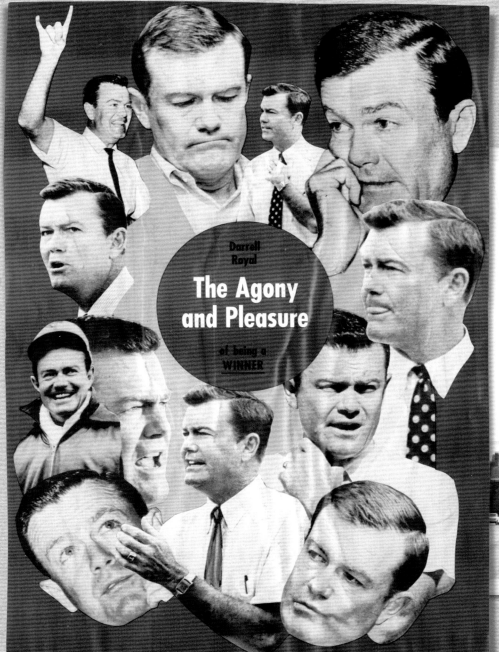

Darrell
Royal

The Agony
and Pleasure

of being a
WINNER

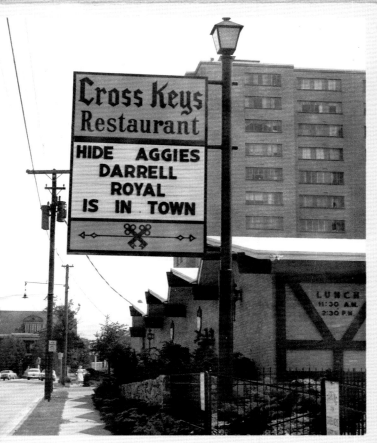

During his tenure at Texas, Darrell Royal
owned the Aggies, winning seventeen of
twenty meetings. (Royal Family Archives)

"If you walked a mile in my boots today,
it would probably be boring. But it was
a hell of a ride up to here. You should
have caught me earlier."

—Darrell K Royal

Appendix B
ROYALISMS

Darrell Royal is one of the most-quoted coaches in the history of sports; his words show appreciation for a uniquely phrased sentiment, and he usually chose the shortest—and most colorful—route to making his point. Many of his Royalisms have been sprinkled throughout the preceding pages; here are some more.

Philosophy

"If you feel like celebrating, wait until the other ten get there and celebrate together. You didn't do it by yourself."

"Football doesn't build character. It eliminates the weak ones."

"Confidence is contagious. So is the lack of it."

"It's like golf. It's not how you shoot, it's how many." After an ugly win over A&M in 1960

"If worms carried pistols, birds wouldn't eat 'em."

"It's like having a big ol' lollipop in your mouth and the first thing you know, all you have is the stick." On losing a game in the last minute

"Luck never jumped on anybody sitting in the shade."

"You've got to be in a position for luck to happen. Luck doesn't go around looking for a stumblebum."

"You got to think lucky. If you fall in a mudhole, check your pockets. You might have caught a fish."

"Breaks balance out. The sun don't shine on the same dog's rear every day." Warning about trouble ahead with the rest of the 1961 schedule despite getting off to a 4-0 start

"There is no such thing as defeat except when it comes from within. As long as a person doesn't admit he is defeated, he is not defeated. . . . He's just a little behind and isn't through fighting."

"Next to weather, there is no equalizer like two fired-up football teams."

"When it gets down to the wood chopping, it is most important to have that deep confidence that your team is going to win and that you represent the best."

"Football's like Russian roulette. Most of the time, the firing pin hits an empty chamber, but you never know when the big bang is coming." On his theory that most football games are decided with a few big plays

"They talk about the new era of football, but it's still offense, defense, and defeat the guy in front of you."

"I've always said nobody will ever have any trouble getting me out of the party. If I see a yawn, I hit the door real quick. I didn't want to stay here until I wore out my welcome, and I don't think I have." Response to writers wanting to know why Royal was retiring, 1976

"To be successful as a team, you must bring all the parts together and play as one heartbeat."

Coaching

"Winning coaches must treat mistakes like copperheads in the bedclothes—avoid them with all the energy you can muster."

"Well, yes. You'd much rather see that ball in a quarterback's hand than lying there on the grass." When asked in 1957 whether his first job would be to find a good split-T quarterback

"You can't invent a feeling." On why he doesn't give fiery rah-rah speeches

"The foremost rule is be natural. If you're not completely natural, you couldn't convince your players Doris Day is a girl."

"You can't kid a kid. If you're not completely honest with your players, you're kidding yourself."

"Anyone in athletics is a bit of a ham. . . . It all starts from the time you earn your first letter. And it carries into coaching."

"Give me an O.J. Simpson, and I'll show you a coaching genius."

"One player was lost because he broke his nose. How do you go about getting a nose in condition for football?" When asked whether the an abnormal number of injuries one season resulted from poor conditioning

"The only way I know to keep football fun is to win. That's the only answer. There is no laughter in losing."

"A football coach is nothing more than a teacher. You teach the same subject and you have a new group of guys every year."

"I'm not married to any one philosophy or any one idea. You have to break the pattern enough that people don't have you completely zeroed in." After surprising fans in 1962 by using a pass-oriented quarterback

"I know this about coaching: you don't have to explain victory, and you can't explain defeat."

"I'm so far in debt that I'll never get out of it, so I might as well be in debt where it's warm." Tongue-in-cheek response to the rumor that he would take a coaching job with the New York Giants

"You're what-iffing now, and anybody can what-if."

"I don't know. I never had one." Answer to Mack Brown, then coach at North Carolina, when Brown asked Royal how he handled a losing season

"I do not believe in retiring jerseys."

"I could write a good first grade reader. It would go, 'See Texas run. See Texas fumble. See Texas run and fumble.'" After Texas lost three fumbles against Rice in 1970 but still won 45–21

"I always said I'd never be a teacher and I'd never be a politician. And I look back on my twenty years and see that I wasn't anything but both of them." To John Wheat in *Coach Royal: Conversations with a Texas Football Legend*

Defense

"Defense is more a test of courage and determination than of technique."

"At Texas, we just like to line up in a balanced defense, matching strength against strength, and start cracking walnuts."

"It was one of those old steady-knucks-down-type of goal-line stands." After stuffing Alabama quarterback Joe Namath on fourth down to seal a 21–17 victory in the 1965 Orange Bowl, the first bowl game played at night

"Great teams make goal-line stands."

"When you have them on the two and you can't take it away from them in eight minutes, the only thing you can do is meet them in the middle of the field and shake hands with the better team." After watching USC go 74 yards at the game's end to pull ahead of Texas, 10–6

Offense

"Football games are decided from the twenty-yard line on in. All that other running and panting out in the middle of the field is just entertaining spectators and wearing out grass."

"We're not exactly a rolling ball of butcher knives."

"We've had an awful lot of 'whoa' but not much 'go.'" On watching the Horns try to move the ball in 1979

"As soon as we got a little money in our pockets, we walked off the job until we were broke again." Complaining about inconsistent play in the 1965 victory over Indiana

"[Commentators] talk about the wishbone, say that you can't come from behind with two minutes to go. My rebuttal to that is you're supposed to be doing something the first fifty-eight minutes. The object of your game is to not be behind with two minutes to go."

"We were not happy with what we had been doing . . . so we circled and we exed and we sucked up our guts and went with it." On designing the wishbone offense, 1968

Kicking Game

"You'd have thought we'd be on it like a hen on a June bug." On the Horns poor coverage of a kick

"Maybe socialism has infiltrated college football. [The touch-back rule] is the only time a team is awarded for doing nothing. The defending team is actually given twenty yards for refusing to play!"

Players

"Fat people don't offend me. What offends me is losing with fat people."

"Our faces were so long we could have eaten oats out of a churn." On the OU players after the 1948 Senior Bowl loss

"A confused player cannot be an aggressive player."

"He's quicker than a wink." On Walter Fondren, his first quarterback at Texas

"He's quick as a hiccup." On Fondren

"Oh, he's grasshopping it around." On a player hobbled with an injury

"He was like a rubber balloon blown up and turned loose, swirling and darting helter-skelter all over the room until finally collapsing with a whoosh." On James Saxton

"He runs faster than small-town gossip, although his compass sometimes goes batty." On Saxton

"He's like a balloon full of air; when you turn him lose, there's no telling where he's going." On Saxton, 1959

"When he's going at an angle out there and he's got room to cut back, you can't hit him with a handful of rice." On Saxton

"Tacklin' him's like trying to catch a minnow in a wash pot." On Saxton

"He was panting like a lizard." On Saxton during the 1959 Oklahoma game

"Look at him rumblin' down the field . . . looks like a grizzly bear haulin' a walnut." On a Baylor tight end

"Once you cross the 50, you feel like an unbridled horse."

"He couldn't play first jumper on the Vassar quoits team."

"The mark of a great player is one who has his best games against great teams." Referring to linebacker Johnny Treadwell in 1962

"Oh, I've had worse cuts than that on my eyeball." To a player complaining about an injury

"He doesn't have a whole lot of speed, but maybe Elizabeth Taylor can't sing." On junior running back Harold Philipp, who replaced Ernie Koy in 1963

"How long is a *piece* of rope?" Response to a sportswriter asking how much a particular player meant to the success of UT's team

"I'd hate to see people coming to the stadium expecting to see a water-walking act." Trying to counteract national publicity of sophomore "Super Bill" Bradley in 1966

"His heart was as big as a No. 3 washtub." Complimenting Bill Bradley's courage on playing against Arkansas with a badly injured and taped knee in 1966

"Usually a lineman will slow down like a piano fell on him after [running] about 30 yards."

"Watching Chris run is like looking at a filmstrip with several frames missing. You see him hit a hole here and all of a sudden he's way over there, and you didn't see him get way over there." Bragging on Chris Gilbert's amazing quickness

"Duffy, you don't want my offense. You want my fullback, and he's busy for two more years." Referring to Steve Worster in response to Duffy Daugherty's question about the fullback's role in the wishbone offense

"You take the guys with the stats. I'll take Eddie [Phillips]."

"He'd stick his head in a buzz saw." On Tommy Ford, 1963

"He'd be a six-footer if he hadn't played football." Referring to five-nine battering ram Tommy Ford

"He looks like he needs worming." On all-American end Cotton Speyrer, 1968

"A boy shows how much he wants to play in the spring, when it's tough, and during two-a-days, when it's hot and tough. I don't count on the boy who waits till October, when it's cool and fun, and then decides he wants to play. Maybe he's better than three guys ahead of him, but I know those three won't change their minds in the fourth quarter."

"When Earl ran, snot flew. I haven't seen any snot fly yet." When asked to compare running back Butch Hadnot to Earl Campbell

"I think Cleveland forgot his game plan." Watching Cleveland Williams fight Muhammad Ali in 1970

"He's as smooth as smoke through a keyhole." On Oklahoma running back Joe Washington

"He's having a little trouble getting disciplined, but he'd be the best sandlot player on our team. He'll tackle anything that comes through the door." DKR on Ray Dowdy, 1970

"That's art." On watching Eddie Phillips run the wishbone against UCLA

"If Sisemore's mother had been more thoughtful, she'd have had triplets." On all-American offensive tackle Jerry Sisemore, 1972

"I thought we were going to have to light pine knots to smoke them out at the half." On the Horns' lackadaisical first-half effort against Wake Forest, 1973

"You spend your time waiting for these promising boys to deliver; pretty soon you're wearing a straw hat to Christmas." 1957

Opponents

"They get a yellow dog running downhill and they'll strap him real good. I want to see that they earn what they get with some bumps and bruises." Before the 1958 game against the Sooners, who had been running up the score on inferior teams

"Our statistical days are about over." Warning that trouble lay ahead for the undefeated Horns after beating OU 28–7 in 1963

"They cut us up like boarding-house pie, and that's real small chunks." Warning sportswriters in 1961 not to be complacent about the upcoming game with Rice, reminding them of what Rice did to the 1958 Longhorns

"We're scratched up a little, but we're not gushing blood." Meaning that in spite of settling for a tie with Rice, Texas was in good position to win the Southwest Conference in 1961

"It's a hoss and a hoss." Rating an upcoming game as even

"There was a hornet's nest waiting for us in Houston, and we were walking into it like Little Red Riding Hood with jam on her face."

"They're like a bunch of field mice." On SMU's shifting defense

"To say we were the only ones aggressive would be like a skunk telling a possum his breath smells."

"You always get a lift when you're going to the chair and somebody gives you a reprieve."

"This is for all the marbles, the whole bag." To sportswriter Gary Cartwright, November 30, 1963, on the team bus to Kyle Field to play the Aggies in what amounted to the national championship game for the Longhorns

"That was for the whole load of watermelons." On Texas' failed two-point conversion that gave Arkansas a 14–13 victory over the Horns in 1964 and the national championship

"I had hoped God would be neutral." Upon seeing a sign in Fayetteville that read: "Darrell Royal, cast not thy steers before swine," December 1969

"They're gonna come after us with their eyes pulled up like BBs."

"Lady Luck was on our side, and we welcomed her in."

"They'll be higher than a Georgia Pine." On the upcoming Arkansas game

"We're hurt and without that little lizard running around." Lamenting Chris Gilbert's shoulder separation against SMU in 1967

"They were on us like white on rice, and that's completely covered." Complimenting the 1969 Sooners' effort, in which future Heisman Trophy winner Steve Owens stung UT's defense for 123 yards, though Texas ultimately triumphed, 27–17

"UCLA brought some good people to town and they came in a bad humor." After the 20–17 win over UCLA in 1970

"But I've been sucking my thumb for three days." Response to writers who asked Royal after the 1973 OU game whether he was contemplating quitting after his third straight loss to the Sooners, 52–13

"Both sides joined the national giveaway program." On the thirteen turnovers—five by Texas—in the 1975 Arkansas game

"I don't think they've used up their only bullet. They've got one left in the chamber for us." On lowly TCU after the Horned Frogs surprised Texas Tech 31–7 in 1972

Random Royalisms

"He was as quiet as a mouse pissing on cotton."

"His finger was throbbin' like a sick robin's ass." On a friend who got a nail driven through his finger

"It's as near nothing as a grapette."

"He's so rich he could burn a wet elephant."

"He didn't know me from a bale of hay." Referring to Julio Iglesias, who was recording an album with Willie Nelson

Dear Mr. Royal,

    My name is Sandra and I'm 13. Mr. Royal I think that the boys would and could have played better if you hadn't walked up and down the side lines and had smoked that gum so bad, when you do that it show ~~make~~ you are nervos and becauce your nervos it make the boys nervos and so they make mistakes. So stop walking up and down the side lines. OK. OK.

                    Love,

1 ✝

A young fan named Sandra wrote to Royal to enlighten him on the cause of the Longhorns' loss to Penn State in the 1972 Cotton Bowl. (Royal Family Archives)

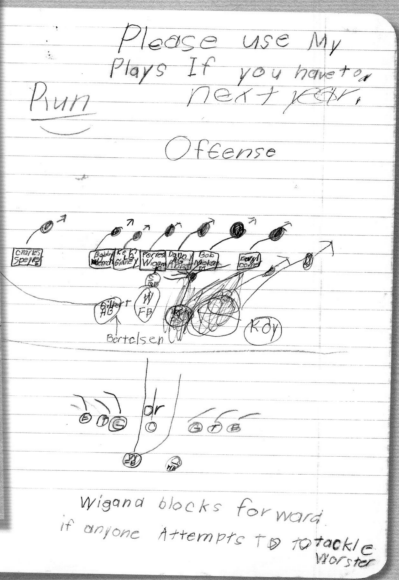

Royal's young admirers were not shy about sending him special plays to run. (Royal Family Archives)

▼

Appendix C

LETTERS TO THE COACH

Edith Royal's bookshelves are lined with album after album, each one filled with photos and letters from both the famed and the unknown. In keeping with her role as family historian, she kept every piece of correspondence: the mean and the meaningful, the inspirational and the scary.

Thumbing through one scrapbook, she uncovered a letter from "Just a Fan" complaining about Royal's decision to play Mike Cotten instead of Bobby Lackey. Another letter insists Donnie Wigginton should start in place of Eddie Phillips. Another anonymous letter from 1973 lists all the recruits Royal missed out on that year and begged him to consider a computerized recruiting system. Edith remarks, "At first he didn't want me to keep the bad stuff. He was so sensitive. But I just told him I was going to keep it all: the good, the bad, and the crazy."

They did receive "the crazy." In 1961, a forty-two-year-old man whose return address listed the YMCA in Long Beach, told Royal he was "over 200 pounds and 6′ 1½ inches tall and I want to play varsity football. I have one to two years of eligibility left, and I am getting a statement from my psychiatrist, saying I am healthy and can play." An inmate wrote from the Val Verde County jail: "If you'll come down here after me, I'll help recruit for you." A yellow Post-It note stuck in an envelope said, "You need not to let Texas Be without me sir. You may NOT believe this. That's your problem. I can give Tx our champenship back for a long time. Proving by results. Money is no problem. I promise you first year 6 of 10 or better. No Drugs. No Alchol. My name should not be spoken."

Royal's magnetism and his genuine interest in people made him approachable, and young fans loved him. Royal's secretary, Blanche Rhodes, kept every note and drawing he received. Boys and girls were inspired to write to him, send him their artwork and poetry, and tell him their secrets.

December 28, 1971

Dear Coach Royal,

I am eagar about the Cotton Bowl to see who is going to be on top. Penn State seems pretty good but Texas can beat them any day.

Even though I am 11 yrs old and going on 12, I make big bets with some of my friends. I won $1.50 on 2 bets. That's how much I depend on Texas winning. My average on bets is 75 cents.

I started betting at the age of 7. The most I have betted is Texas by 20 over Baylor, last year. I won 50 cents on that game. . . . Could you send me a list of the top high school prospects. Please send me information.

A big fan of Texas

An 11-year-old entrepreneur wrote a clever poem about the 1969 Big Shootout with Arkansas, and mailed it to Royal with this note attached:

Dear Mr. Royal,

Would you send me a note on how many their is on your team. Please figure up the total amount of money and send me a check. I will ask you to pay five cents a copy. Please send me a picture of your team and a team football and longhorn stickers.

Your friend,

D.W.

Hopeful recruits furnished their vital statistics and their punt, pass, and kick scores.

Dear Coach Royal,

Thank you for the autographed picture. Please do not get any more players because I do not want anyone to take my locker.

Dear Sir:

I am 12 years old, 5 feet 6 inches tall, and weigh 168 pounds, also a loyal Texas Longhorn fan. I am to big for definsive halfback or safety, to slow for linebacker or end, and I don't like to play defensive tackle. Could you tell me (a.) What position should I play, and (2.) What the heck happened against Notre Dame?

In the days before the Internet made online shopping possible, young fans hungry for anything burnt orange wrote the coach and asked for sideline passes, autographs, pennants, jerseys, and team photos.

Dear Mr. Royal,

I would like for you to send me a football jersey any number you would like for me to have. If you can't give me one, please don't feel bad about it, because if you can't you can't. Please write me back and don't let any ol' secretary answer this letter for you.

Dear Sir: [Read this one first!)

Your my favorite team. My father and I had a bet on your game against Ohio University, naturally I won. I would like to know if you would *please* send me a "jersey." At first I was going to send you a letter with lies in it so you would send me a "jersey", but I thought to myself and I decided it would be wrong. For the heck of it I'll send you the letter with the lies too. Since I been truthful with you now will you please send me a "jersey". I'm 13 years old basketball is my favorite sport. I would write more but I have to hurry.

Your great friend, truthful kid.

M. R.

The coach took an interest in many of his young correspondents and encouraged them to study, sent them books, and visited their schools.

Coach Royal,

Let me know if these notes take up too much of your time. I know you are very busy, but Rene responds to your attention so well; he is really getting a great deal out of knowing you.

Rene is working very hard at school this year. We are working especially in reading because he has been behind in that area. Encourage him to read anything, please. He has already made great strides this year, but he has a long way to go.

Rene wanted you to see some of his work. He made 100s on both papers . . . he wants you to be proud of what he does. I want you to know your influence on Rene has improved his behavior in the classroom.

Thanks for helping us,

Mr. H. F.

Royal corresponded regularly with many of his young fans, including a young man named Billy, whose address was listed as the State School in Austin, and a boy named "Chocolate," whom Royal mentored. He and Edith took this responsibility seriously, and each letter received a personal reply. "I'm sure many of these could be answered with a form letter," Royal said, "but if they've taken the time to write me, I feel I need to take the time to write back."

Read more letters to the coach at www.burntorangebooks.com.

Page 1

Wellcome to
Austin. Where
Texas vs. A+M.
A+M has one the
toss. And they
aleket to resyv.
And there's the
kickoff. fumble
Texas gets the ball
on the 50. In
come's Edy Fillups!

Dear Coach Royal
We watched your team beat the
Bear Monday. I'm a Texas
Fan. I am in the 2nd grade
and play on the 3rd and 4th
grade team at Wathall Academy.
The reason I wrote is to
ask you for a used practice
Jersey or anything with the
University Of Texas on it.

You and Your teams Superfan

P.S. I saved up 2 dollars
so I could get a #1
practice Jersey are
something. I was Born in
Texas But live in Misso now.

Blanche – I took good care of him – Thanks
Rooster, this letter has been answered, Rooster
we told him his 1st 2.00 would be sent to
you and you'd send him a jersey
P.s – Please let me have the letter back. Thanks
Blanche

Bevo's gallery—gifts from DKR's youngest fans (Royal Family Archives).

UNIVERSITY OF TEXAS
LONGHORNS

BEVO

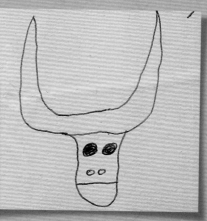

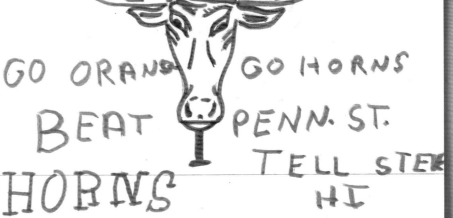

TEXAS

GO ORANGE GO HORNS
BEAT PENN. ST.
HORNS TELL STEK
HI

Going Orange & Going Great

Texas

Longhorns

TEXAS is the best!

TEXAS

TEXAS LONGHORNS!

Texas LongHorns

Sorry Aggies

Hook'em Horns

SELECTED SOURCES

Baldwin, Pat. "Always the Coach." *Private Clubs Magazine*, July–August 2004.

Banks, Jimmy. *The Darrell Royal Story*. Austin: Shoal Creek, 1973.

Buchholz, Brad. "Running Buddies." *Third Coast: The Magazine of Austin*, September 1986, 43–45.

Crouch, Donia Caspersen. *Texas Twosomes: Married for Life*. Austin: Eakin, 1998.

Freeman, Denne H. *Hook 'Em Horns: A Story of Texas Football*. Huntsville, Ala.: Strode, 1974.

Grimsley, Will. *Football: The Greatest Moments in the Southwest Conference*. Boston: Little, Brown, 1968.

Gwynne, S. C. "Come Early. Be Loud. Cash In." *Texas Monthly*, November 2008, 142–147.

Herskowitz, Mickey. "College Football." *Houston Chronicle*, September 15, 1996.

———. "Royal T." *Houston Chronicle*, September 15, 1996.

Little, Bill. "Darrell Royal." *Longhorn Album Magazine*.

Little, Bill, and Jenna McEachern. *What It Means to Be a Longhorn: Darrell Royal, Mack Brown, and Texas's Greatest Players*. Chicago: Triumph, 2007.

MackBrown-TexasFootball.com

Maysel, Lou. *Here Come the Texas Longhorns, 1893–1970*. Fort Worth: Stadium, 1970.

———. *Here Come the Texas Longhorns, 1970–1978*. Austin: Burnt Orange, 1978.

McEachern, Jenna Hays. *100 Things Longhorn Fans Should Know and Do before They Die*. Chicago: Triumph, 2008.

Ramsey, Jones. *The Memoirs of Jones Ramsey*. 1990.

Reid, Jan. "Coach Royal Regrets." *Texas Monthly*, December 1982.

Ross, Steve. "Darrell Royal: The Transcendent Figure in a Classic Rivalry." *Barking Carnival*, October 13, 2009. http://barkingcarnival.fantake.com/2009/10/13/darrell-royal-the-transcendent-figure-in-a-classic-rivalry.

Royal, Darrell, with Blackie Sherrod. *Darrell Royal Talks Football*. Englewood Cliffs, N.J.: Prentice-Hall, 1963.

Royal, Darrell, with John Wheat. *Coach Royal: Conversations with a Texas Football Legend*. Austin: Univ. of Texas Press, 2005.

Horns Hook It: No. 1!

Texas Is Crowned National Champ